Bob Bly does a fantastic job of summarizing al
keting success. When you follow Bob's "Silvei
better position with prospects because they will be calling YOU. I built
my own business over the past 14 years using many of the same tips and
insider secrets that Bob shares in his book. I recommend it highly.

—Stewart Gandolf, CEO of Healthcare Success, LLC

Businesspeople have too many hats that they need to wear.
Bob Bly's book on content marketing is a simple, practical, usable
gold mine full of tips, ideas, and strategies that help any business
owner wear the marketing hat.

—Jim Turner, president of ESSC Inc. and MedixSafe

With *The Content Marketing Handbook*, Bob achieves what many
have unsuccessfully attempted. He shows businesses how to blend
content and copywriting to create content marketing plans
that produce bottom-line results.

—Keith A. Trimels, registered engineer and copywriter

The Content Marketing Handbook provides a simple step-by-step
approach to using your knowledge, experience, and expertise for positioning, credibility-building, and profit. As with Bob's many other books
and information products, no stone is left unturned. This isn't theory; as
a client of Bob's, I can tell you he practices what he preaches.

—Andrew Gardner, owner of Care & Comfort Products Ltd.

In *The Content Marketing Handbook,* Bob Bly offers marketers at all levels a deeper understanding of the difference between content copy and professionally crafted direct response marketing copy. I understand content copy specific to my field but always look to those few rare experts who know how to create that "extra edge" that makes all the difference. What makes this book so different (and special) is Bob lays out a concise blueprint of the inner workings of creating that "extra edge" and specifically how to deploy in a truly omni-present marketing manner; done so, in a way I've never seen revealed so transparently.

—MATT ZAGULA, FOUNDER OF THE SMART ADVISOR NETWORK

THE
content
marketing
HANDBOOK

How to Double The Results of Your Marketing Campaigns

ROBERT W. BLY

Entrepreneur Press®

Entrepreneur Press, Publisher
Cover Design: Andrew Welyczko
Production and Composition: Eliot House Productions

This publication is designed to provide accurate and authoritative information
in regard to the subject matter covered. It is sold with the understanding that the
publisher is not engaged in rendering legal, accounting, or other professional services.
If legal advice or other expert assistance is required, the services of a competent
professional person should be sought.

Entrepreneur Press® is a registered trademark of Entrepreneur Media, Inc.

Library of Congress Cataloging-in-Publication Data
Names: Bly, Robert W., author.
Title: The content marketing handbook : how to double the results of your mar-
    keting campaigns / by Robert W. Bly.
Description: Irvine, California : Entrepreneur Press, [2020] | Summary: "Content
    can be an effective and economical tool to add to your marketing strategy. But
    content marketing is most effective when integrated into a multi-channel cam-
    paign that not only educates consumers but offers that content with various
    direct response methods, online and offline, to generate leads, prospects, and
    direct sales. Having written more than 90 books during his forty-year career in
    content and direct marketing Robert W. Bly has more than a few strategies to
    help readers get the highest ROI on their content"-- Provided by publisher.
Identifiers: LCCN 2019041075 (print) | LCCN 2019041076 (ebook) |
    ISBN 978-1-59918-660-3 (paperback) | ISBN 978-161308-417-5 (ebook)
Subjects: LCSH: Marketing.
Classification: LCC HF5415 .B4846 2020 (print) | LCC HF5415 (ebook) | DDC
    658.8/02--dc23
LC record available at https://lccn.loc.gov/2019041075
LC ebook record available at https://lccn.loc.gov/2019041076

Printed in the United States of America

24 23 22 21 20   10 9 8 7 6 5 4 3 2 1

To Matt Zagula—a true marketing pro and master of his field

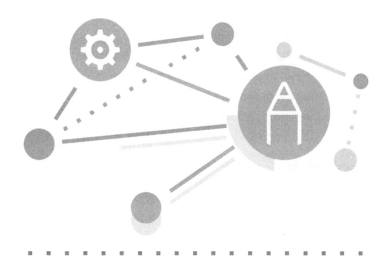

Contents

CHAPTER 2

How to Write Compelling Content 29

CHAPTER 3

Planning Your Content Marketing Campaign 63

CHAPTER 4

Integrating Content with Selling 73

PART II
Implementing Content Marketing Tactics

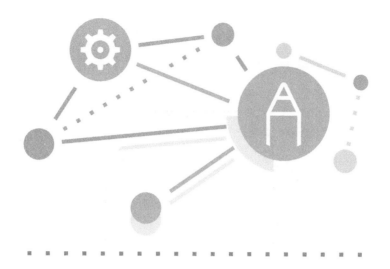

Acknowledgments

I thank my agent, Bob Diforio, for finding a home for this book. I also thank the team at Entrepreneur Press—Jennifer Dorsey, Corbin Collins, Karen Billipp, and Vanessa Campos—for making this book much better than when the manuscript first crossed their desk, as they have done for all my books with Entrepreneur Press.

Thanks also to my vendors, colleagues, joint venture partners, and clients, all of whom have contributed to my education in content marketing in a multichannel world. Some of the material in this book appeared, in slightly different form, in articles I have written for publications, including *Target Marketing* magazine, my enewsletter *The Direct Response Letter,* and my earlier book *The White Paper Marketing Handbook.*

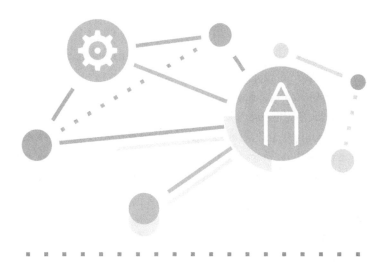

Preface

Of the megatrends in marketing today—which include search engine optimization (SEO), online video, social media, mobile marketing, ad retargeting, and infographics—content marketing is emerging as the new "killer app" in the marketing world.

Although content marketing has been used profitably for more than a century, its popularity has exploded in the past couple of decades: According to the Content Marketing Institute (CMI), as of 2017, almost nine out of ten B2B companies were using content marketing.

The CMI also says corporations spend more than one-quarter of their promotional budgets on content marketing. According to market research company Forrester, in 2016, U.S. businesses spent a total of $10 billion on content marketing. Content marketing was forecast to be a $300 billion industry in 2019.

Yet many content strategists and advocates get one part of marketing entirely wrong: They tell unsuspecting businesspeople that it is no longer effective to sell or persuade, and instead advise them to think of themselves as publishers instead of marketers.

The error in this method, of course, is that businesses exist to sell customers products and services they want and need, and for which they will pay a price that allows the seller to make a profit. Businesses' purpose is *not* to give away free information, which is essentially what content marketing is.

Content marketing is not an end unto itself. It is a *means* to an end—to sell products. Content is not the be-all and end-all of marketing, either. It's just one of many methods that can be used to get customers, orders, and sales.

Content marketing is most effective when it's integrated with a multichannel campaign that not only educates consumers (with content) but also offers that content with various direct response methods both online and offline to generate leads, prospects, and sales. This is the approach you will read about in this book.

In this handbook, I share lessons from my four decades of experience planning and producing hundreds of content marketing campaigns. In these pages, you will discover:

- Why content marketing is so effective and economical
- Which types of businesses and organizations can benefit most from content marketing campaigns
- How to create A-level content that gets noticed, gets read, gets your message across, and eliminates "content pollution"

TIP

URLs change all the time, which means many URLs in published works quickly become outdated and nonfunctional. To keep *The Content Marketing Handbook* as up-to-date as possible, I periodically send the new URLs to my readers. To get them at no charge, just subscribe to my free online newsletter *The Direct Response Letter* (https://www.bly.com/reports/). Another way to find the updated URL is to Google the source by name or even by the old URL.

- How to overcome the biggest weakness of content marketing
- How to double your marketing response rates with lead magnets, bonus reports, and other free content offers
- How to integrate content and direct response marketing to produce greater results than either can generate on their own
- How to use content to build your brand, enhance your reputation, and stand out from your competitors
- How to plan, execute, and measure content marketing in a multi-channel environment
- When to stop giving away content (the easy part of marketing) and start asking for the order (where the money is made)

My aim is to show you content's true role in integrated multichannel marketing campaigns. This book can help you avoid wasting time and money by giving away content with no return on investment, and instead create and offer content that can build trust, stimulate interest, and ultimately get more orders—in a way that creates a stronger relationship with your buyers and helps them get maximum benefit from their purchase of your products.

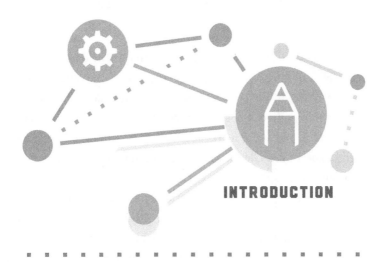

Content Marketing in the 21st Century

Content marketing—giving away free information to build brand awareness, increase response to marketing campaigns, convert more online traffic, and educate prospects on your technology, methodology, products, services, and applications—is one of the hot trends in marketing today. Other marketing methods currently popular include online video, social media, QR codes, search engine optimization (SEO), live online chat, mobile marketing, and infographics. But, as the saying goes, content is king.

More than 8 out of 20 ecommerce shoppers conduct online searches before they make a purchase. And 7 out of 10 cite detailed product content as the number-one reason they buy one product over another. Brands that submit content for SEO can boost their sales more than 25 percent than retailers who just advertise.

Origins of new terms are often murky; *content marketing* may have been coined in 1996 at a roundtable for journalists held at the American Society of News Editors by John F. Oppedahl. In fact, content marketing has been used for far longer than that. It's only the name that is of recent vintage, not the method. I personally have been doing content marketing for four decades, and some marketers have been at it even longer. Online marketing expert Fred Gleeck calls it "edutainment" because the content ideally should be educational and entertaining.

Today, more attention than ever is being focused on content as a marketing tool. For instance, in August 2017, Apple announced the company was making a $1 billion investment in original content for its Apple TV platform; by 2019, a report in the *Financial Times* estimated Apple's content investment at $6 billion. In 2019, Forrester forecasted that by 2023, annual digital marketing dollars spent by businesses will reach $146 billion.

The average American spends almost nine hours a day engaging with digital content, while Millennials spend even more: 11 hours. No wonder 53 percent of marketers consider articles and blog posts their most-used technique for inbound marketing.

I did my first content marketing campaign in 1980. I was advertising manager of Koch Engineering, an industrial manufacturer run by the late David Koch, who at the time was the Libertarian Party's nominee for vice president of the United States, back when he was relatively unknown. Later, of course, he became a household name as half of the infamous "billionaire Koch brothers."

One of the products we sold were various *tower internals*, and one type was the *tray*: circular metal disks with capped openings on their surfaces. The trays were placed inside refinery towers to enhance the distillation of crude oil into kerosene, gasoline, heating oil, jet fuel, and other petroleum-based products.

Specifying the correct configuration of trays for your refinery is a highly technical task, and the engineers in the refineries often needed instructions for how to do it correctly.

To assist them, we produced a technical manual that we dubbed the "tray manual," which cost several dollars per copy to print and bind. It had stiff covers, a spiral binding, and fold-out blueprint drawings showing the configurations of various trays. The tray manual was not my idea; it was already in use when I joined the firm. It was wildly popular—by far our most requested piece of literature. Back then we didn't call it "content marketing." We called it "giving away free information." But the practice was the same. Copywriter Bob Martel says he called it "presales educational writing"—which, he notes, requires you to know something about both education and sales.

Content marketing has been used for more than a century. To test responses to his print ads, Claude Hopkins (1866–1932) offered free informational booklets in many of his ads. And in 1916, Campbell's began promoting its soups with content marketing by offering free booklets of recipes that used Campbell's soups.

Back in those days, this free content was simply called *free booklets* or *free information*. In the latter part of the 20th century, marketers referred to them as *bait pieces*, because they helped "hook" prospects and turn them into leads (see Figure I–1, below).

FIGURE I–1. Free Content Offers Used as "Bait" by Many Marketers to Get Leads

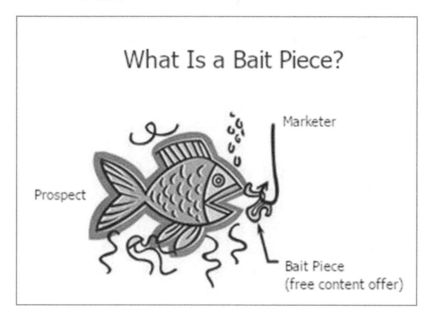

Today, the preferred term for free content is *lead magnet*, the idea being that the tempting offer of valuable free information is like a magnet that draws people into your ad and gets them to request the white paper or other free content. A content offer with multiple components (such as a product sample, brochure, and DVD) is called an *information kit*.

There are all sorts of opinions and tests on the effectiveness of content marketing.

But let me sum up my experience in just two simple points. First, I can't remember the last time I did a B2B (business to business) or B2C (business to consumer) marketing campaign without a free content offer. For B2B, the lead magnet is often the primary offer that drives prospects to respond. For B2C, it is often a bonus report given along with their purchase of the product.

Second, adding a lead magnet to a B2B lead generation campaign can often double (or more) the number of inquiries instead of the same campaign without the free content offer.

In the "good old days" of B2B marketing, our primary offer was a *free color brochure* filled with sales copy about the product. It worked then, but today prospects respond better if you also promise to send them free how-to information, such as a special report or white paper, which will be useful to them in their job, rather than just selling them something. Customers want to get something from their content, and the statistics agree.

For instance:

- ◎ Eighty percent of Americans prefer a series of articles over an ad.
- ◎ Seventy percent say content marketing makes them feel closer to a product or business.
- ◎ Sixty percent credit content marketing for helping them make better purchase decisions.
- ◎ Content marketing costs 62 percent less than outbound marketing and generates three times as many leads.
- ◎ Ninety percent of the most successful B2B content marketers put their audience's information need over the company's sales and promotional messages.

FIGURE I-2. Top Content Marketing Challenges

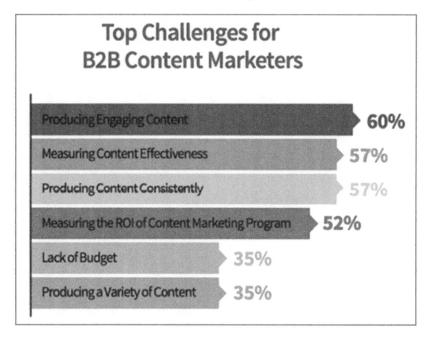

Although a large number of B2B companies use content marketing, it is not in everyone's wheelhouse, and it may not be ideal for you. But if you want to gain content marketing skills, knowledge, and results, this book is a good place to start.

As you can see in Figure I–2 above, three of the top six challenges in B2B content marketing revolve around producing content. Chapters 2 and 3 address this challenge, and Chapters 5 through 14 give detailed instructions for implementing it. Measuring content effectiveness and ROI is covered in Chapters 16 and 17. Budget is discussed in Chapter 3, which is about planning your content marketing campaigns. All the top challenges for B2B content marketers, which I believe apply equally to consumer marketing, are covered in this book. Let's get started!

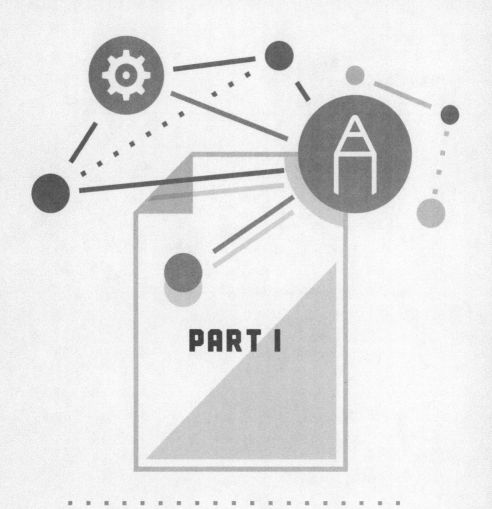

PART I

The Foundations of Content Marketing

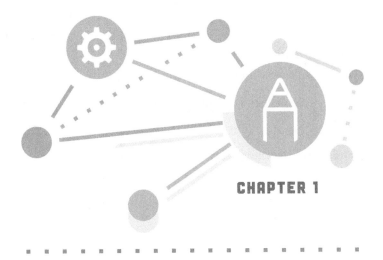

CHAPTER 1

Setting Yourself Up for Content Marketing Success

What is content marketing? Simply put, content marketing is any marketing activity that helps sell a product, service, or organization with the offer of free information.

Content marketing is a powerful way to engage your industry, generate leads, and close deals. Marketers in countless industries are now creating valuable content for their prospective and current customers. You can do the same with content. Here are some examples:

- A social media post talking about attending a business conference
- A trade journal article on industry trends
- A recorded webinar with valuable information about specific technology
- A blog post with tips on tackling a new challenge

3

- A white paper explaining an important concept in your application or niche market
- An enewsletter with tips and reminders

Table 1–1 below lists some of the more popular formats for content marketing.

TABLE 1-1. Content Marketing Formats

Content Formats	
Tip sheets	DVDs
How-to sheets	CDs
Booklet	Webinar
Article	Teleseminar
Enewsletter	Flashcard
Column	Software
Monograph	Games
Mini-report	Ebook
Case study	Print newsletter
Mobile apps	Use cases (applications)
White paper	Streaming video files
Slide guide	Online audio files
Selection guide	Paperbound books

As you can see from this list, content marketing is not just another term for ads for your products. Instead, it provides valuable how-to or reference information to prospective or current customers. Content marketing educates your customers to help them do their job better and faster. But the content, naturally and sometimes subtly, influences them to favor your methodology, your brand, and your products.

Content Writing and Copywriting

The power of your content lies in the writing. *Content* does not explicitly sell your product but rather helps sell it indirectly by educating your prospect.

Syms, a New Jersey-based clothing retailer, ran radio commercials in the 1980s with the slogan "An educated consumer is the best customer." That is content marketing in a nutshell. By educating prospects on your methodology or technology, you increase, for reasons you'll discover later in this book, the chances they will buy from you instead of your competitors. But it's a soft sell—you are giving them information to help them do a task better, rather than blatantly selling your product or brand.

Copy is text about a specific product or brand that openly sells the product to customers. *Content* achieves a number of objectives, including building brand awareness, educating the marketplace, establishing you as the go-to source of information on your topic, boosting search engine rankings, spreading ideas, changing beliefs, presenting a methodology or idea for solving a problem, and persuading people to agree with your point of view.

Direct response copywriting, whether digital or print, is much more narrowly focused. The prime objective here is generating and improving response, including increasing open rates, click-through rates, conversion rates, list building, generating leads, qualifying prospects, selling products and services, and cross-selling and updating buyers on your other products.

Where content sets the stage and warms up prospects to accept your offer, it is copy that closes the deal and makes the sale. Order pages, for example, are usually copy, not content.

In addition, offering content as a lead magnet virtually always increases response rates to direct response promotions, including email and direct mail. So the two go hand-in-hand: Direct response copy is used in email, direct mail, and advertising to drive traffic to websites, landing pages, and squeeze pages. These pages, in turn, use direct response copy to convert the clicks into either leads or sales. Generating inquiries for lead magnets also helps distribute your content to a larger audience. Figure 1–1 on page 6 shows a simple sales funnel for integrating direct response copy with content, in which:

- Direct response copy is used in promotions that drive traffic. Example: an email that convinces the recipient to click on a hyper-link for more information.
- Content is used in the lead magnet which the email copy offers to the user.

FIGURE 1-1. Integration of Content and Direct Marketing to Form a Sales Funnel

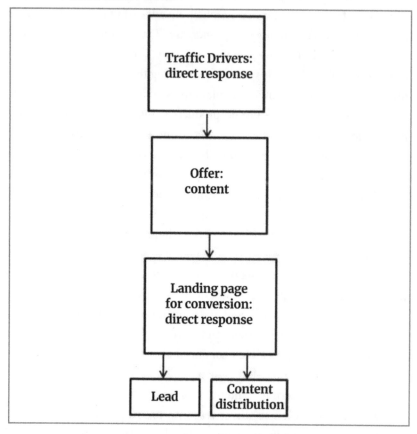

- ⊚ Direct response copy is used on the landing page, which converts visitors who land on the page by persuading them to complete and submit the landing page form to download the lead magnet.
- ⊚ When visitors download the lead magnet, it captures the prospect's name and email address, generates a lead, and helps distribute the content in the lead magnet to a wider audience.

The Seven Fundamentals of Good Content Writing

If you asked me to name the two biggest trends in B2B marketing today, I'd have to say social media and content marketing. And social media seems to work best when it's based on content.

But content marketing isn't just publishing information—there's way too much information available today. Your prospects are drowning in it. What they are starved for is *knowledge*—they want to know how to solve problems and how to do their jobs better.

The following list walks you through seven guidelines that can help set up your content marketing campaign and make it more productive and effective.

TIP

You're not in business to publish free content—you're in business to sell your products and services. Unless publishing content helps you achieve that goal, it's a waste of your time and money.

1. Narrow the Topic

There is no benefit to cramming every last bit of information about a subject into your white paper or other content marketing piece; the prospect can easily find that data through Google.

Content marketing works best when you narrow the topic. The more precise the topic, the more in-depth and useful your content can be. For instance, let's say you are an industrial gas manufacturer creating a ten-page white paper on safety for plant managers. If your title is *Plant Safety*, you cannot hope to cover that topic in even the most superficial way; entire books have been written on that subject.

On the other hand, you could produce a very useful white paper called *Safety Tips for Handling Compressed Gas Cylinders*. That's a topic plant personnel want and need to know more about. And with your experience, you can probably offer some methods that are new to the reader.

2. Target the Prospect

The more narrowly you target the audience for your content marketing piece, the better able you are to deliver truly useful content. For our example of the white paper on compressed gas cylinders, are you targeting plant managers or plant operators? Managers might be more interested in cylinder inventory and control, whereas operators would want nuts-and-bolts tips for handling the cylinders. A CFO would want to look at reducing costly gas cylinder accidents, while a CEO might be more concerned about liability.

3. Determine the Objective

Remember, you're not giving away information out of the kindness of your heart. There has to be a purpose for the content you spend time and money to produce. For instance, a software publisher discovered that it wasn't losing sales to a competitor because their products had better features and benefits. It was because the software in that category was expensive, and even though the prospects wanted the functionality the software delivered, they couldn't cost-justify the purchase. To solve this problem, the company published a white paper titled *Calculating Return on Investment for Purchase of XYZ Software*. It showed that the time and labor savings the software provided could pay back its high cost in six to eight months. Salespeople then used the white paper to overcome the objection that it cost too much.

4. Educate the Reader

Years ago, Duncan Hines ran an ad in magazines about its chocolate cake mix. The headline was "The secret to moister, richer chocolate cake." Why was that headline so effective? Because it implied you would learn something useful just by reading the ad, regardless of whether you bought the product. Generic advice won't cut it in content marketing today. The prospect does not want to read the same old tips they've seen a dozen times before. Chances are you possess proprietary knowledge about your products and their applications. Share some of this knowledge in your white paper. Give your reader specific advice and ideas they haven't seen before. Don't worry that by giving away too much, you'll eliminate the prospect's need for your product or service. It's quite the opposite: When they learn how much effort solving their problem entails, and see that you clearly have the expertise they need, they will turn to you for help.

5. Deliver Value

When you can, include some highly practical, actionable tips the prospect can implement immediately. The more valuable your content is to prospects, the faster your content marketing program will achieve its objective. It's like food vendors giving away samples: the better the free food tastes, the more likely the consumer is to purchase a snack or meal.

6. Set the Specs

Outline the characteristics, features, and specifications the prospect should look for when shopping for products in your category. Of course, the requirements you outline should fit your product to a tee. If you do this credibly, the prospect will turn your white paper into a shopping list.

7. Generate Action or Change Belief

Content marketing succeeds when it gets prospects to take action or change their opinion, attitude, or beliefs about you and your product as it relates to their needs. When writing white papers, I always ask my clients, "What do you want to happen after the prospect finishes reading our white paper?" I often end the white paper with a section titled "The next step," which tells the reader what to do and how to do it.

WRITING TECHNICAL CONTENT

A lot of B2B marketing either promotes technical products, sells to a technical audience, or both. The nature of these marketing campaigns poses a challenge to those who must create them, because the marketers tasked with executing these campaigns often lack a technical background. Therefore, they may have a steep learning curve and difficulty understanding what they are selling and to whom they are selling it.

I have been writing copy to sell technical products to engineers, scientists, programmers, and other techies for more than four

WRITING TECHNICAL CONTENT, continued

decades. Here are seven tricks of the trade that give me an edge in creating copy that pleases the client and persuades the prospect:

1. *Build an accurate "fact bank."* A fact bank is a series of statements describing the product and its features that have been vetted by a technical expert. Before I start writing my copy, I go through the source material for the project and write down five to ten sentences that precisely describe the product, how it works, its major features, and how those features translate into important benefits. I email these sentences to my clients with the request that they review them and make any necessary corrections, additions, or deletions. After they do so, I incorporate their edits. Now I have a set of preapproved sentences I can use to construct my copy, and I know what I am writing is technically accurate. The clients then get a first draft of copy on a highly technical subject that is correct and on the mark.

2. *Buy a children's book on the topic.* If you have to write copy about a technical subject, buy either a children's book on the subject or an adult nonfiction book aimed at a lay audience. For example, when I had to write copy for an aerospace contractor, I was aided by an Isaac Asimov book for young readers about satellites. The children's books especially will provide clear, easy-to-understand explanations of key terms and concepts. The adult books will likely have descriptions of features and functionality you can paraphrase in your own copy. (If I "borrow" from books, I alert the client by adding a footnote and make sure I am not plagiarizing by rephrasing in my own words.) Another good purchase for

WRITING TECHNICAL CONTENT, continued

the high-tech copywriter is a dictionary of industry terms. I have owned at various times dictionaries for computers, telecom, banking, finance, and aerospace.

3. *Ask the client for copies of PowerPoints.* Engineers in particular tend to be visually oriented, so you should have visuals to accompany your text. Rather than draw a lot of charts and graphs, I ask the client for copies of PowerPoints used in presentations by their technical and sales staff. I then paste into my copy whatever visuals I think will work best, carefully noting the name of the PowerPoint and the page number from the source. Sometimes I find an ideal diagram for illustrating my point on a website that is not the client's. If I use it, I add a note explaining that it is for reference only and must be redrawn to avoid copyright infringement.

4. *Understand that graphics have meaning.* Unless you understand what a chart or graph means, don't use it. It is extremely embarrassing to cut and paste a diagram from a client's PowerPoint into your copy, only to be unable to explain to the client why you used it. You should understand each visual so well that you can write a clear, descriptive caption for it—and then do so.

5. *Use email for interviews.* I often interview subject matter experts (SMEs) when writing copy over the phone. But occasionally I get SMEs who cannot express themselves well verbally. In those cases, I offer to email them questions so they can email me their replies. Often technical people who cannot speak English well can still write decently—perhaps a

---

WRITING TECHNICAL CONTENT, continued

result of the rise of email, which forces people to write often. At times, the email replies are so clear I can almost paste them right into my copy. If the answers are still unclear, I rewrite them in plain English and then email my rewrite back to the SME for review. Usually the SME makes a few minor edits, and after that, it is ready to use.

6. *Use Wikipedia—with caution.* You can't wholly rely on information in Wikipedia to be accurate because it is compiled by volunteers. However, I've found that entries on technical terms usually start off with a plain English definition of the term, which can be invaluable. But when you are researching statistics to augment your copy—for example, the date the laser was invented or the speed of sound in a vacuum—most clients want a better source than Wikipedia. Websites are also iffy when you don't know who is running them, as are blogs. I prefer to cite an article in a respected industry or scientific journal.

7. *Get smart.* If you are going to be regularly writing about a product or technology, it makes sense to get some additional education on the topic. One ad agency president told me he assigned an account executive to handle an industrial welding account. On his own, the account executive took night school courses in welding, eventually becoming a certified welder. Smart move!

The Nine Functions of Content Marketing

Content marketing performs nine functions that help B2B as well as B2C marketers generate more leads and ultimately close more sales. Let's explore them:

1. *Sets the specs.* As mentioned earlier, content marketing can educate prospects on what features, functions, and capabilities they should look for when buying a particular type of product or service. Because you have presented your criteria in a white paper or other medium that looks like useful information and not a sales pitch, readers absorb and accept your guidelines. They then use the specifications you have set.

   Say you sell motionless mixers, one of the products I helped market at Koch Engineering. You offer in your ads a booklet called *7 Things to Look for When Specifying Motionless Mixers.* Prospects read it and use your criteria when looking to purchase motionless mixers. And whose mixer fits all seven criteria perfectly? Yours.

2. *Makes the prospect beholden.* This is the principle of reciprocity as described by marketing expert Robert Cialdini in his book *Influence: The Psychology of Persuasion.* When you give somebody something, they feel obligated to give you something in return. Giving a prospect free content does not make them feel obligated to buy your product, but it does make them inclined to give you a little more of their time and attention than they otherwise might.

   More than half of buyers strongly agree that if brands packaged relevant content together, it would help expedite the research phase of the buying cycle. Content marketing includes delivering personalized, segmented, and relevant content to your existing customers. By keeping your current customers engaged and updated with great content, you'll improve your long-term customer retention rates.

   Richie M., one of my newsletter subscribers, told me in an email, "This is just a short note to say that I really enjoy your emails. I can tell when they are commercials, but don't mind them, because you generally also give me worthwhile information. I believe that is why you are successful. When I receive useful information in free emails, I am more likely to purchase additional information—and I have." Richie's response is what you hope for when writing content.

3. *Generates more inquiries.* A lead-generating promotion with a free content offer can produce more than double the response as the same campaign without the free offer. Good content market-

ing is that effective. By publishing new and relevant content on your digital channels, and doing so often, you can increase the likelihood of new customers finding out about your business, its services, and the value you can bring them. Plus, prospects are more likely to return to your website when they know you frequently add fresh content.

4. *Gets you new customers.* Many marketers acquire new customers through their blogs. Whether your content first caught a prospect's eye on Google or a white paper they downloaded on your site tipped them over the edge, content marketing plays an important role in the B2B purchase life cycle.

   Typically, a B2B prospect searching for a product may work through 70 to 90 percent of the product search, research, and evaluation process before contacting the vendor, according to Forrester Research. B2B vendor research happens online, and one thing that can help move the prospect down the pipeline is publishing valuable content on your website, email, search, and social channels.

   For emails sent regularly to your opt-in elist, half or more of the messages should be content, while fewer than half should be sales emails. If you send too many sales pitches and not enough good content, your unsubscribe rate will spike. So will your "mental" unsubscribe rate, meaning that although people won't ask to be removed from your list, they just stop reading or even opening your emails.

5. *Establishes you as the expert.* Publishing content on your industry, niche, or area of specialization helps position you as a recognized authority in your field. And prospects would rather buy from knowledgeable experts than ordinary salespeople. Charging your organization with regularly creating new content fosters a culture of research, innovation, and thought leadership. In a rapidly changing industry, content marketing can help force your team to stay up-to-date on changes and trends, which can become invaluable in your product development efforts.

   It should not be solely the marketing team's job to generate all the material used in your content marketing efforts. Account managers, SMEs, and even long-term clients and site visitors can be engaged to help create great content.

6. *Educates the market.* Content marketing supports your sales efforts, but its first mission is to educate and inform, not make blatant product pitches. Nine out of ten of the top-performing B2B content marketers put their audience's informational needs ahead of their company's sales message, reports the Content Marketing Institute.

One marketer of content management software (CMS) was the first to integrate their CMS with analytics, ecommerce, and other applications. But the market did not yet understand the benefits of this integration. So the marketer published a white paper explaining them, with good results.

7. *Drives sales.* Content can be strategically disseminated at various steps in the buying cycle, helping to accelerate each step and ultimately increasing sales. The sales funnel takes most buyers through four stages: getting their attention, gaining their interest, creating desire for the product, and asking for the order. Each stage can use both selling (copy) and education (content).

8. *Improves search engine ranking and discovery.* Search engines love new, relevant, indexed content. When you host your content on your website—whether through blog posts, white papers, or web copy—you can improve your search engine ranking and the likelihood customers will find your website. According to accounting firm Ignite Spot, a blog on your website will lead to 434 percent more indexed pages on Google and 97 percent more inbound links. By increasing your indexed pages and links, you'll make your site more reputable in a search engine's eyes. Higher search engine rankings mean interested prospects are more likely to discover your site when they search for relevant keywords.

9. *Drives web traffic.* Search engine discovery combined with social posts that point to your site can increase your web traffic considerably. According to HubSpot, if you've got 51 to 100 pages on your website (consider each blog post to be a unique page), you'll generate 48 percent more traffic than if you had under 50. Increased traffic means increased engagement means increased revenue.

Content and the "Silver Rule of Marketing"

My friend, the late consultant Pete Silver, formulated what he called The Silver Rule of Marketing: "It is always better to get *them* [prospects] to come to *you* than to have *you* go to *them*." That's really what these Nine Functions of Content Marketing are all about—I urge you to practice this "Silver Rule." When you go to prospective customers, you convey the impression of needing the sale; when they come to you, they are more qualified. People like to buy from companies they perceive as successful and busy, not those that seem hungry for orders.

Cold calling doesn't do this. Content marketing does. Establish yourself as a recognized expert by giving seminars and speeches, writing articles for publications read by potential clients, or writing books.

When you get an inquiry from someone who subscribes to your enewsletter, you are negotiating from a position of strength—because they came to you, rather than you calling them. When someone approaches you at a conference, says they loved your speech, and asks about engaging your firm's services, you are in a position of strength, because they approached you in response to the good content you just delivered.

Why does Tom Peters get $30,000 or so to give a one-hour speech on business—and have more business than he can handle—while other speakers struggle to get bookings for $2,000 or less? It is largely because, as a bestselling author, he is perceived as an expert. And so prospects come to him, rather than him going to them. He has become a successful marketing consultant simply by practicing the Silver Rule. You can too.

In addition, almost 50 percent of businesspeople use content marketing in their follow-up to event attendees—and two in three of these say this strategy is highly effective in continuing the conversation and leading to new business.

The Ten Steps to Building a Successful Content Marketing Campaign

What makes for a successful B2B and B2C lead-generating content marketing campaign? There are ten key steps:

1. Define the target audience and their information needs.

2. Come up with a strategic or useful content plan.

3. Select a format or medium for your lead magnet.

4. Create a great title for your lead magnet.

5. Research, organize, and write the content.

6. Create a landing page for downloading the lead magnet.

7. Drive traffic to your landing page.

8. Fulfill inquiries.

9. Follow up.

10. Secure an appointment or conversation.

Let's briefly touch on each of these ten steps. If you follow these steps in order and execute each skillfully, you will greatly improve your odds of having a successful and profitable content marketing campaign.

Step 1: Define the Target Audience and Their Information Needs

In B2B, defining the target audience or readership involves knowing the industry, company size, and prospect's title, responsibilities, education, and degree of knowledge in your chosen topic, as well as how they use your type of product in their business. You should also think about the information needs of prospects at the stage of the buying process at which you are reaching them.

In the initial search for solutions, or the *shopping stage*, the prospects for the content management software mentioned earlier needed to understand the unique selling proposition (USP) of the system—the integrated analytics—and the benefits it could deliver. The marketer successfully educated prospects on this front. But when buyers evaluated economic considerations, they felt the high-end CMS was too expensive. They liked the features and what the system could do for them, but they didn't see how they could justify spending that much money.

In fact, a good CMS can quickly pay for itself, so the system was really a profit center, not a cost center. But prospects did not see this. The solution was for the marketer to publish another white paper. This one showed prospects how to calculate the payback period for investing in the CMS, which was in the range of 6 to 12 months. Doing so overcame the price objections for a lot of buyers.

Step 2: Come Up with a Strategic or Useful Content Plan

A *strategic content plan* is one in which publishing and distributing the content solves a marketing problem. In our example of the CMS marketer, both white papers were strategic. The first solved the problem of prospects not understanding the benefits of the integrated analytics. The second solved the problem of "sticker shock"—prospects objecting to the high price.

A *useful content plan* is disseminating information that is of value to the prospect in their job, but is not a sales pitch for your product or service. For instance, a computer reseller might offer prospects and clients a special report on how to prevent data loss or avoid hackers, malware, and viruses. This kind of actionable information doesn't specifically accelerate the steps in the sales cycle or sell the prospect on the reseller or its solutions. But the prospect will appreciate the free tips, and they will reciprocate by viewing the reseller in a more favorable light. It builds goodwill and creates the impression that you are an expert in your field.

Step 3: Select a Format or Medium for Your Lead Magnet

For a long time, the de facto standard in lead magnets for selling hardware and software to IT professionals and executives was the white paper, a downloadable PDF document averaging ten pages in length. But content can be presented in many other formats and media, and your choice can make a big difference in the success of your content marketing campaign.

One effective alternative to white papers is a physical paperbound book. The problem with PDFs is that it is so easy to click away from them. Also, prospects are inundated with white paper offers, so yours won't stand out. When you mail prospects a real book, they take notice. Books also have a higher perceived value than white papers. And while downloaded PDFs can sit invisibly on hard drives, books are right there in plain view, sitting on a nightstand or on a shelf in the office.

There are many other options available to you for lead magnets. You can:

- Offer a free webinar, online course, podcast, infographic, or poster.
- Post a video on your site or YouTube.
- Send an audio CD or a DVD.
- Load useful data and content onto a thumb drive.

The key is to think beyond a downloadable report or white paper. Yes, they are effective. But alternative media, because they are less common, often gain more attention.

SHORT EBOOKS

One of the most interesting lead magnet formats I've seen in recent years is the extremely short book, both in print and ebook format. Short-format books have fewer pages and often a smaller page size. Full-size and short-format books address different purposes. Where an audience is large, and content is both broad and deep, long-form books provide these high-value functions:

- Exploration of multiple concepts
- Case studies
- Credibility
- Supporting documentation

A book with the full story plays a large role in building credibility and authority on an entire body of knowledge or area of expertise. But the best book is not necessarily the most inclusive. If you're trying to show your reader how to look at a specific issue in their life or business with an altered perspective, a full-size book could be too intimidating. Many readers just want to learn the basics in as little time as possible. If they remain engaged, they'll investigate further for more specifics. All you really need to do is build a bridge to your platform. This is where books, training, websites, and/or webinars serve as revenue streams and additional ways for people to connect with you.

Short-format books are optimal as an opening connection to your audience. They serve to deliver the essential "aha" moment that

SHORT EBOOKS, continued

binds them to you or convey that essential knowledge they seek to enhance their skill set.

When your topic is timely but your message timeless, a short book is ideal. The small size and page count makes the short-form book unusual and therefore a real attention-getter. Also, the text is far shorter than a conventional book, so less writing is required. And it's easier and cheaper to produce and distribute. You can easily carry paperbound little books in your bag or pocket and pull one out to read when waiting at the bus stop or bank. It's even more convenient for readers who prefer ebooks, as it can be read with less scrolling. Plus, it can be given away as lead gen or sold for a small price on online retailer sites.

With short-format books, you can attain instant credibility. When you hand someone a little book, you gain the authority of being an author without having to write a full-length book. The book you are reading now is about 80,000 words; the average short-format book is under 10,000 words.

Step 4: Create a Great Title for Your Lead Magnet

Perhaps the biggest factor determining whether prospects will request your free content is the title of your lead magnet. The title is like the headline of an ad or the subject line of an email. In fact, it often *is* the headline or the subject line. The purpose is the same: to grab the prospect's attention, generate interest and curiosity, and compel them to request the lead magnet.

To do that, a great title must stand out, identify the subject of the paper, and suggest who the target audience is. Common title types are shown in Table 1–2 on page 21.

TABLE 1-2. Lead Magnet Titles

Type of Title	Example
List	*The Top 7 Security Problems of 802.11 Wireless Networks*
Active Verb ("ing")	*Managing Large UNIX Data Centers*
Why	*Why Six Sigma Doesn't Work*
Colon	*Defending the Remote Office: Which VPN Technology Is Best?*
How-To	*How to Prevent Machine Parts from Failing Prematurely*
Dramatic	*The Death of Passwords*

Step 5: Research, Organize, and Write the Content

The amount of research you need to do depends on your knowledge of the topic. But even if you know the topic well, do some outside research. Start with searching Google for any white papers on the same topic by competitors. Subscribe to enewsletters on your topic and read trade journals covering your industry. You want to augment your knowledge of the subject with facts, figures, and ideas outside your own. Whenever you use data, graphs, or other content from outside sources, credit the source in a footnote.

Once you've gathered your content, think about how to organize and present the material. Sometimes the content naturally dictates a particular organizational scheme. For instance, if you were writing a guide to vitamins, you might use alphabetical order.

TIP

The cover of the lead magnet should have the title in large type in high contrast, such as big, bold black type on a white background. This way, when the cover image is reduced to fit in an email or landing page, the title is still easily readable. Avoid color schemes like dark blue type on a black background, which may make the title difficult to read.

A booklet on the solar system might cover the planets in order from the closest to the sun moving outward. A history of the semiconductor could be approached in chronological order.

At other times, no organizational scheme seems mandatory or apparent, and it is up to you to select a sensible way to organize your material. Something as simple as a numbered list might do; these are called *listicles*. Or you might choose a Q&A format, as in a FAQ page on a website.

Now that you have your content and a way to organize it, write your document. Start by placing your content and research under the appropriate chapter or section headings. Next, turn the raw material into clear, concise sentences and paragraphs. Remember that small words, short sentences, and short paragraphs make for easy reading. Do not avoid simple writing because you are talking to an educated or technical audience. In four decades of writing for engineers, programmers, scientists, and executives, I have never had someone complain that a document was too easy to read.

Once the document is done, edit to make it tighter, clearer, and better. Remove redundant sentences. Cut unnecessary words. Divide long sentences into two or more shorter sentences, starting the new sentence where a new thought begins. After you are done, give your document to a professional proofreader. Because you have already read the text many times in the writing process, you cannot trust yourself to do the final proofreading, as you will gloss over the copy and miss typos and other errors.

Step 6: Create a Landing Page for Downloading the Lead Magnet

A common mistake in content marketing is driving traffic to your website's homepage

TIP

You can either post your landing page on a URL that is an extension of your main domain name (www.bly.com/dm) or a unique domain name (www.myveryfirstebook. com). The former adds content to your main site, which helps with SEO, but the latter is easier to remember, which is especially useful when you are giving a talk or want to recall the URL when speaking to pros-pects.

and hoping visitors can find the box or link needed to request the lead magnet. Chances are good they will not. In addition, your homepage has lots of options for navigation, so when visitors get there, they will start clicking around and either forget about or never find your free content offer.

A *landing page* is a stand-alone web page where the prospect can request the free bait piece or lead magnet. On a properly designed, effective landing page, there are only two choices: Request the free lead magnet or leave. Therefore, the conversion rate—the percentage of visitors who fill in and submit your form—is much higher on dedicated landing pages than on homepages or any other web pages.

Notice in Figure 1–2 on page 24, that there are three options in the landing page: get the free lead magnet, receive information on the product or service being promoted, or have a salesperson contact the prospect. Also notice that whichever option the visitor chooses, you capture their name and email address. Therefore, in addition to generating qualified leads, this landing page also helps build your opt-in email list!

The visitor can choose one, two, or all three. Those who request product information or a call by a salesperson are generally better prospects than those who ask for the lead magnet only. Having said that, there will be visitors who want only the lead magnet but, upon follow-up, convert into buyers—so don't discount or neglect them.

Step 7: Drive Traffic to Your Landing Page

The success of your content management campaign depends on two factors: traffic and conversion. *Traffic* is the number of people who visit the landing page. *Conversion* is the percentage of those visitors who fill in and submit the form.

How do you drive traffic to your site without burning through your available cash in a couple of weeks? Here are seven cost-effective ways to get hits on your site:

1. *Google.* The world's largest search engine, Google facilitates 3.5 billion web searches per day for its users. As an advertiser, you can buy higher rankings in Google's search engine, based on keywords, on a cost-per-click basis.

FIGURE 1-2. Landing Page Offering Free Lead Magnet

New Free e-Book Reveals 30+ Years of Tested B2B Marketing Secrets

Since 1979, freelance copywriter Bob Bly has written hundreds of winning B2B promotions – including landing pages, white papers, e-mail marketing campaigns, ads, and sales letters – for over 100 clients including IBM, AT&T, Praxair, Associated Global Systems, Intuit, Ingersoll-Rand, and Medical Economics.

Now, in Bob's 167-page e-book *The Business-to-Business Marketing Handbook,* you'll discover 30+ years of tested B2B marketing secrets, including:

Yours FREE – Bob Bly's B2B Marketing Handbook!

- 10 tips for increasing landing page conversion rates – page 10.
- The 6 key components of effective B2B offers – page 19.
- What's working in e-mail marketing today?—page 112.
- 7 tips for more effective content marketing—page 78.
- Best practices for B2B lead generation—page 54.
- 4 steps to writing SEO copy that both your prospects and the search engines will love—page 49.
- 5 ways to build a large and responsive e-list of prospects--page 29.
- How to write technically accurate copy for high-tech products -- page 143.
- And more....

To see whether you qualify for a FREE copy of The Business-to-Business Marketing Handbook, just fill in the form below and click submit now:

*=Required field

* Please send me:
☐ FREE copy of The Business-to-Business Marketing Handbook.
☐ FREE Copywriting Information Kit with details on Bob's copywriting services including a fee schedule.
☐ FREE no-obligation estimate for a copywriting project.

* Name:

* Title:

* Company:

* Website URL:

* E-mail Address:

* Phone

* Verify BDD85

Submit!

Bob Bly | Copywriter/Consultant | 31 Cheyenne Dr., Montville, NJ 07045 |
Phone: 973-263-0562 | www.bly.com | E-mail: rwbly@bly.com

It could cost you as little as a dime a click or more than a dollar a click, depending on the popularity of the keywords you want to buy. If the cost of a keyword is 30 cents per click, and 100 people click on your site that day as a result of a Google search on the keyword you bought, Google charges you $30. You can limit how much you spend per day, so the cost can fit any budget.

2. *Affiliate marketing.* Find websites that cater to the same market you do, and arrange for them to feature your products on their site

and in their emails. Online ads, email blurbs, and web pages talking about your product link to your site, where the user can purchase the product. In return, the affiliate receives a percentage of the sale, ranging from 15 percent to 50 percent. To recruit affiliates or to make money as an affiliate for other marketers, visit Document76 http://www.affiliatesdirectory.com/.

3. *Co-registration.* In co-registration marketing, a website visitor is served a pop-up window containing a number of special offers; most frequently these are subscriptions to free online newsletters (ezines). By arranging to have your ezine or another offer featured in these co-registration pop-ups, you can capture many new names for your online database at a relatively low cost compared with traditional email marketing. Many digital ad agencies can arrange co-registration deals for you as part of their media buy.

4. *Web-hosted ads.* Including ads on related websites is a reliable way to drive traffic to your own site. Banner ads, inline ads within the text frame, and slide-in ads are just some of the web ad options available to marketers in the ever-crowded online landscape. In an attempt to recapture the attention of the overloaded internet user, animation and other visual effects in online ads have become more sophisticated and dynamic. Banner, inline, and slide-in ads can work but should be tested conservatively and cautiously, and don't get your hopes too high. These types of ads usually supplement other traffic generation methods and are only occasionally a primary source of unique visits. Are there exceptions? Of course.

5. *Email marketing.* Sending individual promotional emails to a rent-ed list of names is an expensive way to acquire new subscribers. Say you rent a list of 1,000 email addresses for $200, get a 2 percent clickthrough rate, and 10 percent of those sign up for your ezine. Your acquisition cost for those two new subscribers is a whopping $100 each. B2C marketers have a better chance of success with careful testing of email marketing, however, since consumer lists are more reasonably priced than B2B ones.

6. *Online ads.* Although sending a solo email to a company's elist can run $100 to $400 per thousand names, a less expensive option is

to run a small online ad in their ezine. The cost can be as little as $20 to $40 per thousand names. The ezine publisher specifies the format and length of your ad, which typically run 100 words long with one URL link. The higher up (i.e., earlier) your ad appears in the ezine, the higher the response will be. Some ezine publishers charge higher insertion rates for ads high up in the newsletter or in other premium positions or sizes.

7. *Viral marketing.* At its simplest, viral marketing entails adding a line to your outgoing email marketing messages that says, "Please feel free to forward this email to your friends so they can enjoy this special offer." To work, the email must contain a special offer, either a free offer (typically free content) or a discount on merchandise. According to Bryan Heathman, CEO of Made for Success Publishing and author of *Conversion Marketing*, 81 percent of viral email recipients will pass the email on to at least one other person.

And there are many other cost-effective ways to get hits on your site, including:

- Postcards
- Sales letters
- Print ads
- Enewsletter ads
- Pay-per-click ads
- Retargeted ads
- Blogs
- Social media ads
- Social media posts
- Press releases
- Articles
- Webinars
- Podcasts
- Facebook-boosted posts and ads

You should test to determine which channels drive the most qualified prospects to your landing page at the lowest cost per click.

Step 8: Fulfill Inquiries

Of course, when a prospect requests the lead magnet, you must fulfill the request promptly. In the pre-internet era, best practices called for fulfilling inquiries within 48 hours, though many companies took much longer. Today you must deliver electronic lead magnets, such as PDF downloads, within seconds or minutes. Physical lead magnets, such as books or DVDs, should be mailed within 24 to 48 hours.

If your goal is just to distribute an ebook, an auto-responder can deliver it automatically and almost instantly to everyone who requests one. However, if your goal is qualified leads, you can review each inquiry manually and deliver the content only to qualified leads, not to unqualified ones, such as your competitors.

Step 9: Follow Up

Though opinions vary, I prefer to require prospects to give both their phone number and their email address to enable salespeople to follow up.

The most effective way to follow up is a phone call. The salesperson should confirm the prospect's receipt of the lead magnet and determine whether they are interested in purchasing or finding out more about the product or service being promoted. If they are, schedule a sales appointment, a phone conversation, or a Skype call (see Step 10).

Step 10: Secure an Appointment or Conversation

Marketers frequently need to be reminded that the ultimate goal of content marketing is not to give away information but to sell something. So eventually, you have to take the next step in the sales process, which is securing an appointment—either in person or on the phone—with the prospect to do some personal selling.

If you've done steps one through nine correctly, you'll have an edge in making that sale, for several reasons. First, by offering a lead magnet, you will have gotten more leads, and thus more sales appointments. The more appointments you have, the more sales you will close.

Second, a well-written white paper or other lead magnet can educate prospects before the sales appointment. So when you have that first conversation with them, they are already predisposed to buying your product.

Third, good content can also anticipate and answer the most common objections prospects are likely to have. When objections are asked and answered before the first sales call, the conversation can focus on positives, because the negatives have already been dealt with and dismissed.

The Hidden Danger of Content Marketing

The one major flaw I see in writers, consultants, and agencies that bill themselves as content marketing specialists is that, although they may be good at creating lots of content, they are often bad at and even afraid of selling, whether via copywriting or in person. Many are also inept at integrating their content into an effective multichannel marketing campaign.

One Fortune 500 technology company I worked with would begin its campaigns with a free content offer. When the lead magnet was delivered, it ended with an offer of more free content. This process went on and on without any effort to move on to the selling stage.

Content is fine, but eventually you have to actually sell something. To quote Thomas Watson, an early CEO of IBM, "Nothing happens until a sale is made." At some point, you have to work up the courage to go beyond handing out free information and sit down with the prospect, make your sales presentation, and ask for the order.

CHAPTER 2

How to Write Compelling Content

C ontent marketing is so much more than just "publishing information." There's way too much information available today. As I've said, your prospects are drowning in information, but they are starved for *knowledge*—ideas for how to solve problems and methods for doing their jobs better. You can add value to your content by not merely presenting information and data, but by analyzing the information and telling the reader what it means.

As shown in Figure 2–1 on page 30, the lowest level of content is pure data. Sometimes there is value in creating content that curates and assembles important subject data in one place, The problem is the reader can get the same or similar data with a quick Google search, so data-based content has limited value or exclusivity.

FIGURE 2-1. Hierarchy of Content Value

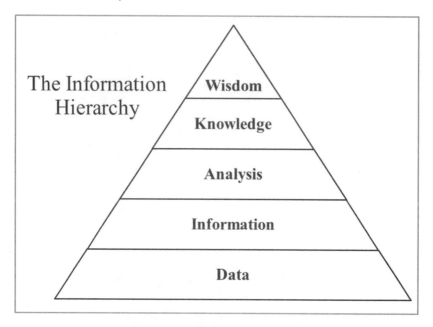

The next level up the content hierarchy is information, examples of which can include what something is, how it works, why it's good, who uses it, and where they use it. More interesting than data, well-crafted informational content can be both useful and engaging to prospects, especially those who are just beginning their search for solutions and need a basic understanding of the topic.

One step up is analysis. Analysis is the interpretation of the meaning, relevance, and significance of the information to your target audience. For instance, if the information is that gold and silver prices move in tandem, the analysis is that because gold prices are rising, silver prices will soon follow.

Knowledge is a deeper understanding of the information and the conclusions reached by the analysis. In our example, the knowledge would be how to take advantage of and profit from a coming bull market in silver predicted by gold moving higher. For instance, should you buy stock in silver mines? Silver coins? Bullion? Silver ETFs? And how can you know whether the current price is low enough to enable a significant profit on your investment or how quickly silver will produce that return?

At the top of the content hierarchy is wisdom, which connotes an extraordinary degree of discernment, insight, and perception. Content with significant wisdom can usually only be prepared by subject matter experts with advanced education and long years of practice and study.

Virtually everyone in a business, industry, or profession has experience and knowledge, but they still find content creation difficult because they withhold their best ideas and methods out of fear prospects will no longer need their services. In fact, the opposite is true. When prospects read truly informative content, it convinces them you know your business, but they lack the skills or experience to feel confident about implementing your ideas. So they conclude that the project is too difficult to do internally and they are better off outsourcing. And to whom do they outsource? The expert who published the content: you.

In this chapter, I'll walk you through some best practices for writing stellar content so you can keep those orders and sales coming in. Let's start with the Five C's.

The Five C's

I love formulas for writing, for two reasons.

First, the best formulas are simple, easy to remember, and rapidly mastered. Knowing them can enable you to create content and copy that's twice as effective in half the time.

Second, the reason they became formulas in the first place is that they work!

Old-timers like me know there are literally dozens of time-tested content and copywriting formulas out there. Yet most of today's newbie marketing writers have only heard of a handful . . . and have mastered even fewer.

Why is that bad? Because if you or your writer doesn't know all the writing formulas, you could be unnecessarily wasting your time reinventing the wheel with each promotion you write. You could also be writing inferior copy that diminishes your sales.

In my day, no self-respecting copywriter or marketer wrote copy without first studying the classic writing formulas and committing them to memory. One of the oldest formulas—and perhaps the most famous—is AIDA. AIDA stands for Attention, Interest, Desire, and Action. It says persuasive copy must first grab the reader's attention, then get them interested in what you are selling, then create a desire to own the product, and finally ask for action.

AIDA is one of my absolute favorite formulas, and I've been using it to write successful promotions for four decades. Even better, it works just as well for content. Yet in seminars today, when I ask attendees whether they know AIDA, not one in ten people raises their hand.

Less well-known than AIDA, but in its way almost as powerful, is the SELWAB formula. SELWAB is a mnemonic device to remind marketers what's most important to the prospect. It stands for "start every letter with a benefit."

Another useful—and little-known—copywriting formula is Star, Chain, and Hook. It says every letter needs a "star" to capture attention, a "chain" to pull readers along through the sales presentation without losing interest, and a "hook" that holds them until they are ready to take action.

Yet another writing formula I use—one I invented—is the Five C's. It says that every good piece of content is clear, concise, compelling, and credible, and has a call to action. Let's take a look at each element of the Five C's formula in a bit more detail.

Clear

Your writing must be clear to everyone who reads it—not just to you or the client or the marketing director or the product manager. There is an oft-quoted saying I like that defines clarity this way: "It is not enough to write so that you can be understood. You must write so that you cannot be misunderstood."

The typical advice given in writing classes about clarity is to use small words and short sentences, paragraphs, and sections. This is sensible, as they make your content easier to read.

But clear writing stems primarily from clear thinking, and the converse is also true. If you don't really understand what you are talking about, your writing will be weak, rambling, and obtuse. On the other hand, when you understand your subject matter, know your audience, and have a useful and important idea you want to convey, the clarity of your writing will inevitably reflect that.

Concise

The key point is that *concise* and *brief* are not synonyms. *Brief* means "short." If you want to be brief, simply cut words until you reduce the composition to the desired length. *Concise* means telling the complete story in the fewest possible words—no rambling, no redundancy, no using three words when one will do.

Compelling

It is not enough to make the content easy to read. It must also be so interesting, engaging, and informative that the reader cannot put it down—or, at minimum, feels compelled to at least skim it to glean the important points.

A major reason why so much content is not compelling is that it is written about things that interest the marketer, not the prospect. Marketers care about their products, their organizations, and in particular their "messaging"—the key points they want to get across to the reader. Unfortunately, readers aren't interested in any of these things. They care about their own problems, needs, fears, concerns, worries, challenges, interests, and desires.

As copywriter Don Hauptman has often said, the more your copy focuses on the prospect instead of the product, the more compelling it will be. The product is only relevant insofar as it addresses one of the reader's core concerns or desires.

Credible

The late copywriter Herschell Gordon Lewis noted that we live in an age of skepticism. Simply put, prospects are disinclined to believe what you say precisely because you are trying to sell them something.

Fortunately, there are a number of useful tools at your disposal for building your credibility and overcoming the reader's skepticism. Your prospects are wary of salespeople but are more inclined to trust advice from recognized experts in a field or industry. Therefore, you can overcome their doubt by establishing yourself or your organization as a thought leader in your market.

One way to do this is by publishing a lot of content. Prospects distrust advertising, but are somewhat more accepting of information sources such as websites, white papers, blogs, and magazine articles. Become an active publisher of valuable content in your niche. Communicate your key messages in documents that are published in editorial formats, such as webcasts and white papers. Not only will your prospects find the messages more credible, but these publications will also accelerate your ascent to subject matter expert (SME) status in your niche.

Another obvious but often overlooked means of building credibility is to offer a strong money-back guarantee and then, when customers ask for refunds, grant them quickly and cheerfully, without question or argument.

Rude, slow, or unresponsive customer service can quickly destroy any credibility you have gained with your customer. In fact, take steps to resolve customer problems beyond what is required so that the customer feels you personally care about them and that they're getting more for their money than they have any right to expect.

> **TIP**
>
> A proven way to build credibility is with customer testimonials. If you are not using them widely and proactively in your marketing, you are missing an easy and effective means of overcoming skepticism. And don't overlook the opportunity to have customers give you video testimonials at your events, especially seminars you are videotaping. Post these video testimonials on your website and landing pages.

Call to Action

A call to action (CTA) tells the readers what action they should take and how to do it. These CTAs can appear throughout the text, or you can put them in a box or sidebar to make them stand out. Common CTAs include:

- Downloading a free white paper or ebook
- Registering for a webinar or teleseminar
- Getting a password to access protected content on a website
- Requesting a free estimate

- Asking to get a phone call from a sales rep
- Purchasing a product online from a shopping cart
- Subscribing to an online newsletter

Convey Sincerity and Enthusiasm

All these elements of the Five C's can help you create winning content. But there are a couple of other huge factors that will help you get your message across.

Jason Stevens, an insurance agent, emailed me his thoughts about sincerity in marketing:

> When I look at the best copywriters, I see a streak of sincerity that is undeniable . . . from [advertising executive] Bruce Barton's old ads through to [advertising icon] Ogilvy's ads and [famed copywriter] Gary Halbert's best pieces . . . which resonates with my own selling experience that says that people want to buy from real people . . . and that the closer we can get to a person-to-person conversation, the more successful the piece will be . . . especially when the offer is legitimately powerful and is truly newsworthy.

In other words, the key to sincerity is to believe in what you are saying. If you have doubts about the claims you're making, do some research to prove that your skepticism is unwarranted. If you find it impossible to change your mind, switch to a different project if you can.

For this reason, I urge you to write for an employer, client, or product you can really get behind. Something you think is cool or interesting, or that can deliver great value to users. Although it can be done, writing about things that bore you or that you don't believe in is arduous and rarely fun. The more enthusiastic you are about a product, the better your copy will be.

These days, I have the luxury, if you will, of picking and choosing my projects—so I pick the ones I am most enthusiastic about. But back in the day when I had to take on some copywriting assignments on products that didn't get me excited initially, I could still write about them with great enthusiasm.

You can, too, and here's the secret: temporary enthusiasm.

You don't have to love every subject, idea, cause, or technology you write about. What you do in such cases is manufacture *temporary enthusiasm*. You learn through experience to find that kernel of interest, even if you are not a regular consumer of the product.

Here are some of the things I use to create the temporary enthusiasm I need to do the best writing job possible:

- Fascinating technology
- Little-known facts
- Good personal chemistry with the client
- Interesting or unusual marketing challenge
- A product or service that is a new idea
- An innovation that is a game changer
- A new methodology or solution for a pressing problem
- Interesting stories
- News
- Human interest

TIP

Your indifference to or disdain for a product risks you writing indifferent copy. Life is too short to work on projects you loathe.

Of course, if the topic is something you are naturally interested in, your enthusiasm is already present, and does not have to be generated through deliberate effort.

The technique of creating temporary enthusiasm allows you to write the content as if you did love the subject. The attitude only has to last as long as it takes to complete the assignment. After that, it can recede until you need to call on it again.

As for using temporary enthusiasm on products, ideas, and beliefs you actively dislike, I don't do that. Instead, I pass on the project. For instance, early in my career I was offered a lucrative assignment by a book publisher who needed five direct-mail packages to sell five different books. I love books, but when I asked what they were about, the client replied, "Hunting."

Now, I don't think hunting is immoral. If someone wants to hunt, they should go hunt. But because I find it personally unappealing, I knew there was no way I could write strong copy for it. I turned down the job.

Contrarian Content

On the opposite side of sincerity and enthusiasm lies contrarianism. This technique lies in being deliberately controversial: getting attention for yourself, your business, or your product or service by focusing on an emotional, important, or timely issue in your content—and taking sides. It works best if you disagree with popular opinion. Or, as author F. Scott Fitzgerald put it: "The cleverly expressed opposite of any generally accepted human idea is worth a fortune."

Marketing expert Marcia Yudkin gives us a great example of this principle in action. She writes about Bob Baker, who—with three colleagues in the music business—collaborated on a press release titled "What's Wrong with *American Idol*?"

"Their press release," Yudkin writes, "criticized the popular U.S. talent show for misleading aspiring musicians and the public about what it takes to succeed in music. Baker's reward for stirring up controversy: five radio interviews that highlighted his status as an expert on careers in music."

So how can you use this principle in your PR to get media attention? Yudkin suggests taking issue with a survey result, disagreeing with a common belief, counteracting a stereotype, championing an underdog, exposing flaws in something assumed to be beneficial, or describing the dark underside of something popular.

For example, when desktop publishing software became widely available, thousands of businesspeople gained the tools needed to design their own documents. During that time, a graphic design consultant self-published a little book titled *The Awful Truth about Desktop Publishing*. His premise was that amateurs who used the software without proper training in design fundamentals risked producing sloppy, amateurish documents. It gained him significant publicity as well as a number of paid speaking engagements.

In marketing, a lot of consultants make a living selling unsuspecting clients on the hot new technology of the month—sometimes referred to as *bright shiny objects* (BSOs)—even if the technology is unproven and has not generated significant ROI for any of their clients.

Many years ago, I wrote an article for the trade newspaper of the direct-marketing industry, saying that blogs were an unproven marketing medium and nothing to get excited about. Not knowing how many new media evangelists there are, I was completely surprised when my article generated a massive debate in the blogosphere (with most people saying I didn't "get" blogging). Tad Clarke, who was at the time editor in chief of *DM News*, said it generated the most reader response of any article they published that year.

What I discovered (or, more accurately, rediscovered, since I had known it but forgotten it) was the corollary to Fitzgerald's rule about controversy being profitable. I am sure you've heard it many times before: "*Any* publicity is good publicity."

And it's true: If you come out on one side of an issue, half the market will revile you. But the other half will think you're wise beyond your years and strive to do business with you.

Should you worry about half the market rejecting you because of your controversial opinions? Well, if half think you're all wet, and half think you walk on water, that's a 50 percent market share. I'll take that any day of the week.

For the suggested length of blog posts and other online content, see Table 2–1, on page 39.

The Content Writing Process

When you are writing content as part of a team, the project typically has definite steps, some of which are laid out in the content writing flowchart (see Figure 2–2, on page 40). As the writer, I begin by gathering source material on the topic. Today, you can find what seems like an almost infinite amount of content on the web on almost any subject. For instance, I just searched "time management," and instantly found 4.76 billion sources on the web that cover or at least mention time management.

So the idea that you need to read everything in existence on your subject is patently absurd. Instead, be selective. Scan through articles and web pages until you find half a dozen or so that give you what you're looking for.

When you are writing for your employer or a client, they may provide a lot of the source material you need, both from content they have previously published as well as content they have collected. As you read

TABLE 2-1. Word Count for Common Content Pieces

Type of Content	Length
Blog posts (for search engine ranking)	1,500 words
Email subject lines (for open rates)	50 characters or less
Line of text	12 words
Paragraph	4 lines or less
YouTube video (for views)	3 to 3.5 minutes
Podcast	22 minutes
Title tags	55 characters
Meta description	155 characters (maximum)
Facebook post (for likes and shares)	100–140 characters
Tweets (for retweets)	280 characters
Domain name	8 characters or less

Source: *Everybody Writes: Your Go-To Guide to Creating Ridiculously Good Content*, by Ann Handley, Wiley, 2014, p.184

the source material, keep a list of questions that occur to you. Typically your client will arrange to have one or more SMEs provide answers and clarification.

Once you have all the information you need, write a first draft. When you finish, the boss, client, or SME reviews it for technical accuracy.

After you correct any technical errors and add any important missing information, submit the draft to one or more reviewers for approval. These might include the company owner or CEO, product manager, and marketing manager. Make any requested revisions, and the revised document is again reviewed, with the aim of finishing the document and signing off on it.

Once the finished draft is approved, and depending on the format (white paper, data sheet, infographic) and the topic, a graphic designer or someone with desktop publishing skills puts it into a layout. The last step is reproduction, and the method of duplication depends on the size, color, graphics, audience, and number of copies needed (if you are printing physical copies). An internal report for your ten team members can be run off on your printer or copier. A 500-page product guide would go to an offset or print-on-demand (POD) printer. Or you can always choose to go paperless and keep it as a PDF file.

FIGURE 2-2. Content Writing Process Flowchart

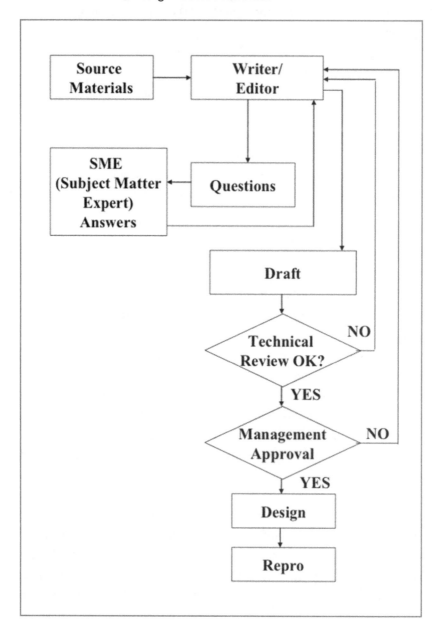

PROOFREADING YOUR CONTENT

Here are seven steps you should take when having your content proofread, based on a list originally published by freelance editor and writer Mark Nichol:

1. Use a checklist, grammar book, or style guide to ensure correct usage of grammar, punctuation, technical terms, and numbering.

2. Ask an SME to fact-check, especially for technical data accuracy, equations, and numbers.

3. Spell check using your computer. However, keep in mind that the spell-checker often does not recognize technical terms. So use an industry-specific dictionary as well.

4. Read the document aloud. This enables you to catch errors you might gloss over when reading silently or that the spell-checker may get wrong.

5. Proofread backwards. This makes you focus on one word at a time, which helps you catch typos you might otherwise skim over.

6. Check formatting, including page numbering, headers and footers, column alignment, typefaces, fonts, footnotes, and captions.

7. Have someone else proofread the document: a colleague, your spouse, or a professional proofreader.

Treasure Your Company's Content Gold Mine

For content writers and marketers, content you have already created and own is solid gold. Much of that content is locked away in your brain in the form of experience, skill, knowledge, and memory. Naturally, your recall and retrieval is imperfect.

But in the digital age, a lot of your knowledge is documented in writing: in emails, enewsletters, blog posts, tweets, articles, books, reports, PowerPoint presentations, and any other written content you have created.

Unlike the content in your brain, your written content can be retrieved in its accurate and original condition, provided it is stored in a manner that allows you to find it quickly, and in a format that makes it easy to use in your new writings.

If content is gold on the internet, your hard drives, network storage devices, and cloud-based data storage are the gold mine. Here are eight tips for using your digital content gold mine to your advantage:

1. Create a digital filing system, with directories and subdirectories organized in a manner that is logical and intuitive to you, regardless of whether it is to others.

2. When you create a document, type the file name in the upper-left corner of the first page. That way, when you have a hard copy, you will know the file name and can quickly search for and retrieve the electronic version from your drives.

3. Save any content related to your niche that you think might be useful someday. This includes your own writings as well as content from outside sources.

4. Always indicate on the file the date the content was created and, if taken from an outside source, details on the source (e.g., name of publication, issue date, page numbers, author, title). Without this information, you may not be able to use the material.

5. Convert materials you may want to use into file formats that are easy to paste into Word documents; for example, charts and graphs from PowerPoints.

6. When you acquire source documents, print and save the document in a file cabinet, but also save the electronic version so you can capture images (charts, graphs, photos, and diagrams) to use in your own writing. Of course you need the author's permission; you can credit them in footnotes or endnotes.

7. When in doubt, clip and save material you might want to refer to someday, but don't be like the infamous Collyer brothers, who saved every newspaper they ever bought in their Manhattan brownstone until it became a rat-infested fire hazard. (One brother died from starvation and the other was crushed when a stack of old newspapers fell on him.) When you want to save something, tear it out and save just the clipping. Make sure the publication name, date, and pages are noted on the clipping, and scan it to save it as a digital file. Similarly, for online content such as articles and posts, print them out and store the hard copy in binders.

8. Back up your entire hard drive to a mirror device (a duplicate hard drive or to the cloud) every 24 hours. I automatically set mine to back up in the middle of the night.

> **TIP**
>
> Your customers are not reading your content for your dazzling prose style. They are reading it for the valuable problem-solving information you provide. To make your writing more useful to these readers, you need solid content. Even if you are a subject matter expert yourself, your writing will be stronger when you augment your own knowledge with additional material. That's why every serious content writer must research and accumulate facts, knowledge, methods, strategies, and ideas to share with their readers.

Content Recycling and Repurposing

One shortcut to keeping up with the constant demand for new content is to recycle and repurpose what you have already created from your content gold mine. *Recycling* means using the same piece of content in different places and ways. *Repurposing* means editing or rewriting the content to update it, give it new life, and allow it to be used in a new campaign.

I have recycled and repurposed much of my content, including transforming:

- trade journal articles into multiple books, ebooks, and special reports
- back issues of my enewsletter into more books
- enewsletter articles into blog posts
- Facebook posts into enewsletter articles
- live presentations into audio and video information products
- webinars into streaming video content
- out-of-print books into ebooks and special reports
- white papers into multiple shorter content pieces

Copywriter Gordon Graham suggest extracting and repurposing content from your white papers:

- Chop it up into three to five blog posts.
- Create an infographic that covers the main points.
- Turn the white paper's content into a slide deck.
- Offer a free webinar based on that slide deck.
- Record the webinar and post it on the web.
- Promote each piece on social media.

All these pieces can be quickly extracted from the original white paper. With minimal research and writing, you get many new pieces of content, all in different mediums, for different channels.

Your content has more than just one life. What other ways can you think of to repurpose content for a bigger audience?

If you create small bits of fresh, relevant content with the latest information every day, you will have plenty of raw material you can easily assemble into various formats.

Writing a 20-page white paper is not easy, but writing short bits of content is quicker and simpler. You can get into this habit by creating a daily or weekly schedule for writing short blog posts, social media posts, and enewsletters, for starters.

The Four Types of Content by Topic and Timeliness

There are four types of content that can be used effectively in your content marketing program: evergreen information, time-sensitive information, branding, and product advances and applications, including case studies. Your ratio should probably lean in favor of the first two types.

1. *Evergreen* means content that doesn't get dated, at least for many years. In the health niche, for instance, examples include the benefits of daily exercise, proper diet, and regular checkups with your doctor. These can be effective as long as they subtly help sell your concept and product, usually but not always early in the buying cycle. For a diabetes product, for example, early evergreen content might talk about the dangers of eating too many carbs because they convert to blood sugar in your body.

    Evergreen content might need updating every now and then, but should stay useful for a long period of time. Some content providers deliver huge amounts of evergreen materials, such as bridal magazines (how many different ways can you write about selecting a wedding cake?).

2. *Time-sensitive* means the content ties into current news, preferably the breaking news of the day. In email marketing, we find a tie-in with major news stories almost always increases open and click-through rates.

3. *Branding* contains messages, some subtle and some more explicit, that educate readers why your approach to the problem your product solves is the right one. For example, diabetics should eat one piece of fruit a day rather than drink fruit juice, since one glass of juice contains the sugar content of five to seven pieces of fruit.

4. *Product advances and applications* are more explicit about how your product or the method of making it specifically reduces or even eliminates the problem. This should be a mix of content and sales copy so it doesn't come across as too much of a hard sell.

How to Work with Experts

Often content writers gather information by interviewing engineers, scientists, doctors, and other technical SMEs. If you are not a techie yourself, this can be a challenging process.

I know of three ways to make technical interviews easier and more successful. First, gather background material, study it thoroughly, and make a list of questions about anything you don't understand.

Second, when techies talk tech, they often speak rapidly, so back up your written notes by recording the conversation. Handheld digital recorders work for face-to-face interviews. For phone interviews, use a conference service such as FreeConferenceCall.com, which offers the option of recording the call. Then hire a transcriptionist to convert the audio file to a written document.

Third, if the SME is distant and travel is either impractical or avoidable, you can conduct the interview with incremental emails, in which you ask one question per email, and the SME replies with an email answering your question. Because the SME took the time to write, the information is usually clearer, more complete, and easier to extract than in an interview. I cut and paste each email answer into the Word document in which I have recorded and compiled my notes.

If you have a technical background, tell the SME this when you introduce yourself. I have found that knowing they are talking to a fellow techie puts the SME more at ease and produces more complete answers. When they give an answer you do not understand, ask for more explanation.

A Collaboration Trick for Working with Senior Management

In addition to interviewing SMEs, also ask brand managers, product managers, marketing managers, and even C-suite executives for a few minutes of their time. Many are too busy to work on content, but others are eager to communicate their plans, visions, and ideas.

When you interview executives and senior managers, your content will reflect

TIP

The SMEs can give you technical knowledge, but the C-level executives give you the "big picture" view. How does this content help the company achieve its strategic goals in response, branding, positioning, and sales? What key points does management want to communicate? These may be points the SMEs are unaware of. By talking to technical SMEs, sales, marketing, *and* top management, you get a more well-rounded briefing. You master both the facts and the strategy so your content better supports the marketing objectives of the campaign.

their views and objectives. This, and the fact that you asked for their opinions, makes them happier with your content and more likely to approve it quickly and with a minimum of edits. They get what they want, and you shorten the rewrite process considerably. You also form a stronger relationship with senior executives so they see you more as a valuable resource than as a low-level scribe.

Implied Content

Remember the Duncan Hines ad I told you about? The headline was: "The secret to moister, richer chocolate cake." It hinted you would gain useful knowledge just by reading the ad: a chocolate cake recipe. When you did read the ad, you discovered the secret was to use Duncan Hines cake mix. Why was that headline so effective? Because it *implied* you would learn something useful just by reading the ad, regardless of whether you bought the product.

Are people put off by implied content? In my experience, no. The editorial nature of the headline prepares them to learn something, and whether the ad is content or copy, they usually do—in this case, how to save time and effort, and how to make a better cake by using a prepared mix.

In a B2B ad selling filters for processing plants, this headline had an editorial and educational feel: "How to Keep Your Products Pure." The ad then explained the best way to maintain purity was to use the company's filters and described the superior design that made them more effective than their competitors'. Yes, it was actually a sales ad, not a content piece. But again, not only did it sell the filter, but it also explained the new design and showed how it could increase yield and ensure product purity in the plant.

Storytelling

Storytelling has been used in marketing for many decades, in part because stories get attention: People love to read and hear stories. "Charts, facts, and figures make good proof, but they don't motivate people," says internet marketing coach Terry Dean. "You can show them charts until their eyes glaze over, but they won't take action on them. Facts simply won't give them momentum to get moving. You have to use true, authentic stories if you want to cut through all the clutter, through the noise, and speak directly to people's hearts."

Public speaking coach Dr. Jim Anderson writes, "The way to convince the skeptic is not through logic. They'll always come up with a way to not believe what you are telling them. Instead, you need to find a way to win their hearts first."

And Stefanie Flaxman, editor in chief of Copyblogger, says that stories are the way to readers' hearts: "Information is simultaneously too much and not enough. Information is impotent to reach the hearts and minds of those who want to run with your idea, product, or service. Story, on the other hand, is virile, rare, unforgettable. And when well-crafted, more true than the mere statement of plain facts."

In a 2019 article in *Target Marketing* magazine, marketing expert Chris Foster identified three types of stories that help build brand awareness: functional, emotional, and moral:

1. *Functional stories* relate how the product or service makes things better, easier, quicker, and faster for a customer. For example, TV commercials for AAA often show a frustrated person stranded by the side of the road with a flat tire or dead battery. But as an AAA member, she makes one phone call that summons immediate assistance and gets the problem fixed so she can continue on her way.

2. *Emotional stories* in marketing are all around us. For instance, the nonprofit humanitarian group Children's International (CI), in its fundraising direct mail, tells the detailed personal story of one impoverished child and how your small donation can dramatically improve their life. In fact, the story is made more real through the marketing: When you donate, you can sponsor a real child, who sends you letters about her life and how your generosity gave her family better shelter, healthy food, clean water, and, for her, an education.

3. *Moral stories* help brands empower you to do good, help others, and make a difference. 4Ocean sells bracelets made from recycled glass and plastic, and for every bracelet you buy, they help fight pollution and protect marine life by removing a pound of plastic from the oceans.

Internet marketing coach Terry Dean shared some thoughts on this topic with me and offered three suggestions to make your stories more compelling and effective:

1. *Is there a story you can share that illustrates your message?* It could be a personal case study or a case study from one of your clients. Or it could be a story about a lesson you learned when you were growing up. Keep your eyes and ears open for the stories that happen all around you: at the restaurant, at the beach, wherever you go. Whenever an idea strikes you, record a voice memo or make a note on your phone. Or you could even go old school and write it in a notebook. When it comes time to write, you'll have a list of ideas and stories to choose from. We live in a culture that is enamored with celebrity. Tell your story. You can be a celebrity no one has ever heard of outside your industry. Get the benefits of fame without the paparazzi.

2. *What contrarian advice can you share?* What mistakes, myths, and misconceptions are common in your market? What are the gurus lying about? What makes you so upset about your industry that you just can't keep quiet about it anymore? In some cases, you may be the only one talking about this. And that's fine. Is there an underlying frustration in your market you can tap into? What truths can you expose to the light? You'll draw an audience when they see you as an individual voice instead of just another echo.

3. *What value can you bring to people's lives?* Filling your head with a bunch of knowledge (i.e., content) doesn't do a lot of good on its own. Sometimes it can even be a problem. If you're stuck in analysis paralysis because there are so many options of shareable information in front of you, adding even more content to the mix isn't going to fix it. Maybe you just need to start with one simple, straightforward piece of content and figure out the rest as you go.

Do these stories have to be true? I cannot give legal advice, but I can say that they must be factually correct. If you say customer X reduced their energy costs by 25 percent using your system, you had better have the documentation to back up that claim, or at least a signed written approval of the content from someone employed by customer X in a professional or management position.

As Terry said, think about how you're bringing value to people's lives. Value is more than content—it's also about inspiration and motivation. Help your audience act in their own best interest.

Curated Content

Curated content is existing content—created either by someone else or by you in the past for other marketing communications or for reference works—which you would like to use as your own content.

I rarely use already-published content "as is" as the basis for my curated content. Instead, I add more information, more recent statistics and facts, and more detail to clarify the concept and its value and use.

For instance, I published an ebook version of Claude Hopkins' classic book *Scientific Advertising,* originally released in 1923, which is now in the public domain. Others have made copies of *Scientific Advertising* available for free download. But unlike them, I expanded mine with updated content. These included copies of ads illustrating his principles, sidebars giving more how-to instructions for implementing his advice, and other

> **TIP**
>
> Your safest course of action is to write to the copyright holder and get written permission to use it in a work you specify in your permission request. Signed permission from the copyright holder is usually but not always sufficient protection to guard you against charges of plagiarism and copyright violation. When you have written permission, you may use the curated content, but only in the manner specified in the signed permission letter.

documents by Hopkins that have rarely been seen. I called the book *Scientific Advertising: Annotated and Illustrated*; while the core is curated, it has been expanded to add value to the original. And you can only get this edition from me.

I cannot give legal advice on the use of copyrighted material, which may include fiction and nonfiction writing, poetry, music, videos, graphics, and artwork; however the topic is addressed in Appendix A.

Some content managers using curated content reprint the text and graphics in their entirety in white papers, on websites, and in other media. More often, though, curated content is only a small part of a longer document where the content is original to you. You can enhance curated content by adding explanations, examples, illustrations, graphs, photos, and commentary that illuminate the curated material and make it more meaningful or clearer to your readers.

Content Syndication

Content syndication refers to posting or linking to your downloadable content (such as white papers, ebooks, webinars, videos, case studies, and articles) on third-party sites and ad networks. The metrics by which content syndication success is measured are cost per lead, lead quality, and the rate at which leads are generated.

The syndicated content is most often placed on a "gated" download page, meaning the user has to enter some personal information—at minimum, name and email address—to download your content.

The advantage of syndication is your content is seen by fresh traffic—the visitors to the third-party site—most of whom would otherwise never encounter it. And by putting it behind a gated page, you capture new names and email addresses and grow your list with a fresh crop of new subscribers.

Some third-party site owners may accept a content swap: They display your white paper on their site, and in exchange you offer their content on yours. In cases where the other party has no interest in swapping, they will most likely charge you

TIP

Do not ask for too much information about the prospect on your registration form. Rather, the sales copy on the download page can to a degree qualify leads for you. If the headline is a free white paper on how to make product prototypes on 3D printers, only people working in design or manufacturing would be likely to download it.

a performance-based fee: You pay a small fee per click or per lead your content gets from their site.

Syndication partners rarely ask for an exclusive deal to post your content on their site, and if they don't ask, don't offer. You want to get your content offer on as many relevant sites as possible. For white papers, one of the bigger syndication sites is Bitpipe (https://www.bitpipe.com).

Setting Expectations for Your Content Team

In the 21st century, many vendors and employees are under increasing pressure to deliver a product or service of top quality, fast, and for the lowest possible price. Content writers are no exception, as shown in Figure 2–3 below.

The problem is that in most cases it is not feasible for vendors to deliver on all three promises. If you work cheap and fast, your product is

FIGURE 2-3. The Triad of Requirements for Content Writers

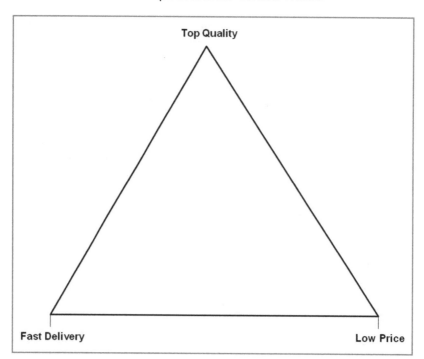

unlikely to be the best quality. And if you deliver premium products and services while meeting extremely tight delivery schedules, you will want to (and should) charge a premium price. If you deliver a product with perfection and care, your price is likely to be higher and you cannot do it quickly, because it takes more time to make.

In the 1970s, many workplaces displayed posters showing the triangle seen in Figure 2–3. The caption simply said "Pick any two."

But because so many executives and professionals view writing as a commodity instead of a valuable skill or profession, they expect their content writers to deliver all three points on the content triangle: high quality, fast turnaround, and cheap prices. This is seldom possible in any activity, and if you attempt it, the work will be subpar, the deadline blown, and the budget exceeded.

Why do content writers, in the words of Rodney Dangerfield, get no respect? Unfortunately, writers are often low on the totem pole in the corporate world, and content writers are near the bottom of that pole, kept there by the false notion that "anyone can write."

True, the vast majority of people can write. But only a few can write *well*, which is one reason we need professional writers and editors. The other reason is that for many corporate employees and entrepreneurs, writing is not the highest and best use of their time. Calling on staff writers or freelancers to do the writing for them allows them to focus on their core business competencies.

If your primary job function is something other than writing, these are the expectations you should be prepared to meet:

- ◉ Be able to write your own content when needed.
- ◉ Evaluate the skills, experience, and work of content writers.
- ◉ Review content submitted to you by others with a more objective and educated eye.

On the other hand, if you are a professional writer, the expectation is that you are capable of creating content that is clear, engaging, and fresh, and that supports important aspects of your marketing campaigns, including SEO, customer education, brand awareness, and increasing click rates, conversions, and other important metrics.

More Tips for Making Your Content Easy to Read

This section offers some more juicy tips on making your copy reader-friendly.

Avoid Big Words

Technical writers sometimes prefer to use big, important-sounding words instead of short, simple words. This is a mistake; fancy language just frustrates the reader. Write in plain, ordinary English, and your readers will love you for it.

Here are a few big words that appear frequently in content; the column on the right presents simpler options:

Big Word	Substitution
terminate	end
utilize	use
incombustible	fireproof
substantiate	prove

Use Shorter Sentences

Shorter sentences are easier and more inviting to read than long sentences. How do you know whether a sentence is too long? Use the "breath test."

How it works: Without taking in extra breath, read the sentence aloud at a normal conversational volume and speed. If you run out of breath before you get to the end of the sentence, the sentence is too long.

Solution: Read the sentence again. As soon as you come to a place where a new idea is introduced, break the sentence into two or more shorter sentences. For example:

Lengthy sentence:
Systems shall be established and maintained that provide control of all functions affecting the quality of raw materials, supplies, services, and products to assure conformance to order, code, and specification requirements.

<u>Broken into two shorter sentences:</u>

Systems shall be established and maintained that provide control of all functions affecting the quality of raw materials, supplies, services, and products. Their purpose is to assure conformance to order, code, and specification requirements.

Prefer the Specific to the General

B2B readers are interested in detailed technical information—facts, figures, conclusions, recommendations. Do not simply say something is good, bad, fast, or slow when you can say *how* good, *how* bad, *how* fast, or *how* slow. Be specific whenever possible.

General	Specific
a tall spray dryer	a 40-foot-tall spray dryer
plant	oil refinery
unit	evaporator
unfavorable weather conditions	rain
structural degradation	a leaky roof
high performance	95% efficiency

Break the Writing Up into Short Sections and Paragraphs

Long, unbroken blocks of text intimidate and bore readers. Breaking up your writing into short sections and paragraphs makes it easier to read.

In the same way, short sentences are easier to grasp than long ones. As noted, a good guide for keeping sentence length under control is to write sentences that can be spoken aloud without losing your breath (do *not* take a deep breath before doing this test).

Find an Organizational Scheme that Fits the Material

Poor organization stems from poor planning. Computer programmers would never think of writing a complex program without first drawing a flowchart, but they'd probably knock out a draft of a user manual without making notes or an outline. In the same way, a builder who requires detailed blueprints before he lays the first brick will write a letter without really considering his message, audience, or purpose.

TIP

Before you write, plan. Create a rough outline that spells out the contents and organization of your paper or report.

Your outline need not be formal. A simple list, doodles, or rough notes will do. Use whatever form suits you. If the format isn't strictly defined by the type of document, publication, or editor you are writing for, select the organizational scheme that best fits the material. Some common formats include:

- *Order of location.* An article on the planets of the solar system might begin with Mercury (the planet nearest the sun) and end with Neptune (the planet farthest out).
- *Order of increasing difficulty.* Instruction manuals often start with the easiest material and, as the user masters basic principles, move on to more complex operations.
- *Alphabetical order.* A to Z is a logical way to arrange a booklet on vitamins (vitamin A, B, B1, and so on) or a directory of company employees.
- *Chronological order.* This presents the facts in the order in which they happened. History books are generally written this way. So are many case histories, feature stories, and corporate biographies.
- *Problem/solution.* This is another format appropriate for case histories and many other types of reports. The problem/solution format begins with "Here's what the problem was" and ends with "Here's how we solved it."
- *Inverted pyramid.* The inverted pyramid style of news reporting has the lead paragraph summarize the most important points of the story, and the following paragraphs present the facts in order of decreasing importance. You can use this format in journal articles, letters, memos, and reports.
- *Deductive order.* Start with a generalization, then support it with particulars. Scientists use this format in research papers that begin with the findings and then state the supporting evidence.

- *Inductive order.* Begin with specific instances, and then lead the reader to the idea or principles the instances suggest. This is an excellent way to approach trade journal feature stories.
- *List.* A list article might be titled "Six Tips for Designing Wet Scrubbers" or "Seven Ways to Reduce Your Plant's Electric Bill."

Use the Active Voice

In the active voice, action is expressed directly: "John performed the experiment." In the passive voice, the action is indirect: "The experiment was performed by John."

When possible, use the active voice. Your writing will be more direct and vigorous; your sentences, more concise. As you can see in the samples below, the passive voice seems puny and stiff by comparison:

Passive Voice	Active Voice
Control of the bearing-oil supply is provided by the shutoff valves.	Shutoff valves control the bearing-oil supply.
Leaking of the seals is prevented by the use of O-rings.	O-rings keep the seals from leaking.
Fuel-cost savings were realized through the installation of thermal insulation.	The installation of thermal insulation cut fuel costs.

Copywriting 101 for Content Writers

Virtually all multichannel campaigns today combine content marketing with copywriting, so a content marketer or writer should learn at least the fundamentals of copywriting. Below are a few tips to get you started.

Write a Killer Headline

The headline is the first thing your reader sees and the most important part of the promotion. The headline's main job is to get the prospect's attention in a way that makes them want to know more about what you are selling. The more specific your headline, the stronger it will be. In his classic book *Scientific Advertising*, Claude Hopkins wrote, "Platitudes and generalities roll off the human understanding like water from a duck." Ford had little success with its "Quality Is Job One" campaign—because *quality* is about as general as you can get. By comparison, David Ogilvy's classic ad for Rolls-Royce, created in the late 1950s, worked because it was specific; many consider it one of the greatest car ads ever written. The headline: "At 60 miles an hour the loudest noise in this new Rolls-Royce comes from the electric clock." (When an engineer at Rolls-Royce saw the ad, he commented, "It's about time we did something about that damn clock!")

Put the Prospect First

Don't start with the product—its features, quality, craftsmanship, and design. Start with the *prospect*—their needs, desires, fears, concerns, problems, headaches, and dreams. People care much more about themselves than about you, your company, or your product. They are only interested in what your product can do for them.

Stress the Benefits

A *feature* is something the product is or has; a *benefit* is what that feature does to help the user. For instance, a watering can has a spout; that is a feature. The spout allows you to direct water to the houseplant so you don't spill it all over the windowsill or table—that is a benefit. Buyers need to know both features and benefits, but benefits are usually more important. Copywriters are told that every consumer listens to a radio station in their head with the call letters WIIFM, which stands for "What's in it for me?" Car manufacturers used to advertise "rack-and-pinion steering" in automobile brochures, but no one understood what it was or what it did—so it had no impact on sales. By comparison, Michelin tire TV spots showed a cute baby sitting inside a Michelin tire. The message was clear: The technology in our tires can keep your family safe when you drive.

Find the Product's USP

Even if your product offers great benefits, so do your competitors' products. You need to tell consumers why your product is different and better than the competition. This is called the *unique selling proposition*, or USP. For instance, holding a piece of chocolate for any length of time will cause it to melt. M&M's solved this problem by placing a hard candy coating around the chocolate. Its USP is now famous: "M&M's melt in your mouth, not in your hand."

Most people know that when you get to the bottom of a pot of coffee, the dregs are bitter, and you should make a fresh pot. Maxwell House claimed it had developed a coffee that stayed fresh-tasting from the first cup in the pot to the last. Its USP: "Good to the last drop."

Give Proof

When you make a claim in advertising, the more proof you back up that claim with, the more believable and effective your advertising will be. For instance, years ago, Krazy Glue claimed its glue was far stronger than other glues. To prove it, a man wearing a hard hat put a drop of glue on top of the hat and pressed it against a T-shaped platform above him. The glue held the hat firm while the man dangled in midair below. Another example of proof can be seen in commercials for various cleaning products, such as sponge mops, stain removers, and cleaning fluids. Two dirty surfaces are treated side by side, with the product being advertised and a competitor. The surface treated with the advertised product comes out clean and shiny, while the competitor's surface is still somewhat dingy. With paper towels, the advertised towel absorbs more fluid, while the competing product can't handle the spill and falls apart.

Remember Your Primary Objective

For your copy to truly succeed, it must persuade consumers to part with their hard-earned money and buy your client's product or service. Selling should be your number-one priority at all times.

Establish Value

Even if you convince consumers that a product delivers benefits they desire, is superior to other brands, and does what you say it will do, one problem remains: persuading them they need the product badly enough to part with their hard-earned cash. In essence, you need to demonstrate that the price you are charging is a pittance compared to the incredible value the product delivers. Here's an example: Your client sells a thermostat that can cut energy bills by 10 percent. Your prospect's monthly gas and electric bill is $300, so a 10 percent reduction is a $30 savings. If the device costs $30, it will pay back its own cost within a month, and give them an ROI of more than 10-to-1 within a year.

Ask for Action

After reading the copy, what do we want the prospect to do next? The next step may be to request a free estimate, visit the dealer's showroom, or apply for a mortgage over the phone. Identify the next step, and, in your copy, tell the prospect to take it. If you don't tell people what to do next, they'll do nothing.

Give a Gift

Free is the most powerful word in the English language. People love free stuff. Giving a gift with an order is a proven response booster. For example, if you are selling subscriptions to a magazine on personal finance, you can get more orders by offering a bonus gift such as a free special report about the best mutual funds to buy now.

Create a Sense of Urgency

Successful salespeople know it is important to close the sale now, not later. Why? Because a decision deferred is a decision not made. It seems sensible, even kind, to let the prospect walk out of your showroom, go shop around, and come back later. But if you do that, your competitors will say anything to get the sale. So you must give the prospect a reason to act now. There are many ways to create a sense of urgency in your copy, but the easiest is to add a deadline to your offer. If you are having a sale on patio furniture, say in your ad that the sale ends Saturday at midnight. And when midnight arrives, remove the sale tags and lock the showroom door.

Urgency + Credibility = Better Response

The usual techniques for adding that sense of urgency that will get the prospect to act now are OK as far as they go—typically a deadline or limited-time offer. However, these methods are much stronger when you give the reader a legitimate reason why these deadlines are real, not just pulled out of thin air. Credibility plus urgency equals a better response. The following are just a few of the credible-urgency techniques you can use:

- *A walk through the warehouse.* We just inspected our warehouse, and inventory levels are low. And we won't be getting a new supply for weeks. So you had better act now while we still have some in stock. Otherwise you may miss out.
- *Rising cost of raw materials.* The cost of the raw materials used to make our product are increasing. That means we will soon have to raise prices. But act now, and you can still pay the lower rate.
- *Limited supply.* Only a few units are left, and after they're gone, it's too late. No more will be made. (I use this with hardcover books, which I have usually bought at low remainder prices. When they are gone, no more will be printed.)
- *Limited production capacity.* Because our production process is slow and exacting, our capacity is small and we can only take 100 new customers or orders. So this offer is limited to the first 100 people to respond.
- *Ingredient availability.* You can use this one for nutritional supplements, for example: The growing season for the main ingredient is almost over, and for the rest of the year, that botanical is extremely difficult to get.
- *Legal status.* We don't know how much longer the government will continue to approve the selling of this product. And once they ban sales, it's too late.
- *Scarcity.* A hurricane, flood, freezing weather, or other conditions have destroyed the bulk of this year's crop. So our supply is dwindling fast, and when it's gone, it can't be rapidly replaced, if at all.
- *Popularity.* Customers love our product so much that it is flying off the shelves, and demand is only increasing, risking short supply.

- *Expertise.* Our experts who do the manufacturing and testing are a small staff, and therefore we do not have enough people to keep up with the orders. Because their skills are specialized, additional qualified staff is difficult to find.
- *Limited resources.* So many customers have joined our auto-ship program that you should join now before we are filled to capacity and can accept no more new members.

CHAPTER 3

Planning Your Content Marketing Campaign

This chapter addresses how to plan a sound, sensible content marketing program that:

- is a series of coordinated content presentations in a logical order that satisfies prospects' information needs at each stage of the product evaluation and buying cycle
- delivers genuine information to your target audience and builds a positive relationship with them
- effectively integrates with your other digital and offline marketing channels to increase brand awareness and response rates
- helps move the prospect through the sales funnel (see Figure 3–1, on page 64) from complete stranger to qualified prospect to first-time buyer to loyal customer

FIGURE 3-1. Sales Funnel

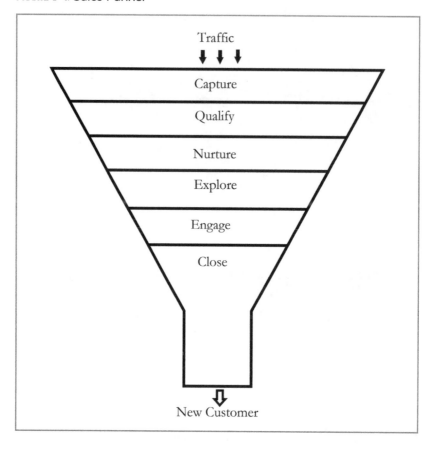

Many of these steps combine both copywriting and content writing, while some have only one or the other. For instance, you might get people to enter your sales funnel with a short online article. In the article, you can include links to more detailed information on the subject, at that point introducing a product that helps implement the ideas in the article. A white paper might help prospects explore various options for solving their problem, and a landing page gets the lead or closes the sale. These are just a few possibilities.

So how much of your sales funnel should be supported or driven by content? According to B2B marketing site Demand Gen Report, 95 percent of customers buy from vendors that gave them content at each stage of the buying process.

The Content Matrix

A useful tool for identifying the elements you need in your content marketing campaign is the content planning matrix, shown in Table 3–1, below. It focuses on tailoring content based on two variables: where your prospects are in the sales funnel and which groups of prospects you are targeting. In the far left column are the steps in the sales funnel your organization uses.

Horizontally across the top are the people the content should target: In this example, those are the CEO, CFO, end user of the product, and technical buying influences. Keep in mind, these are people at the potential customer's company, not yours. Approximately 90 percent of the top-performing B2B content marketers put their audience's information needs ahead of their company's sales message, according to the Content Marketing Institute.

Planning the Individual Pieces of Content

The content matrix shown in Table 3–1 is a useful tool for determining the tactics you need to conduct a complete and effective campaign. You

TABLE 3–1. Content Planning Matrix

Job Function				
Sales Cycle	**CEO**	**CFO**	**End User**	**Technical**
Lead			+	
Fulfillment	+			
RFP				✔
Close		*		

* Cost/Benefit ROI Analysis

+ Problem/Solutions

✔ Selection Tips

don't have to develop content pieces to fill the entire grid; often that is unnecessary overkill. But you should have a tactic for every step in the funnel—that is, at least one piece of content for all the tasks in the left-hand column. As we said earlier, customers like to buy from companies that supply continuous, fresh content.

So we have the grid in Table 3–1 on page 65 to help plan the campaign. What about planning the content pieces themselves? For this, we use the SAP (subject, audience, purpose) formula for writing strategic content:

- *Subject*: What the content is about
- *Audience*: Who the target audience for this content is—and how they can use the information
- *Purpose*: Usually, to move the prospect further down the sales funnel

As for format, your choices are many, and you should think beyond text. Content can include white papers, streaming videos, webinars, ebooks, blog posts, and a wide range of other print, audio, and video content:

- *Length.* Anything from brief Facebook or blog posts to an article or video to a full-length book or online class.
- *Information density.* Is it light, a bit weightier, highly technical, or complex content that some people will have to slog through?
- *Objective.* What do you want the prospect to do, think, learn, feel, or believe after seeing your content?
- *The next step.* What action should the prospect take, and can you include a call to action to get them to do it?
- *"Edutainment."* Combines the words education and entertainment. Master marketer David Ogilvy said "You cannot bore people into buying a product; you can only interest them in buying it." Can you make dull subject matter interesting and even entertaining?
- *Repurposing.* Can this same content be reformatted, edited, or rewritten for use in another area of your sales funnel, for another audience, or elsewhere in your marketing?

Later chapters in this book look at how these guidelines can be modified for each content format you are likely to use—from social media and blog posts to online newsletters and case studies.

Another consideration when writing content is: How useful and specific is this content to your readers. There are four levels of content utility (see Figure 3–2).

The lowest levels is content explaining why the reader should do something; e.g., install a fire suppression system in the company's data center. "Why-to-do-it" content is useful in alerting the prospects that they should be considering a solution to the problem your product solves if they are not already searching for one.

Above the "why" level is the "what" level. In our fire suppression example, the content can tell them what kinds of fire suppression systems to avoid and what type are best. In a data center, for instance, sprinklers are not the optimal solution, as the water can damage expensive electronics.

> **TIP**
>
> Avoid joking, cutesy, and over-the-top writing that is too clever for its own good—and yours.

The next level up is guidance on "how" to implement the solution. For a fire

FIGURE 3–2. Content Utility

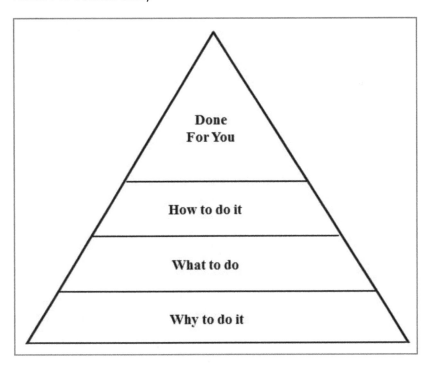

- Done For You
- How to do it
- What to do
- Why to do it

WHY YOU NEED A LOT OF CONTENT

There's an old joke that says, "If self-help books really worked, there would only be one." But of course, that's not quite true, even in content marketing. One of the primary reasons your marketing campaign must deliver multiple pieces of content and copy to your prospects is that a single communication won't get you anywhere close to the same results. In his 1880 book *The Art of Money Getting*, circus impresario P.T. Barnum wrote:

"A French writer says that 'The reader of a newspaper does not see the first mention of an ordinary advertisement; the second insertion he sees, but does not read; the third insertion he reads; the fourth insertion, he looks at the price; the fifth insertion, he speaks of it to his wife; the sixth insertion, he is ready to purchase; and the seventh insertion, he purchases.'"

Concludes Barnum: "Your object in advertising is to make the public understand what you have got to sell, and if you have not the pluck to keep advertising, until you have imparted that information, all the money you have spent is lost."

Substitute *content* for *advertising*, and you see one reason why you need multiple pieces of content: Repetition helps people learn.

A second reason to have multiple content pieces is that you can emphasize different aspects of your message in varying degrees of detail. For instance, if you write a "listicle" (list article) with seven points, you may want to expand one or more of the points with their own fact sheets or short articles.

The third reason to have multiple pieces of content is to tailor each so it moves the prospect forward to the next step in the sales

WHY YOU NEED A LOT OF CONTENT, continued

funnel. At the top of the funnel, you might explain why plastic gears are better than metal; at the bottom, you might give technical details on gear design and selection.

suppression system, this could cover everything from choosing the correct chemicals to determining at what points in the room the suppressant dispensers should be positioned.

The highest level of content is "done for you." The done-for-you fire suppressant content might include detailed blueprints, wiring diagrams, and installation guides that spell out all the particulars. So the reader just follows the instructions step by step, just as a child would when assembling a plastic model car or airplane.

Scheduling Content Distribution

A typical content marketing plan has a publishing schedule—usually monthly, sometimes weekly or quarterly.

The format for a one-month plan)as shown in Table 3–2 on page 70) displays just four pieces of information for each content initiative or piece: the type or format of content, the product or service it supports, the proposed topic or title, and a one-paragraph description of the information to be included. The three content promotions in Table 3–2 are all scheduled for the same month, which is the first month of the 12-month plan.

Sourcing Your Content

When taking a statistic, graph, quotation, fact, or other material from another source, credit the source in an endnote or footnote. You can use traditional footnotes, though more and more content writers and copywriters are using the URL where they found the material.

You may at times use photos and other visuals in your content publications. Many photo and artwork sources specify whether and

TABLE 3-2. One-Month Content Publishing Schedule

Content Publishing Schedule: Month 1			
Type of Content	Service/ Initiative	Topic/Title	Description
White paper	FlexiTray	How algorithms can help support the complex task of designing trays for refinery distillation towers	This paper will examine how the use of smart algorithms can maximize the performance of distillation towers in crude oil refineries.
YouTube video	Tower maintenance	Are your distillation towers suffering from corrosion and aging?	This video will give tips on how to perform visual inspections of refinery tower interiors to determine corrosion and other structural issues that may require maintenance or repair.
Article	Our line of tower internals includes the new FlexiPack loose packing	7 things your refinery can't survive without	This article will talk about 7 ways to address refinery yield and performance with proper selection of tower internals with a focus on the pros and cons of trays vs. packing.

GAIN A COMPETITIVE EDGE WITH UP-TO-DATE CONTENT

Out-of-date and inconsistent content has resulted in 58 percent of global B2B firms having to deal with dissatisfied customers or returns, while 51 percent report that poor product content is the biggest barrier to effective stocking and distribution, per a study by inRiver and Savanta. Additionally, 28 percent find it difficult to meet content standards for new channels and markets. On average, 45 percent of businesses spend six to 11 months creating and updating product content when entering a new channel or market. The best way to meet this requirement is to create a 6- to 12-month content schedule (see Table 3–2 on page 70 for a sample one-month content schedule) and meet all deliverable deadlines within the schedule.

how you must credit them as the source, which may include both the information and format of the footnote. You should follow these instructions to the letter. If the visuals are provided by your employer or client, ask them how the credit should read, if one is needed.

Here are four tips for avoiding copyright violations when taking materials from published sources, both online and in print:

1. *Request to use text and visuals from other sources.* Do it in writing, and don't use the material until the copyright holder signs your permission form and returns the signed document to you.

2. *If you don't have permission from the source, don't use the material word-for-word.* Paraphrase in your own words. Sentences and paragraphs can be copyrighted. But data and ideas (unless patented) usually cannot. Rewriting without copying can help you steer clear of plagiarism.

3. *Don't forget about visual content.* Redraw graphs, diagrams, and other visuals so that you are not copying and plagiarizing copyrighted material.

4. *When you incorporate material from other sources into your content, use only short excerpts.* Typically, quoting 50 words or less is safe in a short piece, and 150 words or less in a book-length work. But I am not a lawyer, so I urge you to consult your attorney to confirm this. See Appendix A for more on copyright.

CHAPTER 4

Integrating Content with Selling

In her enewsletter *The CEO's Edge*, business advisor MaryEllen Tribby defined *multichannel marketing* as "giving people multiple ways to buy." I think of it more as marketers—including you and me—integrating multiple marketing tactics, both content and direct marketing, to communicate with our prospects, change their thinking, and generate a response from them, such as downloading a white paper, completing a survey, buying a product, etc.

As we discussed earlier, *content* is informational writing, and *copywriting* is persuasive or sales writing. For instance, the email that drives traffic to the landing page offering a free white paper is copywriting, and the white paper itself is content.

Multichannel marketing increases the number of people who pass through your funnel, a process also called the *customer journey*. It accelerates the speed at which they make this journey from stranger to buyer.

We know that some of the most effective multichannel marketing campaigns are the ones that integrate both content and copy into the sales funnel to generate maximum results in minimum time. In this chapter, we'll look at some of the most common sequences of multichannel marketing campaigns and how to use them effectively.

Keep in mind that there are almost an infinite number of ways you can combine market tactics. We'll be addressing just a few of the most commonly used multichannel marketing funnel sequences.

One-Step Content Marketing

One-step content marketing is a limited campaign in which you essentially deliver a piece of meaningful content to your target audience. That's it.

The classic example of a single-step use of content is writing an op-ed piece or letter to the editor for your local newspaper. You express your opinion in a short article that runs once. There is no explicit call to action (CTA) mechanism for the reader to respond to. No list to join. And no expectation of receiving further content on the subject. The op-ed is designed to influence and educate all on its own. Of course, readers *can* write letters to the editor in response to your op-ed.

These days, reporters' bylines include their email addresses, making it easier for readers to ask questions, point out errors, and voice contrary opinions to them directly as well as in a traditional "letter to the editor."

Multistep Content Marketing

Multistep content marketing, more commonly used to generate leads or sales, typically starts by using copywriting to drive prospects to a piece of relevant content they can read and download. You can add more steps to the sequence to take your prospect from the top of the funnel to the bottom. Your goal is often to capture quality leads for B2B and B2C companies, either to sell a product directly off the web or drive prospects to a brick-and-mortar location for purchase.

At each stage, the content can serve two purposes:

1. To increase conversions, meaning the percentage of people who go on to the next step in the sales funnel.
2. To educate the prospects about your product, including features, benefits, and applications. This answers the prospect's questions, so by the time they get to the funnel, they know most or all of what they need to make a purchase decision.

Increase Lead Flow with Free Content

Never do a lead-generating promotion—postcard, ad, banner ad, email, or direct-mail package—without a free content offer.

The content can be an informative booklet, white paper, or special report addressing some aspect of the problem your product or service helps the reader solve. You offer a free copy of this information to prospects who inquire about your product or service.

You will greatly increase responses to your direct mail and other promotions with the offer of a strong *bait piece*, such as "Call or write us today for a copy of our FREE booklet, *7 Ways to Reduce Energy Costs*."

Conversely, not having a bait piece will significantly lower the response rate to lead-generating direct response promotions, whether B2B or B2C.

To avoid only attracting people who want the free booklet, have both a "hard" and "soft" offer in every lead generation promotion. The soft offer is the lead magnet—for example, "Click on this link to download a copy of our free white paper on internet security." The hard offer is "Call us now to arrange an appointment so we can discuss your internet security needs in detail." Prospects with an immediate need take you up on the hard offer, whereas those who don't need your help right now but might be interested in the future respond to the soft offer.

Years ago, I used direct mail to generate leads for business writing seminars I marketed to corporations. The main offer was "Mail this card for more information on my seminar, Effective Technical Writing."

Then I got smart and added a P.S. that said, "Be sure to ask for our FREE tip sheet, '10 Ways to Improve Your Technical Writing'"—which was a reprint of an article I had published in a trade magazine. As soon as I included this soft offer, my response rates doubled, and so did my sales.

Three Factors That Can Increase Conversion in Multistep Content Campaigns

At the beginning of the funnel, the first conversion is often a free content offer, with ebooks and white papers being popular lead magnets. The following are three things you can do to increase your lead magnet's desirability and generate more downloads:

1. *Titles.* The title should capture the prospect's attention, typically by arousing curiosity, making a big promise (such as solving a pressing problem), or promising to reveal useful information or important news. See Figure 4–1 for an example of a lead magnet cover—in this

FIGURE 4–1. Sample Lead Magnet Cover

case, an ebook cover showcasing keywords that show the reader what kind of information is promised inside.

2. *Perceived value.* Here's a simple trick for establishing high perceived value: Even though you are giving the content away, put a price on the cover (see Figure 4–1). Very few content marketers know this simple technique; if there is no price on the cover, the recipient doesn't think the lead magnet is as valuable.
3. *Table of contents.* Lead magnets of three to four pages or longer should have a table of contents (TOC). The chapter titles in the TOC should be written like bullets in sales copy to increase interest in the contents (see Figure 4–2, below).

FIGURE 4–2. Use a Table of Contents to Sell Your Content

THE BUSINESS-TO-BUSINESS MARKETING HANDBOOK

Table of Contents

Chapter 1	B2B Marketing: 1978 vs. 2008	5
Chapter 2	10 Tips for Increasing Landing Page Conversion Rates	10
Chapter 3	Are White Papers Dead?	14
Chapter 4	The 6 Key Components of Effective B2B Offers	19
Chapter 5	Should B2B Copywriters Avoid Jargon?	24
Chapter 6	5 Steps to Building a Large and Responsive Opt-In E-List of Qualified B2B Prospects	29
Chapter 7	5 Modern Myths of B2B Marketing	34
Chapter 8	Are Businesspeople Devoid of Emotion When Making Buying Decisions?	39
Chapter 9	Marketing with Case Studies	44
Chapter 10	4 Simple Steps to Writing SEO Copy That Both Your Prospects and the Search Engines Love	49
Chapter 11	What Works Best for B2B Lead Generation: Inbound or Outbound Marketing?	54
Chapter 12	Using Web Analytics to Drive Online Sales	59
Chapter 13	5 Ways to Boost B2B Direct Mail Response Rates	64
Chapter 14	A New Copywriting Formula: the 4 C's	69
Chapter 15	What's Working in B2B Marketing	74
Chapter 16	7 Rules for Content Marketers	78
Chapter 17	Business-to-Business Headline Writing Clinic	82
Chapter 18	The More You Tell, the More You Sell	87
Chapter 19	The Trouble with B2B Marketing	92

Center for Technical Communication. ©2018 2

Drip Campaigns

A *drip campaign* is a sequence of emails, direct-mail letters, or other contacts, with the emails delivered via auto-responder on a preset schedule. For beginning a conversation with a potential buyer or conversion to a direct sale, the first few emails in the drip campaign focus on delivering chunks of useful content, typically one per email. Later efforts in the sequence are often a mix of content and a call to action (CTA). The final messages push the prospect to take the desired action, with increasing urgency the further you get in the sequence.

There is no hard-and-fast rule for the optimal number of emails in a drip campaign, but three to seven emails per sequence is common. Some drips have more. One rule of thumb is to measure the conversion from each effort, until the conversion rate drops so low it is clear there is no point in sending more emails in the campaign. It is called a *drip* because instead of flooding the prospects with the content and sales pitch all at once, they are fed to prospects one drop at a time. This enables you to have more frequent contact with them, which usually translates into higher conversion rates.

Urgency

As already noted, adding a sense of urgency increases your response rate. Without a sense of urgency, prospects defer making a decision while they "think it over." And as I've said, a decision deferred is typically a decision not made.

Here are some tactics and phrases that can create a greater sense of urgency:

- *Specific deadline.* This offer expires January 31 at midnight. After that, it's too late.
- *Number of days deadline.* You must reply within the next 11 days to take advantage of this special offer.
- *Reward for prompt answer.* To claim your free gift, you must be one of the first 100 people to respond.
- *Limited-time offer.* But I urge you to hurry. This offer is for a limited time only. And once it expires, it may never be repeated.

⊛ *Limited supply.* Only so many copies of this report will be printed. And no more.

Retargeting

You probably have seen websites where, in addition to the page content, there are small ads at the top or side of the screen. For instance, when you go on msn.com to read the news, you see small ads for merchandise unrelated to the contents of the article you are reading. What gives?

This practice is known as *retargeting*. Here's how it works: When you visit an ecommerce site, that site transfers a "cookie" or small text file (up to 4KB) to your computer. The cookie may be stored in your hard drive either until you close your browser or until a programmed expiration date (the latter is known as a *persistent cookie*). These cookies provide a way for the website to recognize you and keep track of your preferences.

Say you have been shopping at the Mixology Clothing Company website. As of this writing, as far as I can tell, Mixology does a lot of retargeting. After I visited the Mixology site, I went to Foxfire—and ads for Mixology immediately popped up along with the Foxfire homepage. Retargeting can give you many more impressions than just the first visit to a page of products or content.

Google gives internet users more privacy controls by enabling them to see which cookies are tracking them and manually block and delete those cookies if the users so desire.

Content-Rich Websites

Must you have a website highlighting your products and services, capabilities, experience, and skills as a vendor? If you are starting out, yes, you must. Even if you are experienced, I think you should. You can still find a few online merchants and service providers that don't have websites and do OK. But they are increasingly at risk of being branded as obsolete or out of touch.

We live in a digital world. Every client or employer who hires you to write print materials will ask about your abilities and experience in digital marketing, too. If you don't have a website, it raises doubts about whether you're up-to-date—or a dinosaur. Plus you won't show up on a Google search for your type of product or service.

Many potential buyers turn to Google first to search for what you are selling. If you do not have a website, the chances of them finding you are slim at best. Social media content, such as LinkedIn profiles, may give an overview of who you are and what you do, but they only complement websites, not replace them.

What to Put on Your Site

The most important things to put on your website are the facts potential clients feel they must know before they decide to hire you.

To see examples of the various website sections discussed here, go to my writing website (https://www.bly.com/) and select the page you want to see from the menu bar on the left or click one of the links at the bottom of the homepage. (I have listed these descriptions to help make each section easy to find on the site, and they translate easily to services and products besides writing):

- Who you are (your company or individual bio)
- Who your customers or clients are
- What products and services you sell
- A list of clients
- Pertinent experience in your industry or skill set
- Credentials of you and your key team members—including degrees, licenses, and awards

TIP

By using the heading "Clients/Experience" instead of just "Clients," you can include organizations you've worked with for as an employee or volunteer, not just those who are actual clients—a technique that helps make your experience look more well-rounded, especially when you are just starting out.

Perhaps the most important section of your website are the pages that feature your products or services, preferably one per page. In my portfolio on bly.com, I organize my experience and samples of my work by type of writing assignment (such as annual reports and case studies) as well as product or industry (for example, software and trading systems). When you click on the portfolio, you see thumbnails of the writing samples; clicking on the thumbnail expands the image to a size large enough to read the copy.

As for pricing, you can either post your prices on your website or send a price list as a PDF via email to potential clients who contact you. Both of these approaches have pros and cons, but I prefer to send my fee schedule on request, for three reasons:

1. It gives the potential client a reason to contact me, which helps me find out more about their needs and initiate a discussion that can lead to a contract. If everything is already on your website, the prospect may simply skim the site without talking to you, and you'll lose a valuable opportunity to ask them about their problem and propose a solution.
2. It's too easy for prospects to misread or misinterpret your fee schedule; I prefer the opportunity to explain the scope of each service, what I include with it, and its value.
3. I don't want to make it easy for my competitors to see what I charge.

Obviously, for ecommerce sites where consumers can order directly from your site, you must include prices.

More Stuff for Your Website

In addition to the things your clients look for when deciding whether to hire you, you should also post the things you want them to know about you. Include any credentials that give you an edge over your competitors and that might sway the prospect to hire you instead of them.

The most important of these is a page of *testimonials*—comments from your clients, former employers, and others praising you and your work. How many do you need? The longer the better, but your testimonials page should have at least three to five strong recommendations to start. Otherwise, it looks too thin.

Have you won any awards from J.D. Power or other ratings companies? Have articles been written about you and your company? Post links to them. You can also send a press release about your business along with your photo to your local weekly paper. The smaller your town, the more likely it is that the paper will run a short article about you. Posting that favorable press coverage on your site helps build credibility. Many media outlets allow you to submit press releases via forms on their websites.

Choosing a Domain Name

So what makes for a good website name? The debate rages, but here are three criteria that are hard to disagree with:

1. *Memorable.* Why is an online bookstore called Amazon? It sounds exotic, is easy to remember, and reflects the promise of "big" to its customers.

2. *Logical.* Another tactic that works is to select a name that logically ties in with what you do. Examples: printing.com for a printer and flowers.com for a florist. Or simply make the domain name the same as your company name. IBM's domain name is ibm.com.

3. *Short.* Some marketers prefer longer domain names because they can be more descriptive. For instance, one printer has the website www.printingforless.com. It gets its message across and is easy to remember. Although domain names can be as long as 63 characters, shorter ones—like www.printer.com—are better. Think about the URLs you can recall off the top of your head. How many of them are more than one or two word long?

Note: Having the last letter of your first word be the same as the first letter of your last word also creates problems, because people can't figure out whether to use the letter once or twice. To convert my name into a domain name, would people be more apt to try www.bobly.com or www.bobbly.com? I solved the problem by registering the shorter

> **TIP**
>
> A good way to market your business is to write how-to articles on topics related to your services and publish them in trade magazines and online newsletters. Put up an "Articles" page on your website where you post all your articles. Google gives higher rankings to websites rich in content, so having an articles library online can increase your site's organic search traffic.

and simpler www.bly.com. People frequently comment on how easy it is to remember.

Under current trademark law, a domain name is not a trademark. If you intend for the domain name to act as a trademark, you should search trademark records to see whether it has already been trademarked. If not, file a trademark application.

Capturing Leads and Emails

How can you convert traffic on your website to immediate inquiries or prospects who might have a future need for your product or service? I recommend two techniques.

The first is to have a contact form where someone who might be interested in hiring you can request a price quotation from you. If you go to www.bly.com and click on the square in the upper right corner that says "Need Great Copy? Click HERE Now!" it brings you to my contact form. I always had a link to the contact form in my main menu, but when I added the link to the upper right corner of every page, my online sales leads nearly tripled.

Some visitors may not have an immediate need but could still be potential clients. Wouldn't it be nice to capture their email addresses and send them periodic reminders about you and your services? You can do this by offering a free electronic newsletter about topics related to your business. Place a sign-up box on your homepage offering your free enewsletter to anyone who submits their email address.

To build your enewsletter's circulation, create an interesting special report or short tip sheet on business writing or another relevant topic (this can be one or more of your articles formatted as a downloadable PDF file). Offering this information as a gift will greatly increase subscription rates.

For example, sign up for my free newsletter, and you get a library of

TIP

Don't charge for your enewsletter. Give it away for free. That way you build a list of interested subscribers (many of whom are potential customers or clients) who will give you their contact information and permission to send emails to them whenever you wish.

marketing reports with a retail value of $116 for free (hence the term "free on free"). By offering this bribe, I persuade nearly one out of every two people who visit my squeeze page to subscribe to my enewsletter. This is the primary vehicle through which I have built a list of 60,000 online subscribers.

TIP

Here's another subscription-building method that works: Create a separate domain and sign-up page where people can subscribe to your enewsletter and get their gift. This is known in online marketing as a "free-on-free name squeeze page" because it extracts, or "squeezes," new names for your list from web traffic. You can see my name squeeze page at www.bly.com/reports.

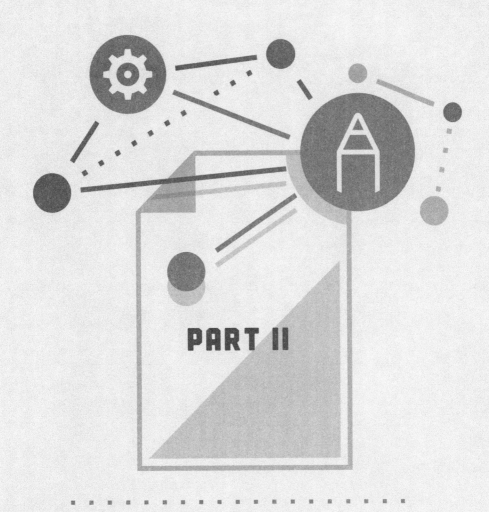

PART II

Implementing Content Marketing Tactics

CHAPTER 5

Marketing with White Papers and Special Reports

White papers, ebooks, and special reports have long been three of the most widely used formats for lead magnets in content marketing, although video (see Chapter 11) is also frequently used today.

In one sense, they are essentially the same thing: multipage texts with useful content. But the label you choose can affect your response. *White papers* are used in multiple industries, and they have become the gold standard in selling enterprise software. People know that white papers are free, so putting a price on the cover is not credible and their perceived value is not high.

Special reports can be given a cover price, as can *ebooks*, because even though some marketers give them away, publishers often sell them for prices ranging from $19 to $49 or even higher. In this chapter, I'll introduce you to all three.

White Papers

Are white papers dead? Is the web so overloaded with free white papers that adding to the pile seems like an exercise in futility?

If a marketing technique is overused, it often begins to lose its effectiveness. When that happens, usage drops off, and prospects are consequently no longer bombarded by the technique. This happened in the 1980s when videocassettes (and later, DVDs) were all the rage in direct mail, but within a year or so, the practice petered out. We saw the same dynamic with other lead magnet offers, such as coffee mugs and golf tees.

After a while, some marketers remember the old technique and decide to test it again. Sure enough, it works, because the market hasn't seen it for some time. Other marketers who follow their lead also start getting good results, and marketing with DVDs becomes popular once more.

Today some marketers question whether white papers are following this same pattern and running out of steam. As one skeptic told me, "Prospects already have too much to read; why would they ask for more?"

Yet the numbers tell a different story: namely, that white paper marketing is alive and well. According to EquiNet, 75 percent of B2B buyers would agree to share information about themselves or their company if they were offered a white paper as a lead generator, as opposed to just 49 percent who would do the same in exchange for a video.

Over the years, I've seen a number of direct mail and email tests in which offering a free white paper or other free content increased response rates 10 percent to 100 percent or more. White papers work; a 2016 report from Demand Gen says that 82 percent of B2B buyers use information from white papers when making a buying decision. I do think, however, that we have to broaden our ideas on how to use free content offers, which is essentially what a white paper is: free information designed to educate our prospects and motivate them to inquire about our product or service.

To begin with, I think it's not white papers themselves that are getting tired but the name itself. *White paper* signals to some prospects a document that is an obvious selling tool—and a low perceived value as a giveaway.

The solution is to keep using white papers in your marketing but to call them something else. Mailing list brokerage Edith Roman used to publish a print catalog of mailing lists—basically a massive white paper. But instead of calling it a catalog, they called it the *Direct Mail Encyclopedia*. Offering a free *Direct Mail Encyclopedia* helped generate more inquiries for their brokerage services. Now this same list data is on their website.

Copywriter Ivan Levison calls his white papers *guides*. Marketer David Yale uses *executive briefing*. I'm partial to *special report*. For consumer marketing, marketing expert Joe Polish suggests *consumer awareness guide*, and for a B2B white paper giving product selection tips, I'd change this to *buyer's guide* or *selection guide*. For a white paper giving tips or instructions on a process, I might call it a *manual*. If you publish a saddle-stitched print version that fits in a #10 envelope, you can call it a *free booklet*. The possibilities are endless.

What about the complaint that prospects already have too much to read? Granted, there is more information on the web than you could process in a thousand lifetimes. But good white papers don't merely present information; they offer solutions to business and technical problems. Virtually every B2B sale you make is because someone thinks your product or service is the solution to their problem. A white paper can help clarify the problem as well as convince the reader that your idea or method is the best of many options for addressing it.

Every marketing campaign has an objective, yet if you ask most managers what the objective of their white paper is, they probably couldn't tell you. Too many see white papers merely as an opportunity to collect and publish a pile of research material they found on the web. To make your white paper succeed, you must define your marketing objective before writing a single word.

For example, one manufacturer found that consumers were not buying their do-it-yourself (DIY) underground sprinkler kits because homeowners perceived installing the irrigation system by themselves as too difficult. Solution: a free DIY manual on how to install an underground sprinkler system in a single weekend. Clearly written and illustrated, the manual overcame the perception that this was a tough project by making it look easy.

Formatting White Papers

In the pre-internet era, bait pieces were mainly hard copies. Thanks to the digital landscape, lead magnets can now be produced as PDF files and instantly downloaded online. But at the receiving end, they can still be printed by the prospect and read on paper.

It may be that what's wearing out is not the free content, but the standard white paper format: black ink on 8½-by-11-inch sheets of paper (when printed out). To make your lead magnet stand out, consider alternative formats: DVDs, digital downloads, podcasts, webinars, teleseminars, flashcards, stickers, posters, software, games, and slide decks.

Many white papers are six to ten pages long—about 3,000 to 4,000 words—but you are not locked into that length. You can go shorter or longer, depending on your marketing objective and the content you want to present. Some marketers use short white papers, about 1,200 words long. The lead magnet can be as simple as a list of tips printed on one side of a sheet of paper or displayed as a single page online; this is called a *tip sheet*. Or it can be as long as a physical or ebook.

Choosing Your White Paper Topic

Pick a topic that moves the prospect forward in the buying process. For instance, if you sell valves, your topic might be "How to Size and Select Valves."

Look for fresh territory not already exhausted by other white papers, articles, and websites. If similar white papers are all over the internet, consider a fresh angle, perhaps by narrowing the focus, "How to Size and Select Valves for *Viscous Fluid and Slurry Applications.*"

Favor subjects that lend themselves to quick tips, how-to advice, and easy explanations. Avoid topics that require in-depth analytical thinking, since your reader is not likely to stick with you while you slowly work through the argument. White papers should be quick, scannable reads. Are there exceptions? Of course.

An effective strategy for topic selection is to ask your salespeople what common objections and questions they hear from prospects, and then produce white papers overcoming the objections or answering the questions. Salespeople can use the white papers to support their answers and arguments in a meeting or presentation. Even if the prospect never reads the white paper, the presentation of an official-looking document supporting the salesperson's point can go a long way toward persuading the prospect to accept their claims.

Choosing the Richest Content

The use of white papers as a marketing tool has skyrocketed in recent years—not just for selling information technology (IT), but also for promoting a wide range of products and services beyond hardware and software.

When professional writers or editors are hired to create white papers, they're typically not experts in the subject, which is often both technical and arcane. I've written white papers on everything from measuring ROI in content management systems to promoting bone healing with an implantable electromagnetic generator.

Pre-internet, the greatest challenge for the writer was research. The local public library contained little usable information on the highly specialized topics most white papers covered, and SMEs were often uncooperative about sharing information with writers.

Now we have the opposite problem: too much information. Let's say you are writing a white paper on COBRA administration. A recent search on Google for "COBRA" got 524 million results. If you visit just the top 10 or 20 and save the relevant information, you can end up with hundreds of pages of background information on COBRA.

Therefore, the writer's challenge is not *finding* sufficient content for writing the white paper, but *selecting* from it. How do you know what to include and what to leave out? All you have to do is ask and answer one critical question: "What is the marketing objective of this white paper?" Importantly, *topic* and *marketing objective* are not the same thing.

For a white paper titled *Administering COBRA*, the topic is "how to administer COBRA benefits." But if you are selling software to automate COBRA administration, your marketing objective might be something like: "Get HR managers who need help in administering COBRA benefits to call us and ask for a demo of our system."

Once you have defined the marketing objective, it's much easier to select from your vast library of source material for your white paper, as well as ruthlessly prune research materials that sound interesting but do not help achieve the marketing objective.

There are three categories of content you should include in your white paper. The first is content that directly helps your white paper achieve your marketing objective. I recently wrote a white paper for a client on how to comply with a particular federal regulation concerning data privacy; let's call it "Regulation X." One of the white paper's marketing objectives was to convince readers that they should in fact make Regulation X compliance a priority (many do not).

So I went online and researched whether any organizations or their employees had suffered negative consequences from not achieving full Regulation X compliance. Many of them had, and I added some of that material to the white paper to drive home the point that you can't ignore Regulation X, and doing so would be harmful to both your company and your career.

The second type of content you can add to a white paper is useful tips or how-to information. For the Regulation X white paper, the client provided me with a list from the federal government on "Nine Simple Steps to Achieving Regulation X Compliance."

The list is short and sweet, so I included it in the white paper as a sidebar. The purpose of the white paper was not to serve as an actual how-to manual on Regulation X compliance; that is beyond the scope of any short document. But readers would feel they're getting some useful, actionable ideas from the sidebar, and so would be more inclined to read and keep the white paper.

The third type of content your white paper should contain is information comparing the various options for solving the problem and steering the reader toward yours. In the Regulation X white paper, there were two types of options. Most software companies sold one specific tool to enable compliance in each of the different rules covered by Regulation X. My client, by comparison, sold a single comprehensive tool that covered all areas. In the white paper, we gave a seemingly objective analysis of the two options, which of course concluded that the advantages of the single-source approach outweighed those of the rule-specific approach—which would naturally lead the reader to pick our software over the competitors'.

When there is a ton of information readily available on your topic, it is often tempting to cram as much into your white paper as possible. But that's a mistake, because your readers are busy. If your white paper has the heft of, say, *Moby Dick*, a reader will put it aside. They have limited time, and your job is to be selective: Knowing what to leave out is almost as important as knowing what to put in.

So what should you leave out? To begin with, leave out anything that the reader could just as easily get elsewhere and does not help your marketing objective. In the Regulation X white paper, for instance, the client had initially wanted to include several pages outlining the various sections and subsections of Regulation X. I asked him where he had gotten this detailed write-up. He replied he had lifted it almost word for word from a government website. I suggested instead just summarizing Regulation X, its purpose, and its importance in a paragraph or two, and then including a link to the site for readers who wanted the complete description.

Next leave out extraneous detail. I also asked the client, "Does knowing the full Regulation X requirements line by line help the reader decide which tool to use?" No, he admitted, it does not. Then it should not be included, I replied, because it adds length without adding value.

You should also leave out material that is interesting but irrelevant. I once read a white paper on fuel cells that went into detail on the history of batteries, including the invention of the voltaic cell and galvanic pile. It was fascinating to me (I'm an engineer) but totally irrelevant to the target audience: automakers trying to decide which fuel cell technology to put into an electric car.

Writing Your White Paper

Nick Copley, cofounder of the white paper syndication website Bitpipe, presents the following checklist for writing an effective white paper:

- *An intriguing title.* "Readers typically select white papers from a long list of papers on a single topic, so the title is very much the most important element in attracting readership," says Copley. A good title "unambiguously" identifies the subject of the paper, he says. In addition, the title should suggest who the target reader is and convey a compelling "what's in it for me" benefit.

- *An executive summary.* Like the title, the summary is essentially marketing copy that persuades readers to download the full white paper. This is where you lay out your key message, and it's a good idea to write this copy even before you write the paper itself, just to make sure it's done well. A good summary should be "meaty"—at least several paragraphs long, with enough detail to suggest what the paper covers in more depth. If the paper is more than three or four pages, you should include a table of contents here.

- *A clear story line.* "Many white papers are choppy and hard to follow," Copley notes. "That's usually a sign of a disorganized editorial process, not bad writing. The project is given to a junior member of the marketing group, and then everyone throws in ideas about what the paper should cover. The right approach is to decide upfront what one goal you're trying to achieve with this document. Save all the other nuggets of ideas for other white papers."

- *Competitive positioning.* "It's pointless to pretend that you have the only solution in the market. The people who download white papers are usually doing research and will probably look at several papers at the same time," says Copley. "Instead, start by reviewing competing white papers and make sure that your own document addresses major issues that competitors raise. You want to say, 'Here's our solution to this problem, and here's how it maps against the competition.'"

- *Charts and diagrams.* "If you're trying to get across a complex message, good visual elements always help," Copley says. "But be sure the diagrams actually tie into the text and say something meaningful. If the reader has to figure out the context, then you're just interrupting the flow of your discussion."

- *Third-party references.* "This is something many people leave out," says Copley. "But in fact it helps when you can bring in outside authorities—standards bodies, research firms, experts on best practices, and so forth. These references show that you know what's going on in the market, and they make the paper more credible."

- *Case studies.* White papers tend to address fairly abstract technology issues, but Copley argues that one or two case studies or user profiles (perhaps presented as sidebars) "can bring the paper back to reality." Case studies "also show that you have at least a few customers who are happy to endorse your solution."

- *An author biography.* Another simple way to add credibility is to include a short profile of the white paper's author. "This is always good, especially if the writer is well-known in the field," Copley says. "It helps make the publication look more like an editorial document and less like marketing copy."

- *A call to action.* "What is the reader supposed to do after reading the paper?" Copley asks. "Presumably, you've educated and persuaded the reader, so now you should spell out the next step." White paper readers are generally at an early stage in the sales cycle, he adds, so trying to move them straight to a sale may not be practical. "But you can certainly suggest they get additional information from you: by requesting a personal sales call, signing up for a newsletter, attending a seminar, or even downloading additional white papers. Never leave the reader dangling."

Syndicate Your White Paper for Broader Distribution

You can release downloads of your white paper in several ways:

- Post it on your website.
- Put it on a separate landing page.
- Announce it to customers and prospects via email.
- Run ads online.

Those methods can accurately target the prospects you want to reach most.

Another way to get broader distribution of your white paper is to submit it to websites that make white papers from many different sources and on many different topics available for free download, such as the following:

- Bitpipe (http://www.bitpipe.com/)
- Campaign Insight (https://www.campaignlive.co.uk/insight)

- Computer Business Review (http://www.cbronline.com/white-papers)
- ComputerWeekly.com (https://bitpipe.computerweekly.com/)
- Computing (https://www.computing.co.uk/static/resources)
- eWeek Research Center (http://www.eweek.com/research)
- Find White Papers (http://www.findwhitepapers.com/)
- IndustryWeek (http://www.industryweek.com/white-papers/)
- InformationWeek (http://www.informationweek.com)
- RetailWire (https://www.retailwire.com/resources/)
- SC Media (https://insight.scmagazineuk.com/expert-reports)
- TechRepublic (https://www.techrepublic.com/resource-library/content-type/whitepapers/)
- Toolbox (http://it.toolbox.com)

The advantage of such white paper sites is that they help your content reach people who might otherwise have never seen it. The downside is that they get a lot of visitors who like free white papers but are not good prospects for what you sell.

Special Reports

A *special report* is a promotional piece similar to an article or other short document containing objective, well-researched, and up-to-date information. There are two basic types of special reports: those given away as a free premium in a content marketing campaign and those sold as paid information products.

Free premiums are designed to educate your prospects and motivate them to inquire about your product or service. Marketers have many uses for free special reports, including as online collateral, handouts at trade shows and conferences, support for live presentations, and email attachments.

Printed special reports are used to generate leads, establish credibility, or left

TIP

Many digital marketers use free special reports as downloadable PDFs in their multichannel marketing programs. Free downloadable content drives website traffic, encourages incoming links, and fuels conversion rates.

behind with prospects to help close a sale. You can include a special report in your company's sales packets or send copies as an update to your current and past customers. You can use a special report as the basis of an article for publication in a trade journal or send one to an interested prospect as a follow-up marketing piece.

Imagine the power of a selection guide for a complicated, high-tech product. As we discussed earlier, you can advise the reader or prospect on the important considerations when making a purchase like this—thereby setting the standards by which your competition will be judged. Because you have defined the guidelines, you know your product fits the specs best. Remember, education should be your top priority, so make any specific product pitches very subtle and understated.

> **TIP**
>
> One easy way to create a special report is to interview an expert in your niche. Then you can offer the interview either as an audio file that can be streamed or down-loaded, or transcribe it into a PDF file and offer it as a downloadable report.

People often arrive at your site in search of information regarding your niche or specialty, so a relevant special report can be sent as a premium to visitors who request further information. Or you can send a special report that goes into more detail on a topic in your FAQ, where the short answers you have listed are insufficient to fully answer a specific question.

Whether you intend to sell your special report or give it away, you should always place a price in the upper right-hand corner of the front cover and offer it for sale on your website. Reason: This legitimizes your claim that the price listed on the report is honest. I sometimes say, "And $29 is not just a price we made up. People actually pay $29 to buy the report on our website. But now it's yours FREE." This further establishes value and adds credibility to your cover price. Figure 5–1 on page 98 shows the front cover of a special report.

Special reports can take many forms and be called many things. They don't need to come in the standard vertical format of 8½-by-11-inch vertical pages printed with black ink. Here are some possibilities:

FIGURE 5-1. Special Report

A CTC Publishing Mini-Briefing $7

Marketing to GOM™*
Grumpy Old Men

10 Tips for Selling to the Age
50+ Male Market

by
ROBERT W. BLY
Copywriter/Consultant

Center for Technical Communication
22 East Quackenbush Ave., 3rd floor
Dumont, NJ 07628
Phone: (201) 385-1220 / fax: (201) 385-1138
Web: www.bly.com
E-mail: rwbly@bly.com

◎ Single-page reports are often written in the form of *tip sheets* or *how-to* documents and are generally given away. A tip sheet is often formatted as a numbered list of tips that solve a problem or make your prospect's life easier (e.g., *15 Steps You Can Take to Get Your Home Ready for Sale*). A how-to paper gives detailed instructions on something that might be intimidating to the prospect (e.g., *How to Become a Recognized Expert in Your Field*).

◎ A *booklet* is a little longer, typically several 8½-by-11-inch sheets folded in half and saddle-stitched to fit into a #10 envelope. Or you can fold it the other way and it becomes a digest size,

5-by-8-inches. A booklet usually conveys content—it is not used for product or service descriptions.

- *Articles* can range from 400 to 2,500 words or even longer if the subject warrants. They can be in print form in a newspaper, magazine, or journal, or online in an enewsletter or on a news website or blog.

- A *column* is an article in a series that appears regularly in a publication or on a website. Many enewsletters feature regular columns by recognized experts. Columns typically range from 400 to 1,000 words in length.

- A *monograph* is a report on a single subject, most often written by just one author. It is usually intended to be a complete and detailed treatise on a complicated subject or issue, at a level more in-depth than a general textbook.

- A *mini-report* is a short piece devoted to a specific topic or problem that might be of interest to your target market. A mini-report that might appeal to real estate investors is *What You Should Know Before You Buy a Foreclosed Home*.

- A *case study* describes a success story involving your product.

Why Prospects Love Special Reports

Investors, technical support people, teachers, consumers, small business owners, scientists—anyone with a problem can find a properly targeted special report. And the web is the perfect place for people to find what they are looking for—that's why so many folks turn to search engines when faced with a dilemma. Internet search makes it easy for them to find helpful advice on just about any subject, and this advice often comes in the form of a downloadable special report.

Special reports are widely used in content marketing to drive website traffic

TIP

Customers like vendors who put the customer first—and help them make intelligent decisions. When you provide your customers with the information they need to make the right choice, you become their trusted advisor or "obvious expert."

and increase sales. They are popular because they work. Readers like special reports because the content is focused on a specific topic, and they feel they are getting valuable information without having to make an investment. You are therefore starting your relationship with your prospect on a positive note. Most important, you've created a feeling of obligation because you have given them something of value.

> **TIP**
>
> Use special reports as an excuse to stay in touch with your valuable customers. Periodically send updates. The more information you share with your customers, the more they will look forward to hearing from you.

A successful report is about a single, specific problem, and it gives practical, proven ideas for solving it. It should contain information the reader might have a hard time finding anywhere else. Because most people have limited time, omit all extraneous details and any information that is interesting but irrelevant.

Special reports educate your customers while you build relationships with them and establish yourself as a leader in your field. When you tell your customer exactly what to ask for and do, it helps eliminate hesitation when it comes time for them to buy. You are handling and overcoming objections upfront, so the sales process becomes much smoother and easier. And because special reports tend to have a long shelf life, you can keep your message in front of your most valuable prospects for months or even years.

Focus on a Narrow Topic Targeting a Specific Audience

Your report should focus on your reader's needs—not your marketing problems. Therefore, it is important to decide exactly who your "ideal" reader is before you begin writing. If yours is a B2B topic, decide on the industry, company size, job title, level, and area of responsibility for your reader. Also important: gender, age, and familiarity with your subject matter. Are you talking to influencers or decision-makers, techies or management?

Once you have a clear picture of your ideal reader, review the information you are gathering to make sure they will find it useful. If you think your reader is a high-level manager, you should focus on business benefits. If they are a technical administrator, focus more on processes, procedures, and the other details that are important to this audience. This type of distribution of information to a narrowly defined audience is called *narrowcasting*. It is also called *niche* or *target marketing*.

When you think about topics for your special report, be as specific and focused as possible. One way to do that is to use a numerical organization, such as *15 Things You Can Do to Reduce Employee Pilferage*. A title like this has the added benefit of capturing your target audience's attention. They will be curious to see your solutions—and whether your answers match their own or if you have come up with something they have not considered.

In general, vertical topics—narrowly defined and intended for a specific audience—tend to work better for targeted communications than horizontal topics that appeal to a broad, general audience.

When deciding on a topic, focus on the needs of your target customer. Imagine what your prospects believe—how do they feel about your industry, your company, and your product or service? Then ask yourself what they desire—how would you define their goals and aspirations? What do they want your product or service to do for them? And finally, how do they feel—what emotions can you evoke to connect with your audience? Emotional appeals generally work better than logical arguments.

You undoubtedly know the answers to these questions, because you wouldn't have gone into business catering to these people if you didn't understand your market. By focusing on how the prospect feels instead of on the product, you keep your reader interested and involved in your special report.

Create an Outline Before You Write

To write an effective report, you must know what you are talking about. That means plenty of research. Even if you feel as if you are an expert on your topic, you should do some Google searches to find relevant articles, websites, and documents you can use as source material. Make sure the publication or copyright date on source material is recent to ensure you have the most up-to-date information at your fingertips.

Also consider interviewing other experts in your field. Their positions and information may match yours—or you could find an interesting twist on the subject, something you might not have considered. Quotes from an acknowledged expert also add credibility to your report.

I like to make an outline before I actually begin writing. This is basically to organize my thoughts and to make sure that I cover all the points I want to cover. In the course of actually writing the report, the outline may change, but it helps me get started.

Type the outline in a Word file and then underneath it type your notes. Now, move relevant paragraphs of notes into the sections of the outline in which they can be used.

Do not copy text from the source material word for word. Instead, paraphrase and restate the information in your own words to avoid accidental plagiarism. Use the footnote feature in Microsoft Word to document sources, inserting in the footnote the URL where you found the source material.

Once you have established your table of contents and/or general outline, and filled in your research notes, it is time to begin writing. Because you are working from an outline with content already filled in under each section, you can create your first draft by turning the outline subtopics into heads and subheads. Then edit the raw content under each into clear, well-organized content.

Remember, this is your first draft. The object is to get as much information down on the paper as possible without worrying about punctuation, grammar, and syntax. You don't even need to compose in full sentences. There will be plenty of time for that later as you polish and edit your manuscript. See Appendix B for guidelines on basic grammar and punctuation if you want a quick reference guide or refresher.

Designing Your Special Report

Be sure to carefully format your document. You want it to be easy to pick up and scan or read, so make sure your margins are wide enough. Suggested page margins: left margin of 2.5 inches, a 1.25 right margin, and 1 inch on the top and bottom of the page.

Type size, typefaces, fonts, and line spacing are also important. Many people believe a sans serif font like Verdana, Arial, or Helvetica is easier to read on a computer screen. Some experts recommend putting headlines and subheads in sans serif with body copy in a serif face like Times New Roman or Garamond.

Don't press the space bar twice at the end of sentences as it creates distracting gaps. This is especially true if you are justifying the copy or having each line be of equal length. Most people find it easier to read copy that is set "flush left, rag right."

The type size should be 12 points. Any size smaller or larger will be harder to read. And you'll want 1.5 line spacing to also make reading easier. Your finished product should look like what it is: valuable information, not advertising or marketing hype. Keep it simple and clean. It should look more like an editorial piece or academic paper than a magazine ad or brochure.

In your document layout, organize your material in small chunks using bold-face subheads and short paragraphs and sentences. Bulleted and numbered lists are also good for the casual reader. Illustrations, charts, diagrams, and photos can be used to break up long blocks of copy. However, be sure any graphic elements you use are relevant to the subject and explained in the copy.

Be sure to include a page number on every page to make it easier for your prospects to keep your document in order and to refer to a previously read segment.

Titling Your Special Reports

The title of your report is extremely important because you need to grab the attention of your target audience and entice them to read. To do that, a great title should stand out, identify the subject of the paper, and suggest who the target audience is.

There are a variety of ways to structure your title:

- A list title always works well: *14 Ways to Prepare for the Coming Economic Tsunami, 11 Key Questions Commonly Asked by Internet Entrepreneurs,* or *8 Ways to Lose Weight Without Dieting.* (You'll notice that I've titled quite a few sections in this book using this method.)

- Perhaps a how-to or guide-to title would work better for your project: *How to Profit with Online Seminars, Your Guide to Estate Planning, How to Prepare Your Home for Sale to Maximize Net Profit,* or *How to Buy a Foreclosure with No Money Down.*

- Begin your title with an active verb: *Find the Job That Is Right for You, Write an Effective Resume,* or *Change the Way You Approach Internet Marketing.*

- A good way to start your title is with the word *why: Why Parents Get Gray, Why Drinking Diet Soda Makes You Fat,* or *Why You Should Start Retirement Planning NOW.*

- Compound titles (using a colon) can be very effective and can be used in combination with some of the examples already given: Try *6 Ways to Eliminate Debt: How Changing Your Spending Habits Can Change Your Life,* or *Buying a Foreclosure Is Harder Than You Think: Why Bottom Feeding in the Real Estate Market Isn't for Everyone.*

However you decide to proceed, your title should conform to the rule of the Four U's: It should be *urgent, unique, ultra-specific,* and *useful.* (I talk more about the Four U's in Chapter 9.) You should also boil down your research and thinking to one powerful idea—the power of one. Your title should be about that one idea, well and simply expressed.

One last tip on titles: Digital marketer Fred Gleeck recommends that you combine your customer's greatest need with your product's greatest benefit. For example: *How to Lose 10 Pounds in Less Than 30 Days.* The customer's need is to lose weight, and the product's benefit is fast weight loss.

We will cover ebooks in Chapter 7.

CHAPTER 6

Marketing with Case Studies and Testimonials

You can often gain solid marketing traction by sharing real-life stories and opinions. Real people sharing their stories creates a human connection that bulleted lists and statistics simply cannot. There are two types of content marketing pieces that really help make that connection: the case study and the testimonial.

A *case study* is a product success story. It tells how a company solved a problem using a specific product, process, method, or idea. According to copywriter Heather Sloan, case studies are often more effective than brochures and traditional sales collateral. "Everyone loves a story," explains Heather. "Stories paint pictures. Stories evoke emotions. Stories are memorable. Stories give your presentations sticking power. The easiest way to tell a marketing story is by case study."

A *testimonial* is an affirmative statement about your business, usually from a consumer who has benefitted from the product or service you are selling. It helps put a human face on your business—presumably one that is not invested in its success or failure. Testimonials are typically sourced from happy customers, trusted colleagues in your industry, or influencers who help create brand awareness.

For the most part, case studies and testimonials are not overly technical. Case studies are written in a style similar to that of a magazine feature article, while testimonials are written in conversational language, most often in a positive tone. The intent of a case study or testimonial is not to present in-depth details and analytical data, but to briefly describe how a product or service can effectively solve a particular problem. In this chapter, I'll introduce you to the power of using case studies and testimonials as content that you can widely market.

Case Studies

As with other marketing techniques, case studies fluctuate in popularity. While almost any company can profitably market with case studies, an informal survey of B2B websites shows that most don't take full advantage of their power.

Case studies need not adhere to any one formula, but we can talk about general guidelines. The average case study is relatively brief: one or two pages long, or approximately 800 to 1,500 words. More complex or in-depth case studies can run 2,000 to 2,500 words.

An effective case study makes the reader want to learn more about the product it features. It's a soft sell designed to lure your prospects into requesting more detailed information. If you've mirrored the reader's problem successfully, the case study will propel them deeper into the sales funnel and closer to buying.

You needn't be overly creative or reinvent the wheel when writing a case study. Most follow some variation on this outline:

1. Who is the customer?
2. What was the problem? How was it hurting the customer's business?
3. What solutions did they consider and ultimately reject, and why?

4. Why did they choose our product?

5. Describe how they implemented the product, including any problems and how they were solved.

6. How and where does the customer use the product?

7. What results and benefits are they getting?

8. Would they recommend the product to others? Why?

"We didn't have formal guidelines for case studies," said Mark Rosenzweig, editor in chief of *Chemical Processing*, a trade publication that has been running case study articles for decades. "Generally we were looking for a relatively recent installation, say within the last two years, of innovative technology. What issues prompted the installation? What did it involve? What results have been achieved? Average length was 1,500 to 2,000 words."

Because case studies are told as a story, readers are more inclined to take an interest—especially if it holds some sort of benefit for them. Unlike sales presentations, case studies are all about showing, rather than telling, how a product or service works. Instead of presenting a pile of facts and figures, you tell an engaging story that vividly shows your product's effectiveness. And by using a satisfied customer as an example, you can demonstrate how well your product works. Since its benefits are being extolled by an actual user, the claims are more believable.

An equally strong selling point is the level of empathy a case study creates between your prospects and your satisfied customers. Prospects feel far more at ease listening to their peers than to a salesperson. They relate better, because they often share the same issues and problems.

Readers also believe case studies more than other types of marketing. They are skeptical of ads and emails full of puffery, and even podcasts and company blogs can seem self-serving. But in a case study, a customer who has no ulterior motive or financial incentive to praise the product does so anyway, creating instant credibility.

Case studies appeal to marketers and B2B prospects alike because they're based on real-life experiences. As such, they are seen as credible third-party endorsements with a high degree of believability, giving them a big advantage over traditional advertising, which consumers often view skeptically.

Relating your customers' positive experiences with your product is one of the best ways to establish credibility in the marketplace. Giving your customers confidence in what you're offering dramatically increases the likelihood they'll do business with you.

One of the best sources of candidates for case studies is your sales force. However, salespeople prefer to spend their time selling. They are often indifferent to marketing communications and view participating in case studies as aggravating and unrewarding.

TIP

Get salespeople excited about finding candidates for case studies by offering them cash, merchandise, or a travel incentive if their customer is chosen for a case study. When offered a nice incentive, salespeople suddenly get enthusiastic about the process. The incentive does not have to be huge, but it should be desirable—a new iPod, for example.

Writing the Case Study

To prepare for the case study, the writer interviews the person in the customer organization who is most involved in working with the product. For a small service business, this may be the owner; for a large manufacturing company, this person could be the plant manager or an engineer. Before the writer calls, the vendor salesperson or account manager handling that customer should contact them to make sure the customer is willing and even eager to participate. Case studies written about reluctant or hostile users rarely succeed.

During the interview, get as many good quotations as possible, include them in the case study, and attribute them to your interviewee. Quotations in published case studies can later do double duty as customer testimonials.

Often prospects answer questions vaguely, and it is up to the interviewer/writer to wring the specifics out of them. Whenever possible, get the subject to give you exact numbers so your claims and results can be specific. For instance, if they say the product reduced their energy costs, pin them down: "Did it reduce energy consumption by more than 10 percent? More than 100 percent?" They may give you a guesstimate, which you can use as an approximate figure: "The XYZ system reduced the plant's energy consumption by more than 10 percent."

Before you can release the case study, the person you interviewed must approve and sign off on it. Keep these signed releases on file. If the subject takes a job with a different company, you may lose track of them, so you can't afford to lose track of their signed permission form. If your authorization to use the case study is questioned and you can't produce a signed release, you may have to remove it from your site.

Ask subjects of case studies whether they are willing to serve as reference accounts. That way, a prospect with similar needs can speak directly to the product user in a case study. Go through your reference account list periodically to make sure names and numbers are current, and update as needed.

Using Case Studies in Marketing Campaigns

"Few marketing tools are more effective than an anecdotal customer success story," says Casey Hibbard of Compelling Cases, a marketing firm that develops case study materials for technology companies. "Yet companies usually multiply the value of a good customer story by using it in many different ways." Here are some of her suggestions:

- *Treat case studies as fresh news.* "Before a case study is republished on your website or distributed to sales reps, pitch it to the trade press," Hibbard advises. "In fact, many publications now have sections called 'Case Studies' or 'Technology in Action' specifically for this purpose—and many readers regularly troll these publications for real-world business and technology solutions."
- *Post them on your website.* "Websites are an obvious place to post case studies," she notes. "But it pays to put some thought into where and how you present them. The best approach is to feature product-specific cases among other product information on your site, along with white papers and brochures that highlight each product. You can even go a step further by allowing visitors to search for case studies by industry to find one that best matches their situation."

- *Add a short version to the company newsletter.* Case studies are popular content for enewsletters. In fact, Hibbard says one large software company with more than 300 products publishes an entire newsletter filled with customer stories. "Newsletter stories educate customers and prospects about the many ways that other people are using the product successfully," she says.

- *Create slides for sales presentations.* "To punch up sales presentations, give the sales team slides with highlights from successful client implementations," says Hibbard. "That can be even more effective than using printed case studies as leave-behinds—handouts you leave on the table after a presentation or meeting."

- *Enter them in awards events.* "One CRM software vendor submitted a particularly compelling case study for Aberdeen Group's annual 'Top Ten CRM Implementations' list," she recalls. "The company was honored as one of the top ten and was then mentioned in at least a dozen follow-up stories."

- *Use them as customer references.* If reference customers get too many calls, they're likely to get irritated. "To give your references a break, hand out case studies," Hibbard suggests. "While it's not as informative as a person-to-person discussion, a case study can often provide enough specifics to make a call unnecessary."

- *Add testimonial quotes to your sales materials.* "Make sure that quotes within the case study can stand by themselves if you choose to pull them as testimonials on your website or in collateral materials," she says. "I've also seen sales materials that feature 'snapshots' of success stories, and that's very powerful."

- *Use them in press releases.* A case study can be quickly abridged and reformatted into a press release. Be sure to note that a longer, more complete version is available. Editors might pick it up and use it for publication.

- *Distribute them to prospects and customers.* This is a terrific way to keep in touch, raise awareness about a new product or service, and even convert prospects into customers.

- *Give them to your salespeople.* Salespeople like case studies. They use them in presentations, to illustrate key points, and as testimonials. A case study is often more convincing than a brochure.

- ⊙ *Present them.* If your executives speak at meetings and conferences, a case study makes an excellent presentation. The content can easily be converted into slide decks, and the printed case study itself can be used as a handout.
- ⊙ *Use them in lead generation programs.* A case study makes a terrific "free giveaway" in an ad, email, or direct mailer, as well as on a website.
- ⊙ *Hand them out at trade shows.* Case studies are a great way to break through the clutter of fliers and brochures that permeate trade shows. One marketer even had a case study enlarged and printed on a trade show exhibit wall!

Testimonials

Using *testimonials*—quotations from satisfied customers and clients—is one of the simplest and most effective ways of adding punch and power to a marketing campaign. Here are some tips for using testimonials for maximum impact.

Always Use Real Testimonials

Even the most skilled copywriter can rarely make up a testimonial that can match the sincerity, specificity, and credibility of praise from a real customer or client. If you ask a customer for a testimonial and they say, "Sure, just write something and I'll sign it," politely reply, "I appreciate that, but would you mind just giving me your opinion of our product in your own words?" Testimonials written by the advertiser or their copywriter usually sound phony; genuine ones invariably have the ring of truth.

Use Longer Testimonials

Many advertisers are hooked on very short testimonials. For instance:

". . . fabulous! . . ."
"truly funny . . . thought-provoking . . ."
". . . excellent . . . wonderful . . ."

I believe when people see these ultra-short testimonials, they suspect some skillful editing has masked a less favorable comment. Longer testimonials—say, two or three sentences instead of a single word or phrase—come across as more believable. For example: *"Frankly, I was nervous about using an outside consultant. But your excellent service has made me a believer! You can be sure that we'll be calling on your firm to organize all our major sales conferences and other meetings for us. Thanks for a job well done!"*

Sure, it's longer, but it seems more sincere than a one-word superlative.

Be Specific and Detailed

Upon receiving an email or letter of praise from a customer, many people's initial impulse is to find the single sentence that directly praises the company or product in glowing superlatives. This usually produces a bland bit of puffery such as: *"We are very pleased with your product."*

Testimonials are stronger if we included more of the specific, detailed comments our client has made about how our product or service helped him. After all, the prospects we are trying to sell to may have similar problems to the one our current customer solved using our product. If we let Mr. Customer tell Mr. Prospect how we came to his rescue, he'll help us make the sale. For instance:

> We have installed your new ChemiCoat system in each of our bottling lines and have already experienced a 25 percent savings in energy and material costs. Thanks to your system, we have now added an additional production line with no increase in energy costs. This has increased profits 15 percent and already paid back the investment in your product. We are very pleased with your product.

Again, don't try to polish the customer's words so they sound like professional ad copy. Testimonials are usually much more convincing when they are not edited for style.

Use Full Attributions

We've all seen ads with testimonials from "J.B. in Arizona" or "Jim S., Self-Made Millionaire." I suspect many people laugh at such testimonials, thinking they are phony.

To increase your testimonials' credibility, attribute each one. Include the person's name, city, and state, and (if a business customer) their job title and company (e.g., "Jim K. Redding, vice president of manufacturing, Divmet Corporation, Fairfield, NJ"). People are more likely to believe this sort of full disclosure than testimonials that seem to conceal the identity of the source.

Group Your Testimonials

There are two basic ways to present testimonials: You can group them together on one page of your website or scatter them throughout the site. I've seen both approaches work well. But all else being equal, I prefer the first approach. When a prospect sees a large number of testimonials, one right after another, they have more impact and power than when the testimonials are separated and scattered throughout. Have a button on your site's main menu that says "Testimonials," which links to the testimonials page.

Get Permission

Make sure you get permission from your customer before including their testimonial in your copy. I suggest you send a letter quoting the lines you want to reprint and ask permission to include them in emails, websites, landing pages, and other materials used to promote your firm. Notice I'm asking for a general release that gives me permission to use the quotation in all current and future promotions, not just a specific ad or letter. This lets me get more mileage out of the testimonial and eliminates the need to ask permission every time I want to use it in a new ad or letter.

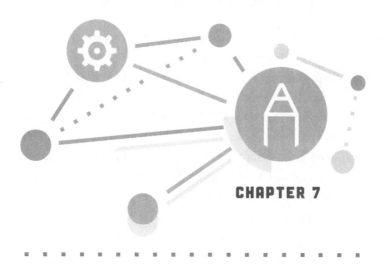

CHAPTER 7

Marketing with Books

Today there are a number of different options for publishing a book. The classic method is to sell it to a traditional publishing house. This can be a major, big-name publisher or a small press; I have sold books to both types of companies. You can also self-publish, which I will cover later in the chapter.

The big-name publishers ostensibly carry more prestige; they certainly pay larger (though usually far from lavish) advances. You usually cannot sell to them unless you have a literary agent representing you. Since they publish many books each season, marketing and PR for your book is likely to be perfunctory.

Small presses *will* look at books submitted directly by an author and do not require a literary agent. In fact, some prefer that an agent not be involved. Their advances are usually nominal. However, since they publish fewer books per year than the big presses, each receives a bit more editorial, marketing, and PR attention.

For self-publishing a physical book, you can use a short-run book printer or *print-on-demand* (POD) publishing service. POD has a higher manufacturing cost per unit but requires no minimum print run. The company will print the books one at a time as they are ordered, meaning you don't need to shell out thousands of dollars for a first-run printing of a book, and you don't need to warehouse copies. You can also opt for a short-run book printer, though the minimum print run is likely to be at least 500 to 1,000 copies. And you will need to arrange for storage, either in your warehouse or at a fulfillment house, which will charge a monthly warehousing fee.

Of course, your book does not have to be published as a physical book at all. You can self-publish it electronically as an *ebook*, such as a downloadable PDF file or a password-protected digital file, which offers you some level of protection for copyrighted material. For the self-publisher, the advantages of an ebook include no printing or binding costs, no inventory to store, and no shipping or fulfillment costs. Plus, it may be a more convenient way to offer the book for free as a lead generation tool.

Whether you choose to offer a free ebook, place your book with a traditional publisher or small press, or self-publish, there are plenty of ways to use books to generate leads. In this chapter, I'll introduce you to the various options available to you when it comes to marketing with books.

Books Have Benefits

Many content marketing campaigns feature the offer of a free book. But in an age where it seems everybody and his brother are publishing books, is it still an effective offer? In my opinion and experience, yes. Let me share why.

A book, no matter the format, still has a perceived value that many other lead magnets do not. For instance, the price tag of white papers is zero, and people tend to value free advice according to what they paid for it—nothing. I actually don't believe that free white papers and special reports have no value, but their perceived value is low. A book, by comparison, can sell for anywhere from $10 to $40 or more whether it is a physical copy or ebook. So when you offer prospects a free book, they grab it, because people like getting something of value for free.

A colleague of mine, marketer and copywriter Jeffrey Lant, famously said that "A book is a brochure that will never be thrown away." People delete white papers and round-file catalogs without a second thought, but they have a harder time tossing a book in the trash, because they hesitate to throw away something of value.

Also, despite the explosive increase in the number of published books and ebooks, writing a book gives you a certain cachet that authoring a white paper or technical paper does not. But which is best—giving your book away for free either as an ebook or printed copy, using a traditional publisher to reach a wide retail audience, or self-publishing your ebook or physical book for sale? Each method has its pros and cons.

Free Books

Free books (ebooks in particular) can be short and focus on very narrow topics. When you offer them in emails, banner ads, landing pages, and other promotions, you can get a significant number of inquiries and downloads. The request for the book is fulfilled right away, so prospects don't have to wait for their content.

The strategy that works best with free ebooks is to take a lot of short documents, put book covers on them, and offer them through an online book retailer as separate books. When a prospect searches your name on the bookseller's site, it looks like you have written a ton of books, which impresses them. They don't stop to realize that many of them are just a few pages long.

The advantage of offering a free physical book is that it is a physical object you can hold in your hand. Between an ebook and a physical book, a physical book is more impressive and prestigious, and has greater impact. When you send a prospect a book, they see you as a "real author," which helps establish you as an expert in their eyes.

Here's an example. Back in the days when electronic data interchange (EDI) was a significant technology, a major bank hired an EDI consultant to write a short paperback book on how to get ready for EDI. The bank

THE **CONTENT MARKETING HANDBOOK**

then prominently featured an image of the book in its print ads with the headline, "Electronic data interchange from the folks who wrote the book on EDI."

All else being equal, customers like to hire the vendor who "wrote the book" on the service or technology. The late publisher Edward Uhland observed, "Just because a person wrote a book, people assume he or she is an expert on the topic." Authors may in fact not be the top experts on their subjects, but because they wrote a book, people perceive they are.

Now here's the drawback of using a book as a free lead magnet in your marketing: When you run an online ad or send an email promoting the book rather than your product or service, you will often double or even triple the number of inquiries you get. But up to 90 percent of respondents are replying only to get the free book and may have little to no interest in your product or service.

Is this necessarily a bad thing? No, because 10 percent or more of respondents will also inquire about your product or service. Ten percent of a lot is still a pretty good number. In one free book campaign we did, we spent $1,000 on an ad, which generated more than 100 downloads of our PDF ebook, at a cost of less than $10 each. Of those inquiries, about 10 percent were good leads for our service, so the cost of these leads was about $100 each. That's a reasonable amount to pay for a qualified lead when you are selling a service that costs $3,000 to $5,000.

> **TIP**
>
> On the landing page for your free book offer, give the prospect three boxes to click: one to request the free book, another to request literature on your product, and a third to request a call from a sales rep. Allow them to check any or all three of these options. Prospects who want product literature or a call from a rep are the most qualified and the best leads.

Fields on the request form should include name, title, company, phone number, email address, and website URL. The person's job title and company help you determine whether you have a *qualified* lead—someone with the money and authority to purchase your product.

118 ◎ PART II / Implementing Content Marketing Tactics

On the checkbox to request the book say, "Check here to see whether you qualify to receive this free book." That way you are not obligated to send it to students and others who are not serious leads but just want a free book.

Traditional Publishing

A free book is a highly desirable premium and an effective bait piece, but so is a book sold into the retail trade at brick-and-mortar and online stores. I tell virtually all self-employed professionals (as well as many small-business owners) who ask me how to promote themselves as a thought leader in their niche specialty that they should write a book about it, and get it published.

When you write a book that is produced, marketed, and sold by a traditional publisher, your content is vetted and edited by industry professionals. This rigorous editorial process, along with dedicated marketing support from the publisher, can help increase the perceived value and quality of your content, which leads to other benefits down the road. Here are just a few ways you can benefit from writing your own book and having it published by a traditional publisher or small press:

- When writing a book, you must do additional research to flesh out gaps in your knowledge. Your knowledge of your subject therefore increases, making you a better resource for your clients or customers.
- Writing a book requires you to organize your material in a logical sequence. This increases clarity in all your communications, including individual consultations with clients.
- A book can serve as the basis for a profitable seminar or workshop. The chapters of the book become the modules of the seminar.
- Potential clients reading your book call to inquire about the services you offer and may be predisposed to hire you.
- Associations will ask you to speak at their conferences for handsome fees if you are the author of a book that interests their members.
- Listing yourself as the author of a book is an impressive credential on your website, brochure, and other marketing materials. It increases your status.

- You can give copies of your book to potential clients to familiarize them with your methodology and convince them that you are an expert in your field.
- You may be called on to serve as an expert witness on your topic in court cases, at a handsome day rate.
- Editors will ask you to contribute articles to their publications.
- The media will want to interview you as an expert in your field. This can lead to appearances as a guest on radio and TV shows.

A developer in Florida held receptions for groups of real estate investors. To entice them to come to the presentation, the developer offered a free book, *Ten Tips on Buying and Enjoying Vacation Property*. The author, Christopher Cain, was even on hand to autograph the books.

"Books make an outstanding premium for developers who sell vacation property," says Cain. "In four consecutive one-day receptions, we targeted 88 highly qualified buyers, and the developer sold out the first phase of his resort project in record time."

TIP

An alternative is to produce your book using print on demand (POD). The cost per book is higher, but there's no minimum quantity; you can print one book at a time, as you sell them. Your publisher might be able to produce books this way as well.

Conventional books published by trade publishers are typically too expensive to use as bait pieces, but they remain a great way to build your brand. Not only will your name reach a wider audience, but you can also frequently purchase books from the publisher at an author discount to sell at speaking events or to give away. However, that can get expensive. If your hardcover book sells for $25, even with a 50 percent author's discount, copies cost you $12.50 apiece. Therefore, if you are going to use a book strictly as a bait piece, self-publishing (for both physical and ebooks) may be a better option (which you'll read about later in the chapter).

If you choose to publish your book with a traditional publishing house, here are the steps involved:

1. *Come up with a good idea for your book.* If you already have a good idea, move on to step two. If not, analyze your knowledge base, consulting specialties, client base, and service offerings. Which topic is broad enough that thousands of people would buy a book about it? Some first-time authors are intimidated by this step, believing they lack the creativity to come up with good ideas. My experience is that we are all capable of having good ideas, including ideas for books. The actual hard part is writing the book.

2. *Evaluate your book idea.* There are many ideas that sound good but must be rejected because they are not commercially viable. When I ask potential authors why they think a publisher would be interested in their book—and why a reader would want to buy it—many of them answer, "Because it's good" or "Because the subject is important."

    These days, that's not enough. Your book has to entertain or inform the reader—ideally both. A book that does neither is going to be extremely difficult to sell.

    And with so many books published every year on virtually every topic imaginable, unless you can convince a publisher that yours is truly different and better, your chances of selling it to them are slim at best.

3. *Create the content outline.* Once you decide on a topic, I recommend that you develop a content outline. The *content outline* is similar to the table of contents in any nonfiction book, except it is more detailed and fleshed out. Creating the content outline has three purposes. First, it helps you determine whether you can write enough about the subject to fill a book. Second, it is perhaps the single most powerful tool for convincing publishers that your book idea has merit. Third, it will save you an enormous amount of time when you sit down to write your book proposal and the book itself. I always make my content outlines detailed rather than sketchy. I am certain this helps me sell my books to a publisher.

4. *Write your book proposal.* The *book proposal* is often the most mysterious part of the book publishing process, especially to beginners.

You know what books are like, because you've read hundreds of them. But chances are you've never seen a book proposal, so you have no idea what it should look like. It typically contains the following elements:

- *Title page.* The book's title and the author's name are centered in the middle of the page. In the upper left comer, type "Book Proposal." In the bottom right, type your name, address, and phone number (or, if you have one, your literary agent's).
- *Overview.* Include one to two pages summarizing what your book is about: the topic, who will read it, why it's important or interesting to your intended audience, and what makes your book different from others in the field.
- *Format.* Specify approximate word length, number of chapters, types of illustrations or graphics you plan to include, and any unique organizational schemes or formats. (For example, will you divide your book into major sections, or do you intend to use sidebars?)
- *Market.* Tell the editor who will buy your book, how many of these people exist, and why they need it or will want to read it. Use statistics to illustrate the size of the market. For example, if your book is about infertility, mention that one in every eight couples in the U.S. is infertile.
- *Promotion.* Is your book a natural for talk radio or a celebrity book club (be realistic)? Can it be promoted through seminars or speeches to associations and clubs? Give the publisher some ideas on how the book can be marketed. (Note: Phrase these as suggestions, not demands. The publisher will be interested to hear your ideas but probably won't use most of them.)
- *Competition.* List books that compare with yours. Include the title, author, publisher, year of publication, number of pages, price, and format (hardcover, trade paperback, or mass market paperback). Describe each book briefly, pointing out weaknesses and areas in which your book is different and superior.
- *Author's bio.* This should be a brief biography listing your writing credentials (books and articles published), qualifications to

write about the topic (for instance, for a book on global warm-
ing, it helps if you're a climatologist), and your media experience
(previous appearances in the media).

- ◎ *Table of contents/outline.* Give a chapter-by-chapter outline
  showing the contents of your proposed book. Many editors tell
  me that a detailed, well-thought-out table of contents in a proposal helps sway them in favor of a book.

5. *Get an agent.* Although you can sell a book directly to the publisher, I recommend you go through a literary agent. *Literary Market
   Place*, available in bookstores, online, or the reference room of your
   local library, lists agents you can contact. Or visit the Association of
   Authors' Representatives' website (http://aaronline.org).

6. *Send your proposal to publishers and get an offer.* If you have an
   agent, they will approach publishers for you; otherwise you can
   contact publishers directly. Many large publishing houses do not
   look at unagented manuscripts. But small and midsize publishers
   are open to doing so, and some small publishers actually prefer
   authors who do not have an agent.

7. *Negotiate your contract.* If you have an agent, they will negotiate
   the contract on your behalf, with your input and approval. If you
   don't, you will handle the negotiations yourself. Key contract terms
   include advances, royalties, first and second serial rights, termina-
   tion, and copyright. If you intend to use the book as a bait piece,
   negotiate the largest author's discount you can get, and ask if the
   publisher can give an even larger discount if you buy multiple copies at once.

8. *Write and deliver the manuscript.* Follow the outline the publisher
   bought when accepting your proposal. And be on time.

Self-Publishing

Self-publishing is having a huge impact on the book industry. In 1985, only
about 35,000 books were published in the U.S., but by 2019, International
Standard Book Numbers (ISBNs) were secured for more than 1 million
books published that year. And that doesn't even account for all books,
because many are published without an ISBN.

EBOOK KNOW-HOW

If you choose the traditional publishing route, your publisher will likely release an ebook version of your book along with a print version. If, however, you opt to go your own way to create, distribute, and possibly sell ebooks on your own dime, things can get a bit tricky. Why? Because there is much more to creating a professional-quality ebook than slapping together a few text files and selling them as a package deal. Remember: An ebook (even one that is solely used to give away free as lead gen) must look as professional as a traditional book. Otherwise, marketing prospects will see right through your claim of "I have a book" and realize that you didn't take care in editing or designing a quality product. And, if you want to sell your ebook through online retailers, it must meet certain industry conventions to qualify. Here are some tips for making sure your ebook meets the expectations of consumers and online retailers alike:

- As with a self-published print book, make sure you have a good editor review the content and copy.

- Divide the book content into chapters that include major headings.

- Include a table of contents.

- Apply for an ISBN and affix it to the back cover image. You can apply for an ISBN at www.isbn.org.

- Apply for copyright and Publisher's Cataloging-in-Publication (CIP) data at https://www.loc.gov/publish/cip/.

- Use a graphic design program (InDesign is popular in the industry) to lay out your text into a designed book

EBOOK KNOW-HOW, continued

format. You can also use a plug-and-play book design site like Canva or BookBaby.

⊚ Decide whether you want to use a PDF or EPUB file format for your ebook. PDFs are best used for free ebooks that you give away for lead gen because they are easy to create. However, keep in mind that they can also be easily copied or reproduced by outside parties, so you may want to consider making yours password protected. An EPUB file, on the other hand, offers a bit more protection against piracy and better universal text flow on multiple ereader devices because it is often used for ebooks sold at online retailers. So, it has to be secure and able to look good on all kinds of ereaders, tablets, and phones. However, you have to have some coding skills to know how to navigate this file type.

⊚ If you want to sell your ebook in addition to, or instead of, using it for lead gen, you will need to set up a seller's account with each individual online retailer as well as include "Buy" buttons for each retailer on your own landing page.

As you can see, ebook creation is much more involved than giving away a simple text file online—at least if you want to do it right.

Many writers I've met swear by self-publishing. However, an equal number swear *at* it.

In self-publishing, you are the publisher as well as the author. You must pay to have the book typeset, designed, and printed (unless you want to do it yourself, which I don't recommend unless you have experience in book and graphic design). You are responsible for inventory, shipping, distribution, sales, marketing, and promotion. As publisher/ author, though, you get to keep all the revenues generated from sales (less

THE CONTENT MARKETING HANDBOOK

expenses) instead of the 6 to 15 percent of sales a mainstream publisher would pay you.

If your goal is simply to hold in your hands a nicely designed, printed book with your name on the cover or point people to your ebook in your marketing outreach, self-publishing is relatively easy. Anyone can have a manuscript typeset, take it to a printer, and pay them to print the book or hire a designer well-versed in ebook design and conversion to create a book that can be distributed online. But if you want to sell a lot of copies of your book, self-publishing requires a long-term commitment. You must act as warehouse staff, shipping department, accounting department, sales force, publicity department, marketing director, distribution, collections agency, and secretary.

Having your book published by a traditional publisher means you can concentrate on writing, which for me is the part I like best. Self-publishing in essence requires you to form and run a mini-publishing company.

Deciding Which Way to Go

How do you make the choice between self-publishing (and offering your books either free or for a small price) instead of traditional publishing (and selling through a retailer)? Unless you are already dead set in favor of one particular option, here are some guidelines to consider.

You may prefer traditional publishing if:

- ⊙ you believe your idea would appeal to a mass audience
- ⊙ yours is the type of book that would sell well in bookstores
- ⊙ you want the prestige and branding that come with selling a book to a "real" publisher
- ⊙ you do not have the time or inclination to be in business as a small publishing house and would prefer instead to concentrate on your core business
- ⊙ you want to establish your reputation as an expert in your field
- ⊙ you do not have the skills and expertise to self-publish (e.g., book design, marketing, distribution, desktop publishing) and do not wish to acquire them

126 ⊙ PART II / Implementing Content Marketing Tactics

You may prefer self-publishing if:

- your idea appeals to a specialized, narrow target market: parachutists, chiropractors, carwash owners, or other specific audience
- yours is the type of book that would sell well through direct response advertising using magazine ads, direct mail, catalogs, or the internet
- you have the time, talent, and inclination to handle all aspects of the publishing business, like distribution, promotion, and administration, in addition to researching and writing the book
- the "snob appeal" and status of being published in the conventional method is not important to you
- you have been turned down by the major publishing houses, yet believe in the book so strongly that you are willing to act as publisher to get it into print
- you are impatient and want to get the book out right away, rather than wait the 9 to 18 months it normally takes to write a book and get it published through a conventional publisher

Many proponents of self-publishing (and some are valued colleagues and personal friends of mine) are highly critical of traditional publishing. They will tell you publishing houses are book factories that only care about churning out products. They destroy your work in the editing process, and they don't do a proper job of promoting or publicizing your book. they will also tell you books don't sell and most authors don't make money.

But they don't tell you the flip side, which gives you a more balanced picture: that many authors who publish through traditional houses are happy and satisfied, at least most of the time. Their books bring them fame, prestige, and visibility, and enhance their careers. Many have become rich (even millionaires) from royalty payments when their books hit the bestseller lists.

The formula for book revenues is as follows: DBR + IBR = TBR, which stands for direct book revenues plus indirect book revenues equals total book revenues.

Direct book revenues refers to the advance and royalties the publisher pays you. *Indirect book revenues* refers to ancillary income, such as the leads the book generates for your business and the product sales it helps generate. In content marketing, most of the total book revenue comes from IBR, and the DBR is usually modest. You have to decide which matters more to you.

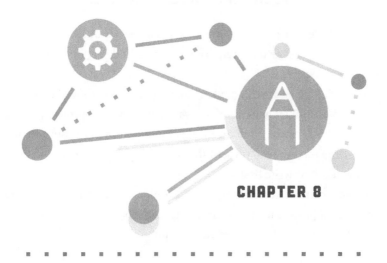

CHAPTER 8

Marketing with Articles and Blogs

You can write articles for traditional print publications such as magazines, newsletters, and newspapers, or write them online for enewsletters, blogs, and websites. Online articles can include a link to your site or landing page, and thus generate many more responses than a print article. On the other hand, publishing an article in a respected academic journal, newspaper, trade journal, or consumer magazine adds credibility and does more to promote you as an expert resource in your field.

Articles are versatile tools in a content marketing campaign. Just one article in a trade journal can bring a company hundreds of leads and thousands of dollars in sales. And with more than 7,000 magazines from which to choose, there's bound to be at least one that could accommodate a story from your company. They work well online, too: Just scan the article and post it on your site or include a link to the journal's website.

In addition, reprints have enormous marketing value. You can offer them as bait pieces, or use them as enclosures in direct mail and inquiry fulfillment packages.

But, although nearly all content marketers know the value of placing trade journal stories, they don't always know how to approach an editor. What's the best way to pitch an idea? Should you present more than one idea at a time? Is it wise to present the same story to more than one editor? Should you call or write first?

This chapter answers those questions and more. It can help you through the process of placing an article in the right journal for your company and reaping the rewards of increased recognition.

Getting Your Articles Published

Chances are you already know which journals you'd like to approach. The magazines that cross your desk every week are strong candidates, because they're likely to cover subjects relevant to you and your competitors. But if you have an idea for an article that is outside your industry, or if you're just not sure which magazine would be most appropriate, *Writer's Market* is a useful resource. It lists thousands of magazines and describes the editorial requirements of each. Because *Writer's Market* is helpful when it comes to finding a home for a full-length feature on your company.

The quickest way to turn off an editor is to suggest an idea that has nothing to do with their magazine. "My pet peeve with people calling or writing to pitch an idea is that they often haven't studied the magazine," says Rick Dunn, a trade

TIP

If you are not familiar with a magazine but think it sounds appropriate for your article, be sure to read a few issues before contacting an editor. Many trade journals will send a sample issue and a set of editorial guidelines to prospective authors upon request. These can provide valuable clues as to style, format, and topics. They often tell how to contact the magazine, give hints on writing an article, describe the manuscript review process, and discuss payment/reprint arrangements.

journal editor. "If they haven't read several issues and gotten a handle on who we are and who our audience is, they won't be able to pitch an idea effectively."

Get to Know the Publication

There's no substitute for knowing the audience and the various departments within a magazine. Editors pay more attention to an idea that is intended for a particular section of their magazine. Every magazine is unique. Study the tone, style, content, and quality of their writing and illustrations to increase your chances of being published.

Offer an editor the type of article they seem to prefer—frequency and length are good indicators of popular subjects—and the odds are more in your favor. Companies can increase their chances for coverage by checking a magazine's editorial calendar on the publication's website for upcoming articles that might mesh with their products or activities. "If people respond to our editorial calendar with ideas for specific issues, great!" says Dunn. "Or if they can provide background for a story we want to do, they'll have an edge in getting into the magazine."

You may even want to suggest feature story ideas for next year's calendar. The trick is to do it tactfully. Don't come across as pushy or demanding. Refrain from saying things like, "This is important to your readers" or "You should run this story."

If your content campaign relates to a new trend in, say, packaging food in plastic containers instead of glass jars, and you can provide statistics and facts to back up your claim, go ahead and contact the appropriate editor. They will probably appreciate your interest and effort. Many publications have response forms on their websites for submitting article ideas.

Do not email your query to an editor unless they have indicated they accept article proposals by email. And do not send an attached file via email to an editor you do not know. Most will delete it without opening, fearing it contains a virus.

The solution? Go to the magazine's website. In most cases, you will find a form that you can use to submit your query letter online. This increasingly is the way more and more editors want you to pitch article ideas to them.

Despite a growing aversion today to using the telephone, it can be a different and perhaps effective way to reach an editor. If she is receptive to the call, you can make your case for doing the article, answer any questions she might have, and often get a go-ahead right on the spot. I write the occasional article for both consumer and trade magazines, and have found that the phone can sometimes get through when online forms and emails are ignored or rejected.

Be Specific

Mentioning certain elements in your initial query—whether via social media, over the phone, or in writing—can sway an editor toward your proposal. For instance, many magazines seek practical information that shows their readers how to save money, time, or labor, or that can help them improve their job performance. Statistics, benefits, examples, and how-to tips can strengthen your case substantially.

Specifics sell a story. You're much more likely to grab an editor's attention if you say, "Our newly developed Dry Scrubber pollution control device saved the Smithson Paper Plant $4,400 a day in fuel costs" than if you say, "Our new product can save paper plants a lot of money." Then go on to explain just how the company has saved money, and be prepared to back up your claim with documented facts.

The more help your idea promises readers, the more likely it is to interest an editor. Specifically, editors want content that helps readers solve specific problems. Ask yourself if the content provides a takeaway that readers can apply to their lives, either at home or at work.

Put yourself in the readers' shoes and analyze their problems, and you will have a better idea of what kind of articles an editor wants. If you read the magazine regularly, you may have a head start in coming up with useful ideas. Also, any knowledge or technical expertise you have will help you "sell yourself" to an editor as an authoritative source.

Most industry-specific editors, for example, want bylines from subject-matter experts to provide the most up-to-date advice and a strong author ethos. Technical/industry knowledge can help you build a bridge to that particular audience, especially if you already speak on that topic elsewhere.

Know Your Topic

But don't despair if you are not a technical whiz or industry "name." Plenty of trade journal authors, including legions of PR executives, aren't either. They get published because they take the time to study a subject they want to write about. That doesn't mean they acquire the same knowledge a technical expert would have, but they know enough to write clearly, concisely, and logically about it. For many trade journals, that's all that's required.

Many editors will consider articles that are short on either writing prowess or technical skill if their full-time staff has those covered. What counts for scores of editors is an article's newsworthiness. Many are particularly interested in new ways of doing things within the industry they cover.

Mark Rosenzweig, editor in chief of *Chemical Processing,* says he looks for "heavy-duty, nuts-and-bolts articles, not puff or promotional pieces. Title or position isn't that important to us—it's whether there's any 'meat' in an idea." Impartiality is another "must" for many editors. Remember, they're not there to praise your company's products; they're there to give readers an objective overview of what's happening in their industry. This can be a sticking point when dealing with PR departments, although most editors recognize the "one-hand-washes-the-other" usefulness of such contacts.

"We're certainly not prejudiced against articles from PR firms," says Rosenzweig. "We just generally have to make more revisions to eliminate their tendency toward one-sidedness. We want all the disadvantages spelled out, as well as the advantages."

Adds Dunn, "If an article is about storage methods, we want to see all 15 methods discussed, not just the ones used by the writer's company or client."

Deliver on Time

Still, the fact that PR people are generally eager to give editors information and can be trusted to produce articles on target and on time endears them to many editors. "We don't have to chase after them," explains Dunn. "They understand our role a little better than most people, they know how we operate, and they tend to give us good service."

So follow the PR agencies' example: Make yourself available to editors when they call, follow their guidelines, and deliver written copy as promised. You'll put yourself in good standing with people who can exert considerable influence on your company's fortunes.

Use High-Quality Visuals

Some editors will kill a feature story simply for lack of photos or illustrations, and many weigh heavily the availability of appropriate graphics. Those visual "extras" can be a deciding factor in choosing one story idea over another. Even though the larger journals may have illustrators on staff to produce high-quality finished drawings, they often work from original sketches supplied by an author.

Professional photographs, while nice, are not necessary for most trade journals. Straightforward, good-quality, high-resolution color photos taken with a smartphone satisfy most trade editors. You can email images to the editor you are working with as an attached JPEG or PNG file. You can also set up a file-sharing account (like Dropbox) where you can leave large image files in a shared folder.

TIP

You can get a good idea of how important visuals are to a magazine before you make your pitch by scanning a couple of issues. Note whether it uses photos or drawings. If photos, are they black and white or color? Is there at least one illustration with every story of one page or more? If so, be prepared to provide the same. Otherwise, your article may land on the reject pile, regardless of its merits.

Follow the Norms of Exclusivity

Never submit the same idea or story to more than one magazine at a time. Only if the idea is rejected should you approach another editor. This is one point nearly all editors agree on: They want exclusive material—especially for feature articles.

If a story is particularly timely or newsworthy and has run in a magazine that does not directly compete with the one you're currently approaching, you may be able to get around the problem by working with the editor to expand or rewrite the piece. But be upfront about it or risk losing the editor's confidence and goodwill.

Many trade journal and consumer magazine editors want articles that are exclusive, meaning the articles as not been published anywhere else. "I'd like everything to be exclusive," says Russo. "That increases its value to us and can sway us toward acceptance if it's a 'borderline' story." Offering *world exclusives* can also make an article more appealing to an editor. That means you promise not to submit the article to any other magazine, even if it's in a completely different field.

Whether you are willing to do that depends on how badly you want a story to run in a particular magazine. You may decide you'd rather try to get more mileage out of the story by submitting it to a number of unrelated publications.

As Dunn points out, "Exclusivity is a quality consideration for a feature article. Editors don't want their readers to pick up their magazine and see something that they've already read elsewhere."

Often the exceptions to this rule are column items or case histories—for example, a problem/solution/result story describing how a customer successfully used a company's product. However, even those stories should not be submitted to competing publications.

Pitch First, Submit Later

Submitting unsolicited manuscripts is always risky—again, with the exception of case histories and short news pieces. Some editors never want to see an unsolicited manuscript; others are willing to review them and may even publish a few. *Chemical Engineering* falls into that category.

"We get hundreds of unsolicited manuscripts every year, but we have the resources to do a heavy amount of rewriting for the ones we use," says Rosenzweig.

Query the editor. Send a synopsis of the content of the article you want to write and why the publication's readers would be interested in it. Many magazine websites have online forms for quick and easy submission of short queries.

In the end, most editors prefer to be asked about story ideas before the author writes the article. It saves them time—they don't have to read a lengthy manuscript to decide whether the subject is right for the magazine. And it saves the author the trouble of researching and writing an article that might never get accepted.

Even if you have a manuscript already in hand, by submitting it "blind" you may lead an editor to suspect you're submitting it to other magazines at the same time. That's not what an editor wants to see. It's far better to query first and then send the story only if the editor expresses interest.

Once your idea is accepted, which is always tentative until final review of the manuscript, you'll need to know any length and deadline requirements. If the editor doesn't volunteer this information, by all means ask to avoid any misunderstandings later.

Adhere to a Publication's Standards

As a rule, be generous with length. Include everything you think is relevant, and don't skimp on examples. Editors would rather cut material than have to request more.

A few magazines, such as *Chemical Engineering*, are very flexible on length. "We run articles anywhere from three paragraphs to 40 to 50 pages long," says Rosenzweig. Most other magazines give authors more specific limits. Check with your editor for the exact range.

Deadlines, too, can vary considerably. Some don't like to impose any deadlines at all, especially if they work far enough ahead that they're not pressed for material. But if the article is intended for publication in a special issue, the editors will probably want the finished manuscript in hand at least two months prior to publication. That allows time for final revisions, assembling photos or illustrations, and production.

Chemical Engineering, for example, has a 6- to 12-month lead time on many of the articles it assigns. In at least one case, the magazine waited for six years for a promised manuscript. Unsurprisingly, the editor had completely forgotten about the story.

Some magazines may send a follow-up email to remind delinquent authors about expected articles, but, as Dunn says: "We won't chase after someone. If we don't hear from a writer in about six months, we figure the article is never going to materialize."

Don't put an editor's patience to the test. You may gain a reputation as being undependable, which can hurt your future chances of being published.

Stay attuned to editors' needs by keeping up with news in their field, as well as your own; staying up-to-date with any changes (in format or content) in their publications; heeding their suggestions; being considerate of their time; and, above all, delivering articles as promised. "The best way to cultivate an editor's friendship is to produce results," advises Dunn, "because the people who are sincerely interested in helping us out are the ones we go back to."

Blogging

"A blog is an online journal," explains blogging expert Debbie Weil. "It's called a journal because every entry is time and date stamped and always presented in reverse chronological order." A blog has a unique URL. It can stand alone or be a section of your main website. For example, my blog is on my website, https://www.bly.com/.

In content marketing, blogging is a powerful communications channel. According to Weil, a business blog is "a platform from which to lobby, network, and influence sales. It's a way to circumvent traditional media and analysts. And blogging can be done instantly, in real time, at a fraction of the cost of using traditional channels."

Today, blogging is heralded as a standard form of content generation in publishing and marketing. It supposedly takes the power out of the hands of the publishing establishment (book publishers, newspapers, and magazines that can accept or reject your work) and puts it into the hands of individual authors and companies marketing their products. This is because anyone can start a blog anywhere, at any time, without approval or authorization from a publisher or anyone else.

Many content writers and consultants use blogging as a free marketing tool. "My blog convinces skeptics that they should hire me to speak," says professional speaker David Meerman Scott.

Consultant Ilise Benun says, "People tell me they read a post that hit a nerve and decided to find out more about how my consulting works."

Content writers and marketing experts also use their blogs as a platform from which to disseminate content as well as develop more substantial writings. "More than anything, it's a container for all the ideas I have and want to write about but don't have time to devote a whole article to," Benun says. "That's why I think a blog is especially good for people who have ideas and like to write. If you're going to struggle with what to say, Twitter is better."

"My blog is my 'front door,'" Scott says. "I test ideas on the blog that go into my books. It gets me new fans who then buy my books."

In this section, I will walk you through some basic need-to-know information about content marketing with a blog.

Blogging Basics

According to Software Finder, there are over 505 million blogs available online. So what does blogging entail? Blogging in its most basic form is journaling online. Merriam-Webster defines a blog as "a website that contains an online personal journal with reflections, comments, and often hyperlinks."

Is there an ideal length and schedule for blog posts? Many blogging experts say once a week is the minimum, while others recommend blogging every day. The length can vary from a few pithy paragraphs to a full-length article.

A number of writers have parlayed their blogs into book deals. The most notorious is Jessica Cutler, who was fired from her job as a Senate aide for writing about her sex life on Capitol Hill and then offered a contract by Hyperion to turn her blog, *The Washingtonienne*, into a book. Other bloggers who have received book deals include Jeremy Blachman (*Anonymous Lawyer*), Wendy McClure (*Pound*), Stephanie Klein (*Greek Tragedy*), and U.S. soldier Colby Buzzell (*CBFTW*).

One big advantage of blogs, according to digital marketer Paul Chaney, is that having a blog can help pull traffic to your website. "The search engines, especially Google, love blogs," Chaney says. "You'd be amazed at how many of your posts will end up in the top ten returns. If search engine optimization is a concern to you, blogs are the best way I know to move up the ladder as well as increase your page rank."

"I confidently predict that blogs will soon be a key piece of an effective online marketing strategy," says Weil. "Ultimately, they're nothing more than an instant publishing tool, one that makes posting fresh content to the web within anyone's reach. No tech skill or knowledge required."

"My argument is that blogging is more likely to raise brand awareness, but that the impact on direct sales will be more difficult to assess," says management consultant and analytics expert Max Blumberg. "Therefore, I don't think it is appropriate to look for a close relationship between blogging and direct sales."

Business coach Jennifer Rice adds, "Blogging is not a direct response vehicle. It's an awareness, visibility, and promotion vehicle that happens to be terrific for those of us selling intellectual capital. It's also extremely useful for corporations to use as a means to connect with customers and get feedback."

I disagree with Ms. Rice: Experience proves that blogs can be an effective direct response tool, as you can link to your conversion and order pages in your posts. Seven out of ten B2B buyers say they read blog content as part of their research when searching for needed products or services, And more than half of marketers have acquired new customers because of their blogs.

In my blog, I post comments on topics that interest me and presumably my readers. To incorporate your blog into a content marketing campaign, it must focus on the same topics as your bait pieces—for example, project management, hazardous materials handling, or whatever you are promoting.

But even more so than a lead magnet, a blog must be educational and informative, not a sales piece. Readers will only stick with your blog if they feel you are being honest and helpful. If you start selling your product on your blog, they will be turned off and leave.

Here are some tips for attracting more prospects and getting wider readership for your blog posts:

- Integrate your blog as a page on your website so the content in the posts boosts your Google search ranking.
- Post titles should not exceed 70 characters.
- Post frequently. Both Google and your readers respond well to fresh content.

- Add YouTube video links to some of your posts.
- Write in a natural, conversational style.
- Write about what you know.
- If you use or reference other people's material, credit them as the source. Keep in mind that most content is copyrighted and some may require written permission to use.
- When relevant, include links to other web pages in your posts.
- Respond politely and intelligently to reasonable comments on your posts.
- Rant against misinformed, critical, argumentative, incorrect, or offensive emails.
- Extract material for your posts from existing copy for paid offers.
- Rewrite private label rights (PLR) content (see tip below) so it's relevant to your blog.
- Answer frequently asked questions.
- Ask interesting questions and invite comments.
- Explain a technology or idea.
- Propose a solution to a common problem or give other useful advice.
- Provide how-to instructions and tutorials.
- Review other people's products, technology, and services.
- Share your favorite resources.
- Highlight a checklist of freebies with links to download pages.
- Share relevant personal stories.
- Be contentious, though avoid insulting those with opposing viewpoints.
- Share your flaws and flubs, and then derive a lesson from them.

> **TIP**
>
> Private label rights (PLR) content is prewritten content that you can gain unlimited rights to and use in your own content marketing for a small license fee. It's useful for covering topics beyond your own knowledge and experience.

Public Relations in Content Marketing

News releases about your products can give you a results-to-expenditures ROI unmatched by any other promotion or marketing tool. By investing a few days' work and often less than $500, you can achieve results comparable to those produced by an advertising or PR agency—for a fraction of what an agency charges.

For marketers, news releases can produce sales leads or inquiries they can follow up on with literature or qualify through calling. For content marketers, articles based on the release guide prospects through the sales funnel while building their brand's reputation.

The key is to target your news release the same way you target mailings to your database. Don't simply email your release to lists of magazines you obtain from standard directories. Screen copies of each magazine to get a feel for its editorial approach, and tailor your release to the needs and interests of its readers.

Six Tested Ways to Produce Inquiries from PR

As with all direct marketing, a lot depends on your offer. Don't just tack a sentence onto the end of your release that reads "For more information, contact . . . " Make your offer specific and tangible, like one of these:

1. *Free booklet or report.* Business prospects are always on the lookout for ideas and information. The offer of a free booklet or report stops busy readers and gets them to act, dramatically increasing lead responses.

2. *Free article reprint.* This is a variation on the free booklet. Trade journal articles by company executives can be reprinted and offered in a news release. Even competing magazines will run the offer. A lengthy article can be called a "special report" or "monograph" and a short one a "tip sheet."

3. *New product.* Short reports on new products, with photos, are published by "product news" tabloids or in new product sections of industrial magazines. The product need not actually be new. New enhancements, features, models, upgrades, or applications will do. Again, for the best response, offer a free brochure or data sheet.

4. *New literature.* New product brochures, catalogs, market surveys, white papers, or other literature can form the basis of a release. You can follow up a new product release in a month or two with a new literature release.

5. *New angle.* Put a new slant on an existing product. The product may not be new, but find a new angle or application and you've got the makings of a news release. Is it newsworthy? That's the key. If it's simply a puff piece disguised as a news release, the magazine, quite rightly, may suggest that you buy an ad. But make it bright, creative, imaginative, and add a free offer, and you'll be surprised at the response.

6. *New online resources.* These are typically either free software tools, online databases, or online searchable content archives. For example, on bly.com, I have a simple tool that tells you the percentage response you need to make money on a direct-mail promotion.

Four Common Myths About PR

The following are corrections to widespread misconceptions about public relations:

1. *Myth*: You can't buy public relations with advertising.
   Reality: In some cases, you can, but not in quality publications with editorial integrity. Small magazines may give advertisers preferential treatment (I have seen it happen many times). But chances are, the quality of responses you get won't be worth the effort.

2. *Myth*: You need "contacts" to get publicity.
   Reality: Yes, contacts help, but you can succeed without them. Every time you get coverage, add the editor's name and email address to your database and send a short, sincere thank-you email to the editor or reporter.

3. *Myth*: Editors want to be wined and dined.
   Reality: It's unnecessary. A few may respond positively to lunch at a posh restaurant or tickets to a basketball game. But most editors prefer to keep PR sources at arm's length. A simple thank-you note is all that's called for.

4. *Myth*: PR promotions don't work without follow-up.
   Reality: Follow-up may get some editors who initially missed your material to reconsider it, but overall, a well-written press

release, targeted to the publication's readers, will do just as well without it.

Publicity has to be managed. Media research, writing, checking, photos, and distribution—all take time and supervision. As a marketer, you may have the clearest insights in your company into markets, applications, customers, and prospects, so regardless of whether you have the time, the responsibility for publicity may fall on your shoulders.

In addition, though some marketers, including me, find paper press releases are effective at getting an editor's attention because they stand out in a digital world, the overwhelming majority of press releases are distributed electronically today. Appendix C lists some online press release distribution services you can use to deliver PR to the media.

Product publicity conversion rates are typically low. Still, because of its comparatively low cost, it can be a very profitable way to generate sales leads.

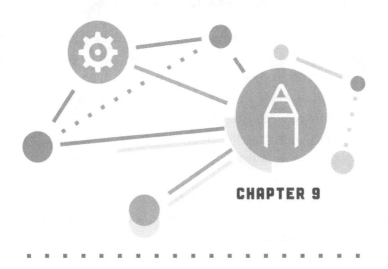

CHAPTER 9

Marketing with Enewsletters and Emails

A s mentioned earlier, marketers are shifting more of their marketing communications budgets from traditional direct mail and paper newsletters to email marketing and enewsletters (electronic newsletter). But if you want to ramp up your online marketing program, your first step, unless you already have one, should be to build a large, opt-in elist of customers and prospects.

That's because without a significant online "house file" (list of opt-in subscribers), you can only reach prospects in your niche by renting other marketers' opt-in elists, which is hardly cost-effective: Each time you want to send another message, you have to rent the list again—and that can easily cost you hundreds of dollars for every thousand names on the list.

145

Some marketers buy databases containing the email addresses of business prospects in their niche market. This can work if you are sending highly targeted emails on extremely relevant topics. But when you send email messages to people who have not opted in, you are mostly asking for trouble. The CAN-SPAM Act, which established the rules for commercial email in 2003, does not prohibit these messages. But people on these lists are much more likely to register spam complaints—and far less likely to buy from you.

So the best online strategy for marketers is to build your own list of subscribers. This eliminates the cost of renting lists and prevents the spam complaints and lower response rates typical of non-opt-in lists.

When you own an opt-in elist covering a sizable percentage of your target market, you can communicate with your prospects and customers as often as you think is appropriate at minimal cost. Being able to send an email to your target market with just a few mouse clicks makes you less dependent on costly direct mail, print newsletters, and other paper promotions.

By using a double opt-in process that requires new subscribers to verify their identity before being added to your elist, you help minimize spam complaints and bounce-backs. In double opt-in, you subscribe using an online form. A pop-up window then appears, telling you to watch for a confirmation email asking you to confirm your opt-in. If you do not confirm, you are not added to the list. This prevents pranksters from registering other people for the list without their knowledge. If they did sign someone up, they might get your emails and complain they are being spammed, which could temporarily shut down your entire email account.

In this chapter, I will give you advice for setting up an email content marketing campaign that you can use for the long term.

TIP

You should spend 10 to 20 percent of your digital marketing budget on building your house opt-in elist. That means finding new, qualified prospects in your industry who will opt into your online subscriber list.

Building Your Elist

Writing great email marketing content is important, but it doesn't do you much good unless you have a dedicated, trustworthy email list in place. This section covers how to build a large, profitable opt-in elist of qualified B2B prospects in your field.

Most B2B marketers drive traffic either to their website's homepage or landing pages relating to specific offers (such as free webinar registration, free white paper download, or a product order page). And a lot of the traffic they drive to these pages is existing customers and prospects who are already on their elist.

There are many online marketing options for building your elist, including pay-per-click advertising, postcard marketing, banner advertising, online ads in other marketers' enewsletters, B2B co-registration deals, video marketing, viral marketing, editorial mentions in trade publications, online article marketing, affiliate marketing, and social media—to name just a few.

Calculate Maximum Acceptable Cost Per New Subscriber

When evaluating marketing methods for elist building, you must weigh the cost of acquiring the new name and the value that new name holds for your business.

To determine value, divide the total annual revenues generated by your online subscriber list by the number of names on that list. For example, if your 20,000 online subscribers account for $600,000 in annual sales, your subscriber value is $30 per name per year.

Say you drive traffic to a landing page where people can sign up to your elist. The conversion rate is 50 percent, so for every two unique visitors you drive to your registration page, you get one new opt-in subscriber.

Using Google ads, you can drive traffic at a cost of $7 per click. Can you afford

TIP

Decide how much you are willing to spend to acquire a subscriber worth $30 per year. If uncertain, use this rule of thumb: List-building campaigns should ideally pay back their cost within three to six months. Therefore, if each name is worth $30 per year, you can afford to spend up to $15 per subscriber to acquire new names.

that? Yes, because that means you get one new subscriber for every two clicks you buy, which works out to $14 per subscriber—within your $15 per new name limit.

Would it make more sense to base the allowable acquisition cost per new name on the *lifetime customer value* (LTCV) of online subscribers rather than just the average one-year revenue per name? Theoretically, yes. But you can only do that if you've been marketing online long enough to have reliable numbers on which to base LTCV estimates. Until you do, stick with the revenue per year per name figure as the baseline.

Publish a Free Enewsletter

The best way to build and regularly communicate with an opt-in list of prospects is to publish and distribute a free enewsletter on a specialized topic that is related to your product line and of interest to your target prospects.

A free enewsletter benefits your online marketing efforts in two important ways. First, it gives you a standing free offer—a free subscription to your enewsletter—that you can use in your list-building efforts. Second, it ensures that you communicate with your subscribers on a regular basis, building your relationship with your online prospects while increasing the frequency of your branding messages and online marketing opportunities. We'll delve further into how to create this kind of content later in the chapter.

Build a Free-on-Free Name Squeeze Page

With the staggering number of free enewsletters competing for attention on the internet, it's not enough to have a simple sign-up box on your homepage for yours. You should offer a bribe (typically known as a lead-gen) to get visitors to subscribe. The best bribe is a free downloadable special report in exchange for opting into your elist.

For instance, if you sell supply chain management software and publish an enewsletter called *The Strategic SCM Partner*, offer a short bonus report called *7 Steps to Improving Supply Chain Management in Your Enterprise* as a premium for new subscribers.

TIP

For an example of a free-on-free name squeeze page, visit www.bly.com/reports.

Drive traffic not to your homepage or a standard subscription form, but to a special *free-on-free name squeeze page*—a separate landing page highlighting this offer. We call it a "name squeeze page" because it extracts or "squeezes" new names for your list from web traffic. "Free-on-free" means you are offering free content (the report) to get them to accept your primary free offer (the subscription).

Capture Email Addresses of Those Who Don't Register

Put in place one or more mechanisms for capturing the email addresses of site visitors who do not buy a product, download a demo, subscribe to your online newsletter, or take other actions that opt them into your elist.

For example, when they attempt to leave the site without purchasing or registering, have a window pop up to capture their email address with the headline, "Wait! Don't leave without claiming your free special report!"

The text explains they can get a free copy of your special report *7 Steps to Improving Supply Chain Management in Your Enterprise* by entering their email address and clicking submit. If you are not proactively making an effort to capture these email addresses, you are leaving money on the table.

Be sure to let subscribers know what they will be getting when they join your subscriber list. What are the free bonus gifts? How many do they get? How many times a week will they get an email from you? And make it easy to sign up. Just ask for their email address and their first name, which you can use to personalize the salutation as well as the subject line.

> **TIP**
>
> For more ideas on building your elist and capturing site visitors' email addresses, go to www.thelandingpageguru.com. You can get in for free with the username *user* and the password *pageguru.*

Publishing Your Own Enewsletter

Whether you are building brand awareness, generating leads, or making direct sales, there are two ways to sell your products and services to your enewsletter subscribers. One is to place small online ads in the regular issues. These ads are usually a hundred words or so in length and include a link to a page on your site where the subscriber can read about and order the product. The other is to send stand-alone email messages to your subscribers, again promoting a specific product and with a link to your site.

My enewsletter, *The Direct Response Letter* (www.bly.com/report), is not the most successful or widely read on the planet. Far from it. But marketing results and comments from subscribers tell me my formula for creating the enewsletter—which, including copy and layout, takes me just an hour or two per issue—works. I want to share the formula with you, so you can produce an effective enewsletter of your own—by yourself, at your computer, in just a single morning or afternoon.

Pick a Formula and Stick with It

When reading a free enewsletter (as opposed to one they pay for), people spend just a little time on it before deleting it. Therefore, I use a quick-reading format designed to allow subscribers to read it online as soon as they open it (see Figure 9–1, page 157).

In this format, my enewsletter always has between five and seven short articles, each just a few paragraphs long. Every article can be read in less than a minute, so it never takes more than seven minutes to read the whole issue, though I doubt most people do. I advise against having just a headline and a one-line description of the article, with a link to the full text of the article. That forces your subscribers to click to read your articles. Make it easy for them.

I do not use HTML—my enewsletter is text only. This way it is easy and inexpensive to produce. Many marketers use HTML enewsletters, which look more promotional and less informational.

When preparing your text enewsletter for distribution, type your copy in a single-column text file, in Times Roman or another easy-to-read typeface. The column width should be 60 characters, so you can set your margins at 20 and 80. However, to make sure the lines come out evenly, you must hit Enter at the end of each line.

Getting Your Newsletter Noticed

There are many services and software programs you can use to distribute your enewsletter and email marketing messages, including

Constant Contact, AWeber, Mailchimp, Keap, Bronto, Pinpointe, and ActiveCampaign, to name just a few. Be aware that pricing, list capacity, and compliance vary widely among services—for instance, one service would not let me distribute business opportunity emails. Check them out carefully and ask about the issues I just mentioned and any others that are relevant to your business. I would include a comparison table here, but by the time this book is printed, it would already be out of date.

Let me show you how distributing an enewsletter helps bring in business for me as a freelance copywriter. I recently gave a speech on software direct marketing that was recorded, so I had the MP3 file burned onto audio CDs. In my enewsletter, I offered the CD free to any subscribers involved in software marketing, because they are potential clients for my copywriting services. Within 24 hours after distributing the newsletter, I received more than 200 inquiries from marketing managers at software companies requesting the CD, many of whom needed copy written to promote their software.

Once you build your subscriber list, you will have an incredibly powerful marketing tool and the most valuable asset your business can own: a database of buyers with email addresses and permission to mail to them at any time.

Monitor the ROI from your enewsletter carefully, especially with respect to the investment of your time spent producing it. Is your free enewsletter delivering a good ROI? If you're spending too many hours or even days every month creating an enewsletter in order to generate leads or sales, and you're not showing a measurable bump in either, then stop the presses.

How much self-promotion or useful how-to tips should you include in your enewsletter? According to Debbie Weil, "Best practice guidelines recommended a 70/30 or even 80/20 ratio of content to promotion for enewsletters."

But if you're giving away too much free content and never "making them ask" for a sale, your readers may not be motivated to buy. Why should they? They've got a good thing going, and they'll enjoy it as long as you'll dish it out. You might need to tinker with your ratio or experiment with gracefully intertwining a promotion with your content. If they're logically related, readers will want to learn more.

As for frequency and consistency of publication, it's all in the eye of your reader. For some people, receiving your enewsletter once a month will seem frequent. For others, that much of a gap between issues means it will lack a recognizable punch. The bottom line is that you'll never make everyone happy. But whatever your publishing schedule, make sure it's consistent, whether it's once a week, twice a month, or even less often.

Newsletter Tips

Copywriter John Forde offers the following tips for writing an engaging enewsletter:

- *Your reader is much smarter than you think.* Even while educating or informing, never talk down to them. And never think they won't notice when you haven't done your homework.

- *Your reader prefers stories to lists of facts.* You'll find it a lot easier to hold on to their attention by putting plenty of human interest angles into the articles you write. For example, marketer Joe Vitale once ran an article called "How Mark Twain Might Write Online." He could have just listed bullet points. But instead, he gave his lesson a face we could all identify with.

- *Your reader expects occasional profundity.* The deeper you can take your reader, the more you can expand their mind, the greater your editor-reader relationship will be, the more they'll recommend your enewsletter to friends, and the longer they'll stay active on your mailing list.

- *Trust encourages action.* Relationships like the ones we've been talking about are built on trust. The more the reader trusts you, the more genuinely they regard your message, and the more likely they are to take the action you recommend.

- *Your reader expects imperfection.* There's a reason we laugh hardest at comedians who aren't afraid to make fun of themselves. Showing an occasional weakness actually confirms your strength of character and gives your writing a personal, human appeal.

- *Your reader expects emotion.* Getting personal means getting emotional. But be careful in two ways. First, realize that even zealots can only go so far. Be passionate about your position, but not crazed. Second, good writers express the full range of emotions over time (fear, greed, anger, desire, vanity, and so on). You can't fake this. But don't suppress it in your enewsletter copy, either.

- *Give both need-to-know and want-to-know content.* No question, the most valuable enewsletters educate readers. But remember, your subscribers will want to be entertained as much as they'll want to be informed. Think of it like the difference between the college professor who bores listeners at a cocktail party and the master storyteller who builds a circle of guests around him, all leaning in to hear more.

- *Reinforce the old, introduce the new.* When you're writing an enewsletter, you're almost always "preaching to the choir." That means a lot of your copy will appeal to the opinions and principles you and your readers already share. But just as much, you have to make sure you introduce, amplify, and illuminate a new direction for them to take. By repeating core ideas, you reinforce your readers' good feelings about your enewsletter. By saying something new, however, you also provide understanding.

Article Ideas for Company Newsletters

Here's a checklist of article ideas to stimulate editorial thinking and help identify topics with high reader interest that can promote your company or educate prospects:

1. *Product stories.* New products, improvements to existing products, new models, new accessories, new options, and new applications.
2. *News.* Joint ventures, mergers and acquisitions, new divisions, new departments, and other company news. Also, industry news and analyses of events and trends.

3. *Tips.* Tips on product selection, installation, maintenance, repair, and troubleshooting.

4. *How-to articles.* Similar to tips, but with more detailed instructions. Examples: how to use the product, how to design a system, or how to select the right type or model.

5. *Previews and reports.* Write-ups of special events such as trade shows, conferences, sales meetings, seminars, presentations, and press conferences.

6. *Case histories.* Either in-depth or brief, reporting product application success stories, service successes, etc.

7. *People.* Company promotions, new hires, transfers, awards, anniversaries, employee profiles, customer profiles, human interest stories (unusual jobs, hobbies, etc.).

8. *Milestones.* "1,000th unit shipped," "Sales reach $1 million mark," "Division celebrates 10th anniversary," etc.

9. *Sales news.* New customers, bids accepted, contracts renewed, and satisfied customer reports.

10. *R&D.* New products, new technologies, new patents, technology awards, inventions, innovations, and breakthroughs.

11. *Publications.* New white papers, new ad campaigns, technical papers presented, reprints available, new or updated manuals, and announcements of other recently published literature.

12. *Explanatory articles.* How a product works, industry overviews, and background information on applications and technologies.

13. *Customer stories.* Interviews with customers, photos, customer news and profiles, guest articles by customers about their industries, applications, and positive experiences with the vendor's product or service.

14. *Financial news.* Quarterly and annual report highlights, presentations to financial analysts, earnings and dividend news, etc.

15. *Photos with captions.* People, facilities, products, and events.

16. *Columns.* President's letter, letters to the editor, guest columns, and regular features such as "Q&A" or "Tech Talk."

17. *Excerpts, reprints, or condensed versions of larger works.* Press releases, executive speeches, journal articles, technical papers, company seminars, etc.

18. *Quality control stories.* Quality circles, employee suggestion programs, new quality assurance methods, success rates, and case histories.

19. *Productivity stories.* New programs, methods, and systems to cut waste and boost efficiency.

20. *Manufacturing stories.* New techniques, equipment, raw materials, production line successes, detailed explanations of manufacturing processes, etc.

21. *Community affairs.* Fundraisers, special events, support for the arts, scholarship programs, social responsibility programs, environmental programs, and employee and corporate participation in local/regional/national events.

22. *IT stories.* New computer hardware and software systems, improved computing and its benefits to customers, new applications, and explanations of how systems serve customers.

23. *Overseas activities.* Reports on the company's international activities, profiles of facilities, people, markets, etc.

24. *Service.* Background on company service facilities, case histories of outstanding service activities, new services for customers, new hotlines, etc.

25. *History.* Articles about company, industry, product, and community history.

26. *Human resources.* Company benefits program, announcements of new benefits and training and how they improve customer service, and explanations of company policies.

27. *Interviews.* With company key employees, engineers, service personnel, etc.; with customers; and with suppliers (to illustrate the quality of materials going into your products).

28. *Forums.* Top managers answer customer complaints and concerns, service managers discuss customer needs, and customers share their positive experiences with company products/services.

29. *Gimmicks.* Contents, quizzes, puzzles, games, and cartoons.

And here, from business advisor MaryEllen Tribby, are ten more ideas you can use in enewsletters and blog posts:

1. Step-by-step how-to instructions
2. Top ten tips
3. News stories
4. Controversial essays
5. Responses to criticism
6. Top mistakes to avoid
7. Useful resources
8. Case studies
9. Product reviews
10. Excerpts from your longer works

Content: How to Write Tips Your Readers Will Love

Tips are short items that give valuable and actionable advice in compressed form, usually just one to three paragraphs. How do you write these mini-articles for enewsletters, as well as other content formats? Here are some suggestions from marketing expert Ilise Benun of Marketing Mentor (www.marketing-mentor.com):

- Think of yourself as a conduit. Your job is to pass useful information along to those who can use it.
- Pay close attention to questions, problems, and ideas that come up when you're doing your work or interacting with customers.
- Distill the lesson (or lessons) into a tip that you can share with your network via email, snail mail, or even in simple conversation.
- State the problem or situation as an introduction to your tip. Distill it down to its essence.
- Then give the solution. Tips are action-oriented, so make sure you give a couple of action steps to take. Readers especially love something they can use right away.
- Describe the result or benefit of using these tips to provide some incentive to act. If there are tools they can use to measure the results, give them a link to websites offering these tools.

- Include tips the reader can use without doing any work: phrases they can use verbatim, boilerplate clauses, checklists, forms, and so on.
- List websites and other resources where readers can go for more information.
- Put your best tip first, so in case people don't read the whole issue, they get at least one good idea.

Figure 9–1 below shows you a portion of an issue of my monthly enewsletter, *The Direct Response Letter*. Note that the articles, mostly tips, are only a few paragraphs long, and you can read any article in less than a minute.

FIGURE 9-1. Sample Enewsletter

Stop Retail Customers from Haggling

To stop retail customers from haggling over price, do not use handwritten price labels, says consultant Bob Clements.

Reason: A handwritten label says to the customer that you made up the price and therefore you can change it.

Solution: Get printed price labels from the manufacturer. These say to the customer that the price has been set by someone other than you, the retailer, and therefore you cannot change it.

Best Time of Day to Send B2B Emails

My colleague Amy Africa's consultancy tracks the results of billions of emails a year—so she knows what works in email marketing better than most.

FIGURE 9-1. Sample Enewsletter, continued

According to Amy, the best times of day to send business-to-business (B2B) email marketing messages are one hour before lunch . . . and one hour before quitting time.

"People spend more time interacting with emails then," says Amy.

Time-limited offers also work well: early bird specials, moonlight madness deals, one-hour lunchtime bonanzas, etc.

Add Visual Interest to Your Marketing Materials

As entrepreneurs, most of us can't afford the expensive graphic art studios Fortune 500 companies use, yet we want our marketing materials to have visual appeal.

Here are five low-cost/no-cost graphic design techniques you can use to liven up your print and online promotions:

1. Use sidebars . . . these are short bits of text placed in a box.

2. Make bar charts or pie charts from numerical data.

3. Use pull quotes . . . these are quotes printed in large type and placed in a box.

4. Use cheap, royalty-free stock photos or digital clip art . . . like www.dreamstime.com.

5. Use a variety of different bullets . . . solid circles, solid squares, arrows, check marks.

Source: Newsletter Formula, Vol. 1, Issue 1, p. 12.

Tweet Your Way to Success

Perry Belcher, a successful Internet marketer with more than 80,000 Twitter followers, uses this formula for successful tweeting:

FIGURE 9-1. Sample Enewsletter, continued

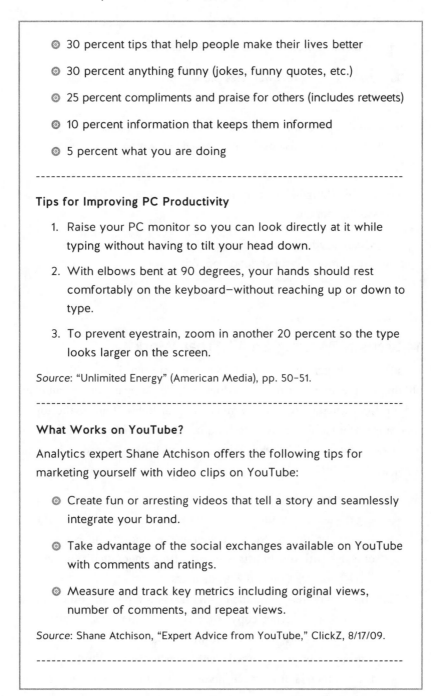

⊙ 30 percent tips that help people make their lives better

⊙ 30 percent anything funny (jokes, funny quotes, etc.)

⊙ 25 percent compliments and praise for others (includes retweets)

⊙ 10 percent information that keeps them informed

⊙ 5 percent what you are doing

Tips for Improving PC Productivity

1. Raise your PC monitor so you can look directly at it while typing without having to tilt your head down.

2. With elbows bent at 90 degrees, your hands should rest comfortably on the keyboard—without reaching up or down to type.

3. To prevent eyestrain, zoom in another 20 percent so the type looks larger on the screen.

Source: "Unlimited Energy" (American Media), pp. 50-51.

What Works on YouTube?

Analytics expert Shane Atchison offers the following tips for marketing yourself with video clips on YouTube:

⊙ Create fun or arresting videos that tell a story and seamlessly integrate your brand.

⊙ Take advantage of the social exchanges available on YouTube with comments and ratings.

⊙ Measure and track key metrics including original views, number of comments, and repeat views.

Source: Shane Atchison, "Expert Advice from YouTube," ClickZ, 8/17/09.

FIGURE 9-1. Sample Enewsletter, continued

How to Increase Renewal Rates in a Recession

During a recession, renewal rates plunge for subscription-based services, especially high-priced annual contracts.

To solve this problem, Dataprise, a technology company serving small and midsize businesses, offered clients a monthly contract option.

Result: Renewal rates climbed to 95 percent and new business increased 25 percent.

Action step: If your product or service is sold on an annual fee, test quarterly or monthly subscription options.

---

14 Steps to Writing Emails That Work

Email typically generates a response rate between 1 and 20 percent, although some do better and a few do worse. The copy in your email plays a big role in whether your message ends up at the bottom or the top of that range. Here are 15 proven techniques for maximizing the number of email recipients who click through to your website or respond in some other way:

1. The email "From" line identifies you as the sender if you're emailing to your house file. If you're emailing to a rented list, the From line might identify the list owner as the sender. This is especially effective with opt-in lists where the list owner (such as a website) has a good relationship with its users.

2. Some marketers think the From line is unimportant; others think it's critical. Internet copywriter Ivan Levison says, "I often use the word 'Team' in the From line. It makes it sound as if there's a group of bright, energetic, enthusiastic people standing behind the product." For instance, if you are sending an email to a rented

list of computer people to promote a new software product, your From and Subject lines might read as follows: FROM: The Apple Product Development Team / SUBJECT: New Apple iPhone screen is 24% bigger! The Subject line of the email should be constructed like a short, attention-grabbing, curiosity-arousing teaser, compelling recipients to read further—without being so blatantly promotional it turns them off.

3. Despite the fact that the word FREE is a proven, powerful response-booster in traditional direct marketing, and that internet culture is biased in favor of free offers, some marketers avoid putting FREE in the Subject line. This is because the "spam filter" software that screens people's email may identify any message with FREE in the Subject line as promotional and block it.

4. Begin the message copy with a killer headline or lead-in sentence. You need to get a terrific benefit right upfront. Pretend you're writing envelope teaser copy or a headline for a sales letter.

5. In the first paragraph, deliver a mini-version of your complete message. State the offer and provide an immediate response mechanism, such as clicking on a link to a web page. This appeals to internet prospects with short attention spans.

6. After the first paragraph, present expanded copy that covers the features, benefits, proof, and other information the buyer needs to make a decision. This appeals to the prospect who needs more details than your first short paragraph can provide.

7. The offer and response mechanism should be repeated in the close of the email, as in a traditional direct-mail letter. But they should almost always appear at the very beginning, too. That way, busy internet users who give each email only a second or two get the whole story.

8. If you put multiple response links in your email, 80 to 95 percent of clickthrough responses will come from the first two. Therefore, you should probably limit the number of links in your email to three. An exception might be an enewsletter or ezine broken into five or six short items, where each item is on a different subject and therefore has its own link.

9. Use wide margins. You don't want to have weird wraps or breaks. Limit yourself to about 55 or 60 characters per line. If you think a line is going to be too long, insert a character return. Internet copywriter Joe Vitale sets his margins at 20 and 80, keeping sentence length to 60 characters and ensuring the whole line is displayed on the screen without odd text breaks.

10. Take it easy on the capital letters. You can use words IN ALL CAPS but do so carefully. They can be a little hard to read—and in email, all caps give the impression that you're shouting.

11. In general, shorter is better. This is not the case in classic mail order selling, where as a general principle, "the more you tell, the more you sell." With email, readers are quickly sorting through their inbox and don't have time to read a long message.

12. Regardless of length, get the important points across quickly. If you want to include a lot of product information, put it lower down in the message or include a link to a landing page where the reader can find more information. People who need more information can always scroll down. The key benefits and deal should be communicated in the first paragraph, or very soon afterward.

13. The tone should be helpful, friendly, informative, and educational, not promotional or hard-sell. "Information is the gold in cyberspace," says Vitale. Trying to sell readers with a traditional hyped-up sales letter won't work. People online want information and lots of it. You'll have to add solid material to your puffed-up sales letter to make it work online. Refrain from saying your service is "the best" or that you offer "quality." Those are empty, meaningless phrases. Be specific. How are you the best? What exactly do you mean by quality? And who says it besides you? And even though information is gold, readers don't want to be bored. Just like the rest of us, they seek excitement. Give it to them.

14. Including an opt-out statement prevents being flamed by recipients who feel they have been spammed by stating that you wish

to respect their privacy, and making it easy for them to prevent further emails from being sent to them. All they have to do is click on an Unsubscribe link that takes them to a web page where they click on a button to unsubscribe. Example: "We respect your online time and privacy, and pledge not to abuse this medium. If you prefer not to receive further emails from us of this type, click the unsubscribe button below."

WHAT IS SPAM?

The federal CAN-SPAM Act requires that commercial emails:

- Don't use false or misleading information in the "From" or "Subject" lines.
- Identify the message as an advertisement.
- Include your physical postal address.
- Give instructions on how to opt-out.
- Sex-oriented email must say SEXUALLY EXPLICIT at the beginning of the subject line.

Three More Ways to Write Stronger Content Emails

There are always ways to improve your email writing strategy—even if you have been at it as long as I have. In this section, I want to share with you the three most important things I've learned about writing winning email marketing campaigns.

1. Refer to Current Events

The first tip is: When your email copy mentions what's going on in the news the same week—or even better, the same day—you distribute it, your response rates soar.

Financial publishers were probably the first to discover this. Emails that reflect what's going on in the market on the day they are distributed—for instance, "Gold hits $1,500 per ounce . . . should you sell or buy more?"—pull much better than generic promotional emails or those with evergreen content.

For example, the publisher of a financial newsletter boosted subscriptions by referencing the Martha Stewart insider trading case during her trial. The headline read: "Stay one step ahead of the stock market, just like Martha Stewart . . . but *without* her legal liability." The email even included a color photo of Martha looking contrite on the courthouse steps—an image the reader probably saw daily on TV and in the newspapers, and which therefore immediately attracted their attention.

The idea of including news in your copy is not new. But email marketing makes it easier to more precisely coordinate and time your messages with current events.

Of course, some products are easier to tie in than others. A company that sells aluminum siding to homeowners might find it more difficult to link their email copy to the president's latest speech than a company promoting penny stocks. But it's not impossible. And any time your email can reflect news or current trends, readership and response are likely to soar.

2. Give It Away

My second tip for writing winning email messages: Giving away content in the email itself is, contrary to what you might expect, a way to strengthen copy and results. You might think, "If I give the information away in the email, their curiosity is satisfied, and they will not have to click through to find the answers they are looking for."

The trick is to give "partial content"—a sample of the kind of help your product, service, or firm offers. This could be something as quick as a simple how-to tip. Then you promise many more useful tips and advice when the reader clicks through.

This works for two reasons. First, people are trained on the internet to expect free content, so this technique fulfills their expectations. Second, including actual content in your email—not just teasing the reader with promises of valuable content when they respond—demonstrates your expertise and knowledge right there in the message. The reader is convinced you know what you are talking about, and that you may be a resource they want to know better.

3. Be Consistent in Format

My third tip for writing winning email messages: Open rates and clickthrough rates both increase when your email marketing messages match—in look, content, tone, and style—the other emails prospects regularly get from you or the list owner.

For instance, if your email is going to an opt-in list of subscribers to a text enewsletter, the response will be better if you also send a text email, rather than an HTML message. If people on your list are used to extremely short emails, a long blast probably won't work as well as a short teaser linked to a landing page, where they can read the rest of your message.

Take a look at past email promotions sent to the list that worked, as well as issues of enewsletters these readers receive. If they all contain graphs—or technical information, or pictures of pets, or news, or pithy how-to tips, or survey results—then your email probably should, too.

People on a given list are "trained" to accept emails with a similar look and feel to the ones they get regularly. When your email matches their expectations, they believe it's something they usually read and open it. But if it looks wildly different, they class it as spam and delete.

This is contrary to the approach Madison Avenue favors in print advertising, which is to make their ads look different from all others the reader has seen.

The Four U's Formula for Winning Subject Lines

When readers get your email marketing message, they make a quick decision, usually in just a couple of seconds, to open or delete it based largely on the subject line. So how can you convince a busy prospect—in just a few words—that your message is worthy of their attention?

The "Four U's" copywriting formula—which stands for *urgent, unique, ultra-specific,* and *useful*—can help. (You can also read about how to use the Four U's for writing special report headlines in Chapter 5.) Originally developed by my colleague Michael Masterson for writing more powerful headlines, the Four U's formula works especially well with email subject lines. I'll share it with you now.

According to this formula, strong subject lines are:

1. *Urgent.* Urgency gives the reader a reason to act now instead of later. You can create a sense of urgency in your subject line by incorporating a time element. For instance, "Make $100,000 working from home this year" has a greater sense of urgency than "Make $100,000 working from home." You can also use a time-limited special offer, such as a discount or premium if you order by a certain date.

2. *Unique.* A unique subject line either says something new or says something the reader has heard before in a new and fresh way. For example, "Why Japanese women have beautiful skin" was the subject line in an email promoting a Japanese bath kit. This is different from the typical "Save 10% on Japanese Bath Kits."

3. *Ultra-specific.* Boardroom is the absolute master of ultra-specific bullets, known as fascinations, that tease the recipient into reading further and ordering the product. Examples: "What never to eat on an airplane," "Bills it's OK to pay late," and "Best time to file for a tax refund." They use such fascinations in direct mail as envelope teasers and in email as subject lines.

4. *Useful.* The useful subject line appeals to the reader's self-interest by offering a benefit. In the subject line "An Invitation to Ski & Save," the benefit is saving money.

> **TIP**
>
> After you have written your subject line, ask yourself how strong it is in each of the Four U's. Use a scale of 1 to 4 (1 = weak, 4 = strong) to rank it in each category. Rarely will a subject line rate a 3 or 4 in all four U's. But if your subject line doesn't rate a 3 or 4 in at least *three* of the U's, it's probably not as strong as it should be—and could benefit from some rewriting.

A common mistake is to defend a weak subject line by pointing to a good response. A better way to think about it is this: If the email generated a profitable response despite a weak subject line, imagine how much more money you could have made by applying the 4 U's.

One software marketer sent out an email with the subject line "Free White Paper." How does this stack up against the Four U's?

1. *Urgent.* There is no urgency or sense of timeliness. On a scale of 1 to 4, with 4 being the strongest, "Free White Paper" is a 1.
2. *Unique.* Not every software marketer offers a free white paper, but many of them do. So "Free White Paper" rates only a 2 in terms of uniqueness.
3. *Ultra-specific.* Could the marketer have been less specific than "Free White Paper"? Yes, they could have just said "Free Bonus Gift." So I rate "Free White Paper" a 2 instead of a 1 for specificity.
4. *Useful.* I suppose the reader is smart enough to figure out that the white paper contains some helpful information they can use. On the other hand, the usefulness lies in the specific information contained in the paper, which isn't even hinted at in the headline. And does the recipient, who already has too much to read, really need yet another "Free White Paper"? I rate it a 2. Naming the topic would help: "Free white paper: How to cut training costs up to 90 percent with elearning."

I urge you to go through this exercise with every email subject line you write. You can also apply the formula to other copy, both online and off-line, including direct-mail envelope teasers, ad headlines, letter leads, web page headlines, subheads, and bullets.

Rate the line you've written in all four U's, and then rewrite it until you can upgrade your rating by at least one point in two—and preferably three or four—of the categories. This simple exercise may increase your readership and response rates substantially for very little extra effort.

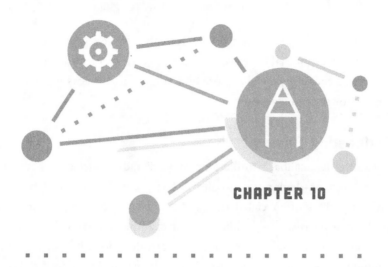

CHAPTER 10

Marketing with Podcasts and Other Audio

Podcasts are popular. According to Edison Research's 2019 "Infinite Dial Study," 144 million Americans over the age of 12 have listened to a podcast. More than 40 percent of them listen to podcasts weekly. Those weekly listeners hear an average of seven different podcasts per week, and 80 percent listen to all or most of each episode.

A 2018 survey of podcast listeners by advertising company Midroll found that 81 percent of them sometimes or always paid attention to podcast ads, and 60 percent had bought a product or service from those ads. Another survey by Edison Research, "The Podcast Consumer 2019," found that 54 percent of listeners were more likely to buy from a company that was a podcast sponsor.

"Podcasting is one of the greatest ways to get your message out, no matter how big your business," says Francesco Baschieri, president of podcasting company Voxnest. "All of your production and distribution needs are right there on your phone. It's infinitely less costly than video, and it's a medium that is perfectly catered to niche topics and audiences."

In this chapter, we will explore how you can use podcasting to market content for your business.

Podcasting Basics

Podcasting is a callback to the glory days of radio—in fact, a podcast is basically an on-demand radio show. There are thousands of podcasts today, which is often called the golden age of podcasting. Technically speaking, a *podcast* is an audio file (for example, an MP3 file) that you make available online so your audience can download it, either to their computer or a mobile device, to listen at their leisure. Podcasts may be hosted by one person or a group of people, and many are interview-type shows between a host and a guest expert.

There are several types of audio files you can use to share your podcast. Many podcasters choose to first record and edit their podcasts using .wav files then later convert them to a more compressed, smaller type like MP3. Compressing files post-recording tends to shrink their size so they can download faster. Most major podcast platforms like Apple Podcasts, Luminary, Stitcher, and SoundCloud accept MP3 and M4A files. Some also support MOV, MP4, M4V, and even PDF files. Why? Because while most podcasts are audio-based, some may include other elements like video and text.

People typically listen to podcasts on their smartphones or play them while driving. You can also play them on your computer. Listeners usually subscribe to podcasts through aggregation apps on smartphones, such as Spotify, Stitcher, Luminary, TuneIn Radio, Spreaker, and Overcast, or via the built-in podcasting apps on iOS and Android. You can also stream many podcasts online directly from websites.

The advantages of podcasting are many:

- It's portable.
- It's personal.
- It's entertaining.
- It's educational.
- It's accessible.

⊚ It's cooperative.

By downloading or streaming your podcast, your listeners have demonstrated a commitment to participation.

The Power of the Podcast

Why should you create a podcast? "To be successful on the web, you need new thinking," says content marketing guru David Meerman Scott. "The web is not about buying lists. Instead, it is about publishing great content."

As we've seen, that content can take many forms: blogs, video, ebooks, articles, enewsletters, and white papers. The more media you use to disseminate your content, the more people you reach, and the faster you establish your reputation as a thought leader in your field.

Podcasting is a medium for publishing and distributing content via the internet. A podcast can serve as a powerful marketing tool for the solo service professional, internet marketer, or small business-owner who might want to do one of the following:

⊚ Create an internet radio show or talk show with content-rich broadcasts for your target market.

⊚ Conduct a tele-class series in which you interview experts who have solutions to problems faced by your target market.

⊚ Promote a printed book, ebook, or CD/DVD series by releasing promotional snippets to a wider audience.

⊚ Provide short, valuable expert tips to your target market.

Podcasting is also used by national and international corporations, such as the media company Bloomberg, the National Geographic Society, and the international assurance and advisory firm EY. Podcasting for these firms targets their consumers or clients as well as their own employees, because many firms use podcasts for in-house training and education.

Your use of podcasting is limited only by your creativity—you certainly don't need to spend a lot of money on your podcast production, just time and energy. Should you have a big budget available, that's OK, too; your productions can be as elaborate as you want. Podcasting can reach people who:

⊚ choose to get their information via audio, as opposed to the written word

- travel or have busy schedules
- like to multitask by playing a podcast while doing other things
- commute to and from work or school
- listen to podcasts as they exercise or do household chores

Podcasting can be used to meet many goals—but they all boil down to one thing: creating a trusted, valued relationship with your listeners. Many podcast publishers use them to engage in:

- brand building
- training
- product information dissemination
- public relations
- stockholder communications
- viral marketing

Whatever your desired outcome, podcasting should be part of an integrated content marketing program. Online radio service Pandora notes, "Digital has mobilized audio, creating new ways for consumers to listen throughout the day and therefore, more opportunities for you to connect with your audience in a moment that truly matters."

Delivering Your Podcast

Should you create a script or an outline for your podcast? I don't mean for you to be rigid in your podcast delivery. What I mean is that you should know the details of how you want to structure—and present—your podcast.

But remember, the show format, topics, and content are not set in stone. Your podcast will likely evolve as time goes on. You will add things and drop things. Eventually you will find your groove and settle into what works well for you—and your listeners.

It's good to start out with an outline so you have an idea of where you're going. It will make the process easier and also make your podcast better. A better podcast means more listeners and more fun for you.

Let's talk about a few things to consider when you choose a format for your podcast. For example, should you be a solo act or, as so many podcasts do today, have a co-host?

You see it all the time on television talk shows—two people share the spotlight. But, just as often, there are those strong, well-loved personalities who can carry the load on their own—however, they always have guests as their platform.

There are a *lot* of solo podcasts out there. Some podcasts have two or more hosts. There are also podcasts with several participants discussing a topic at the same time.

You can even co-host a show with someone who lives in another state or another country. This is often done using internet phone software or by using a conference call service. There are distinct advantages to having a co-host.

Many listeners find the discussion between multiple hosts more interesting than just one person talking. With multiple hosts you can split the work required to produce the podcast, and there are more people to come up with ideas and content for your shows. There are added complications, though, of coordinating the schedules of multiple people, maybe even across time zones. The advantage to going solo is that you're totally in control. You might try it both ways, just to see what you enjoy most and what your listener's responses are to the different presentations.

Strengthen Your Podcast Community

To get the most success out of your podcast, it's essential to not only inform and entertain your audience, but to also give them a sense of belonging and community. Give them opportunities to participate in the creation of your content. Encourage them to communicate and collaborate with each other on your site or through the show.

How can they collaborate on the podcast with you? Provide an easy means for them to communicate with you: At the close of your podcast, give them a URL (keep it short and memorable) to a survey, a forum for open discussion, or your related blog where they can post their opinions, ask questions, or share stories related to the podcast topic. Use your podcast to promote a teleseminar event, and have the sign-up information on your website, blog, or within a forum post.

Make it simple for your listeners to share your podcast with others, using a "send this to a friend" link on your website. Here's how it works: When you click the "share this with a friend" link, you are taken to a page where you can type in email addresses of people you know. When you click "submit," the podcast page is emailed automatically to those people with a short cover note, saying it was sent from the sender.

Audio CDs

Despite digital media's dominance, physical media still reaches a wide audience. By producing your lead magnet content as an audio CD, you can dramatically increase the time people spend with your message and boost its perceived value. There are several reasons for the effectiveness of audio CDs. They are a good alternative to print when your message can be communicated solely in words. When graphics are required as well as text, you can use print or video.

Electronic media are attention-getting because, even today, they are underused. Most white papers and other bait pieces are either printed documents or electronic files (PDFs) that can be downloaded from a website. Offering an audio CD or DVD helps your bait piece stand out. Also, physical electronic media have a higher perceived value, creating a sense that you are giving away something really valuable. CDs have several specific characteristics:

- *They are physical objects.* One of the major challenges of designing direct-mail packages is to get them opened. A CD or DVD is dimensional, so it stands out in the mail. To get the audio CD, the prospect has to provide their street address, city, and state so you get more data than you would by offering a digital lead magnet.
- *They are tangible.* Your prospect is flooded with electronic marketing. An audio CD stands out from the rest. Prospects notice it. Yet it mails flat, so it's easy and inexpensive to ship. I often put a teaser on the outer envelope that reads: "MAGNETIC MEDIA ENCLOSED. DO NOT BEND." A single audio CD weighs just ounces, so when you are mailing, the added weight of the CD is negligible in terms of postage costs.
- *They are not overused.* Personalized sales letters, laser-addressed envelopes, letters, 800 numbers, buck slips (inserts in direct-mail packages), lift letters, and other attention and involvement devices are all overused to some degree. But not one inquiry fulfillment

package in a hundred contains an audio CD. This adds to the CD's attention-grabbing powers.

- *They have high perceived value.* The retail price of a CD, depending on whether it is audio or software, ranges from $10 to $50 or more. Because their perceived value is higher than a brochure or email sales letter, the mailroom is less likely to screen mail containing CDs, and prospects are less likely to put them in the trash.

Another advantage of using audio CDs is their low production costs. Professional studio recording and editing isn't usually necessary. Excellent results can be achieved with a digital recorder in your office, or by recording a live presentation at a meeting or seminar. Or you can use a podcasting microphone and record it with your laptop.

Purists will argue that recording live seminars produces low-quality audio that presents a poor image of the advertiser, but I disagree. There is something vibrant and energetic about most live recordings of seminars and speeches that makes for a pleasant contrast with the stilted dullness and lack of enthusiasm found in many professional, "slick" audio productions. I have gotten excellent sales results using recordings of live presentations, seminars, demos, and similar events as inserts.

You don't need to be a professional actor to narrate your own audio CDs, but you must have a clear, pleasant, and resonant speaking voice. If you have a strong accent, mumble, or are otherwise difficult to understand, consider using someone else as the narrator.

Vendors who can record and duplicate seminars for you are listed on the Vendors page of my website (https://www.bly.com/). Or you can search Google local audio or sound recording studios. In addition, some organizations that sponsor conferences and meetings routinely record speaker presentations and sell the recordings to their members. Make it a condition that you retain the rights to the audio file and get a free master copy. This eliminates the cost of paying a professional or buying your own taping equipment.

Audio Content That Works

Here are a few approaches to creating audio content:

- *Message from the CEO.* One way to gain the prospect's attention is to have someone important talk to them. Have the message narrated by your CEO or another high-level executive. If you're selling a technical product to a technical buyer, have the message presented by a credible expert the prospect will respect.

- ⊚ *Commercials.* A number of direct marketers use audio to present short commercials. Essentially, they take the promotional copy from their sales letter or brochure, condense it, and present it as a sales pitch on CD or online in an MP3 file.

- ⊚ *Explanation.* When the message is complex, it can sometimes be made more palatable in verbal form. People who are intimidated by a prospectus or detailed technical paper can often better understand the same material if it is clearly explained by a narrator.

- ⊚ *Demonstration.* Audio can be used to demonstrate products, especially those that have an audio component. For instance, if you sell enclosures designed to dampen the clatter of noisy computer printers, your recording can present the sound of a printer before and after your enclosure is installed.

  One music publisher selling musical arrangements includes a demo CD in its mailings. School and church music directors can thus hear the arrangements played by a full orchestra or sung by a full choir before they buy.

- ⊚ *Dramatization.* Audio, like radio, is often overlooked as a dramatic medium. Instead of a monologue, a dialogue between two actors, or a complete scenario with multiple characters and sound effects, can add drama, interest, and entertainment value to what otherwise might be a dull presentation.

- ⊚ *Informational audios.* An underused approach—and perhaps the easiest to implement—is to send the prospect an audio CD that is informational rather than promotional. This works well for service firms, manufacturers, and any other B2B marketer selling to an audience that seeks solutions to problems, answers to questions, or just more information about the product or service.

Audio CDs can be your secret weapon in boosting response rates. Telecommunications company US West, in a mail campaign to sell disaster recovery services, used an audio CD to dramatize what would happen to the prospect's company if they were unprepared for a communications disaster.

The mailing pulled a 50 percent response, generated millions in sales, and won a gold award from the Direct Marketing Association (DMA).

Audio CDs work. They have worked for others; they can work for you.

Five Ways to Create Audio Content Quickly and Easily

Though online video is becoming perhaps the dominant format for digital content, 81 percent of marketers say they find video to be the most difficult type of content to produce.

Audio, on the other hand, is relatively simple to produce. Here are the four most common methods of creating audio content:

1. *Studio-recorded.* Go to a professional recording studio with a script and read your audio content into the microphone. The studio will give you a digital audio file you can either post online or burn onto a CD.

2. *Office- or home-recorded.* Today the prices on high-quality digital audio recorders have fallen so almost everyone can afford to buy one. So you do not even need to find a recording study. Just get a digital recorder and produce your audio content in your home or office.

3. *Interview or discussion format.* Much more interesting to listen to is audio content with two speakers. The speakers can have a lively and engaging discussion on the topic, or one who serves as the host interviews the other who is the subject matter expert, similar to a podcast. Again you can do this on a digital recorder at home or the office.

4. *Podcasts and radio shows.* Whenever you are invited to be a guest on a podcast or radio show, tell the producer you will do it provided you are given a copy of the recorded interview and may use it however you wish. If the host or producer refuses, I personally would pass on the interview, unless it is a show or podcast with a huge audience.

5. *Speaking.* When you speak at association meetings, they often record the audio and then offer it to their membership. Ask for a copy of the recording and the right to use it however you wish. If it's a small meeting of a local chapter of the association, these talks are often not recorded. Ask permission to bring in a helper and equipment to record it yourself, and again you also ask for the rights to use the audio content however you wish.

How to Be a Great Podcast Guest

Kanika Tolver is a serial podcast guest—and I mean that in a good way. As a career coach, IT professional, and author of *Career Rehab: Rebuild Your Personal Brand and Rethink the Way You Work* (Entrepreneur Press, 2020), Kanika builds her brand by showcasing her knowledge and her content. Below are her top tips for being a great podcast guest:

- To get a great pod guest spot, pitch related topics that align with your personal brand, products and services. When you pitch topics to the podcast, make sure your topics clearly align with your expertise, books, articles, products, and services. Reference your content: case studies, surveys, statistics, books, and articles that are related to the topic you and the podcast show host agreed on.
- Research the podcast show's mission and the podcast show host's personal brand. This will help you make a connection with the purpose and mission of the show. When you appear on the show, display natural enthusiasm and appreciation for being a featured guest.
- Make sure the podcast show interview feels like a natural conversation. Before the interview, listen to a few podcast episodes to get a feel of the format and vibe of the show. This will help you develop a path for how you would like to communicate with the host. I recommend a natural conversation with the podcast show host so listeners feel the engagement throughout the duration of the show. It's perfectly fine to ask for the podcast show interview questions in advance before the interview.
- Make sure you and the podcast show host mention your product/services information and website and where listeners can learn more about you. Also, always mention your social media handles and hashtags so the listeners can follow the marketing of your online content, products, and services.

CHAPTER 11

Marketing with Videos and Apps

The other day a client and I were discussing plans to create a video for her firm—their first venture into this medium. At the end of the conversation she asked, "Do you have anything you can send me so I can read up on the subject?" I didn't then. Now I can send her this chapter to answer some of her questions about content marketing with videos.

Video is increasingly important in content marketing.

- When video and text are both on a product page, 72 percent of people would rather watch the video than read the text.
- YouTube has more than 1.5 billion users per month and plays over 1 billion hours of video daily to its users.
- 85 percent of American internet users watch online video monthly.
- 54 percent say they want to see more video content from the brands and businesses they support.

- The average American adult watches almost 5.5 hours of videos daily.
- 87 percent of marketing professionals use video as a marketing tool.
- Video marketers get 66 percent more qualified leads and a 54 percent increase in brand awareness than marketers who do not use video.

In this chapter, we'll talk about how you can market your content using videos and interactive apps.

Videos

The average video posted on a site's homepage today is short, running two to three minutes long. B2B videos have an average run time of about four minutes, and about half of viewers watch them all the way through. Videos on second-level pages, especially those dealing with products and their applications, can go to five to seven minutes or longer.

Video sales letters (VSLs), which are posted on separate URLs, can run anywhere from 15 to 45 minutes, depending on the audience and the product. Most marketers today do not make their VSLs pure advertising. Rather, the goal is to educate the viewer in the subject matter (for example, how to combat diabetes) and combine that with information on how the product, typically a dietary supplement, is formulated to slow, halt, and even reverse the effects of diabetes.

As for script length, figure your narration at 120 words per minute. A 10-minute script would then have 1,200 words—the equivalent of about five double-spaced pages in a Microsoft Word document.

Selecting a Topic

The best guideline is: "One presentation, one topic." Your video should only talk about one product, one idea, or one offer. After all, you have a limited time to tell your story before your viewer's attention wanes and they click away.

You can use video to add motion and visuals to many different content formats and subjects, including:

- *Case studies.* Most case studies are still PDF documents. But the subjects of many case studies lend themselves to video—for example, a case study about a farmer using software to make decisions about what crops to plant and when to sell them for maximum profit.

- *Demonstrations.* For many products, technologies, and services, nothing beats video for showing how something works or teaching your viewers how to use it.
- *Tutorials.* Tutorials are relatively short videos that educate people about topics ranging from Medicare coverage to filing tax returns.
- *Message delivery.* CEOs and other C-suite executives often have important information to share with employees and others. Having the executive on video talking about issues, industry news, or company strategies or challenges adds more credibility to the message.
- *Interviews.* Instead of having only the speaker on camera as a "talking head," having someone interview the subject matter expert or executive in a Q&A format or free-flowing discussion livens up the presentation and creates more viewer engagement. You can also do interviews with satisfied customers, third-party industry experts, or your crews or service people in the field who install and maintain your products.

Whether it's marketing or customer care, videos are most effective when they support a sales, branding, or educational objective. For instance, one electronics manufacturer found that customers were damaging its sensitive equipment after purchase by inadvertently exposing it to static electricity. Its solution was to produce a video, shipped with every purchase, explaining how static electricity works, why it is harmful to electronics, and how to prevent it from damaging electronic devices. (The small spark of static electricity that jumps from your fingertip to a metal doorknob after you have been walking on a carpet can carry 3,000 volts or more, as incredible as that sounds.)

Writing the Video Script

Videos have two components: the audio (sound) and the visual (video, including live action, "talking heads," animation, text slides, charts, graphs, and special effects). The traditional video script format has a description of the visual in the left columns side-by-side with the audio script accompanying that visual in the right column (see Figure 11–1).

The script must work for the type of video you are creating; some of the basic formats of videos include the following:

Talking Head Video A: Directing the Visitor Through a Web Page

This is the kind of video the script above would be used for. It should be very short—no more than one minute long—and should have you (or

FIGURE 11-1. Proper Format for Video Scripts

Sample Short Landing Page Video Script	
Opening animation sequence	**Music track A**
Bob is sitting at a desk with a book in his hand, looking directly into the camera	**Bob**: Hello and welcome. In the next few minutes, you can gain access to a powerful secret that can forever change the way your approach online marketing.
Bob looks and points to his right (the viewer's left) where the opt-in form will appear on the finished page	**Bob**: Enter your name and email address here to get instant access to my top-secret proven strategies for maximizing conversion rates with online video.
Bob looks directly at the camera and smiles	**Bob**: See you inside!
Quick fade to black	
Screen with logo and URL	**Sound effect B**

whoever is starring in your video) physically pointing to the elements on the page that you want the visitor to interact with. It should follow the motivation sequence step by step.

Talking Head Video B: Building a Relationship with the Visitor

In this kind of video, your main purpose is to give the page a personal feel and give the visitor the sense that they know you. Remember to keep the message very targeted—you should know what your visitor is searching for before they arrive at your landing page so you can address their specific needs in your message. (Don't try to cheat by creating a generic video to use on all your pages—it simply won't be as effective as targeted messaging.)

Video Testimonial Montage

You may think that you don't need a script for a montage, since you're starting with existing footage. But, even if all your testimonials are already filmed, you need to choose which parts of the testimonials you want to include and what order they should be presented in. You should stick to no more than about 15 seconds from each person, allowing you to include up to eight people in your video.

The script for your montage is really an editing script, rather than a shooting script, and should contain all the notes the editor needs to complete the video. And yes, you should go through this exercise even if you're editing the video yourself, since it forces you to think about what you're going to include.

You may want to be as specific as to include the time stamp where you want to start and end each testimonial, or you might just want to use the first few words at the start and end of the quote you want to use.

Remember to include transitions in the left column of your script. You may want to fade in and out between testimonials to make the montage less choppy. And you should still end with your call to action—you can include it in a closing screen that appears after the final testimonial ends.

If you haven't shot your testimonial footage yet, your shooting script can basically be a set of questions that you'll ask customers to get them talking about your products. You will cut your questions out during the editing process. When filming your clients' testimonials, plan to have them looking at you rather than at the camera. The testimonial will have a much more genuine feel if they're not looking directly into the lens.

One thing about video testimonial montages: Always make sure you have permission from the people who will be appearing in your video. You should have them give you written permission, including their signature, and keep all of these release forms on file.

If your business develops public seminars, boot camps, or conferences, then these are the best places to shoot customer testimonials. That way, you can videotape the customers who have come to the event, rather than travel to see them at their home or place of business. Bringing your videographer to where your buyers have gathered results in huge savings in time and money when shooting video testimonials.

Product Demonstration Video

A script is critical in a product demonstration video, especially if you are not the only person to appear in it. For example, if you're doing a short cooking demonstration, and you have an assistant in the kitchen, you need to make sure you both know what is happening when.

You will also want to include some close-up shots of the product. You can do this even if you only have one camera by filming the close-up shots of the product at the end of the demonstration and editing them into the appropriate spots in the video later. By including the close-ups in your scripts, you'll be sure to remember to take them and get the right close-ups to work with your planned edit.

A product demonstration is the most action-packed kind of video, so it will have more information in the left column of the script than any of the other kinds. Be sure to include detailed information about who's doing what when, and always include what is happening with the product—the real star of the show.

Q&A Video

For a Q&A video to work, you must have two people. You should plan to sit facing each other at about a 45-degree angle, rather than facing each other head-on so that your faces can both be seen by a wide-shot camera. You should look at each other, ignoring the camera as much as possible.

Depending on the effect you're going for, you may not want to write a full script for the answers in your video, but you will certainly want to make sure the "interviewer" is prepared with a well-scripted set of questions. The goal of the questions is to allow you to convey your marketing message. For example, the interviewer might ask what makes your product different from the competition.

For the answers, you can write them out word-by-word if you like, but this may take away from the real "interview" feel of the video, since the person answering will either have to memorize their lines or read answers directly from notes. It's easier to create a few bullet points that need to be covered in each answer.

A good way to end a Q&A video is for the interviewer to thank you for your time, and then deliver the call to action directly to the camera on your behalf.

Photo Montage

You may think you don't need a script for a photo montage video, but it can certainly help in all stages of production—planning, shooting, and editing. By writing out a script, you can plan the image you want first, then look for (or take) photos to work with the script, rather than trying to build the script around photos you already have.

A very basic photo montage can have music as the background, but a vocal audio track is much more effective in leading your visitor through the motivating sequence and stating your call to action.

TIP

Back in the day, the cost of producing your video could range from $800 to $2,500 per minute. For a ten-minute video, that translates into $8,000 to $25,000! Today, with the incredibly high resolution of smartphones, a lot of people buy a $5 tripod and shoot the video with their phone. The factor that raises costs now is extensive on-location shooting, requiring travel to multiple sites. Nevertheless, the trend today is away from whiteboard or sketch formats to full-production videos.

If you're using a vocal audio track, the best way to approach your script is to write the audio track first, in the right column of your script. Then look at what you've written and think about images that complement the message you're trying to convey. Then describe each in the left column.

Showing Your Videos

Here are the four most popular means of showing your videos to your prospects and customers:

1. *Post a video directly on your website.* It will get the most views if it is prominent on your homepage. Secondary videos can be placed on the pages for the products or applications they highlight. Posting videos can help raise your Google ranking.

2. *Post multiple videos on your own YouTube channel.* Should your YouTube channel or even one video get a lot of traffic, or even go viral, you can become a YouTube celebrity pretty quickly, which gives you great visibility and credibility in your field. YouTube is by far the most widely adopted video channel for marketers.

3. *Post video to other sites where you can monetize them.* YouTube isn't the only game in town. You can also post videos on websites where you can either monetize them directly or create channels that reach your intended audience. Some possible sites include Vimeo, Flickr (mostly for photos, but you can post videos shorter than 90 seconds), and Brightcove. You can also post content marketing videos to social media platforms like Pinterest and Instagram.

4. *Produce DVDs.* A number of firms have used video presentations in

> **TIP**
>
> Add graphics, special effects, charts, and other footage for a varied presentation that's more than just you talking behind a lectern. Create a nice label or package as well. Even though you are giving the video away, put a price on the package indicating that the video retails for $29 to $59 or more, just as I advised you to do earlier on PDF lead magnets.

DON'T NEGLECT DVDS

Countless companies are posting videos on their websites and YouTube at a dizzying rate. However, I estimate that not one company in 100 is using physical videos (DVDs) in content marketing. This represents an opportunity for you to stand out from the crowd. In an age when marketers are increasingly searching for something new and different, both DVDs and online videos can add an irresistible attention-getting quality, whether you are communicating valuable content or a more direct sales message.

Right now, DVDs are an underused medium for content marketing. However, unlike YouTube videos, the viewer expects your DVD to have production quality close to what they see on TV. Therefore, have your video edited professionally in a video studio or with editing software.

In addition to sending DVDs to prospects as a cold mailing piece, you can use the video as a presentation aid or a leave-behind by a salesperson. They can also serve as a response piece in advertising or direct-mail campaigns along with the regular inquiry fulfillment package: A package with a brochure, a DVD, and maybe a product sample is effective, and you can increase response rates by promoting it as a "free information kit." The DVD adds another dimension to ordinary print materials and increases the kit's perceived value. Today some vendors even make brochures that, when opened, have small windows that play short video clips when you press a button under them. We call these *video brochures*.

direct-mail promotions. One major computer manufacturer, for example, mailed videos to thousands of firms that used a specific type of computer the company had manufactured years earlier. The DVD explained how these companies could trade in their old computer for substantial savings on a newer model. In addition to the video, the package contained a letter, brochure, and reply element.

No matter what format you choose, both digital and physical videos give you an opportunity to reach customers in a very personal way. By showing them what your business or brand offers and associating imagery with it, you can make an even greater impact on their purchasing decisions.

Marketing with Apps

An app may be something that you've worked hard on so it can meet a need in the market, and you can profit from it. Or it may be a critical part of your overall marketing strategy that you need to obtain user data for more effective market research. For whatever reason you created your app, one thing is certain: For it to succeed, it must be used.

That means you need an effective strategy to market it. You can't just rely on word-of-mouth to promote your app. You need to understand and exploit the mobile marketplace to get people to want, use, and talk about your app. So how do you deploy the right tactics?

Research Your Audience

It all starts with knowing who your app is for. If you don't understand who will benefit most from using your app, then how will they ever find out about it? Be clear about who your audience is, and target your marketing efforts toward them.

Know your demographic as well. Their age, their lifestyle, their spending habits, their recreational habits, and any other factors that help you understand who you are selling to. Do not try to cast as wide a net as possible and say the app is for everybody. An app that is popular with college students may not appeal to retirees.

Give Away Apps with Useful Content or Capabilities

For instance, one app allows smartphone users to quickly locate the nearest public restroom—sometimes a matter of urgency in a place like Manhattan.

Functional apps also work well for marketing. Uber and Lyft give customers an app for requesting a ride, eliminating the need to call the company directly.

Of course, many app developers monetize their apps by selling them directly to consumers. But others give them away freely. They monetize their apps by connecting them to online ad networks (mobile advertising platforms) such as MoPub, Ogury, and InMobi. The ad network pays the app publisher for each ad that is displayed to mobile users through that particular app.

Understand Your Competitors

You should also be looking at what your competitors have been up to and seeing what has and hasn't worked for them. Nothing will hurt your app marketing strategy more than being seen as "late to the party" with an imitation of what's already on the market.

Besides, if you're planning an app, and you see that one of your competitors has already tried and failed, why would you want to court that same failure yourself?

TIP

Knowing your market is not just about knowing your audience, it's also about knowing what your peers and competitors have been doing so you can remain relevant and original.

Market Early

Although it's possible to start your app marketing strategy only after your app is released, it is often better to start earlier than that. Depending on how confident you're feeling, you can even start while the software is in development, releasing things like video development diaries or engaging with potential customers on social media, then running polls and surveys to see what features they'd like to see incorporated.

As the release date gets closer, you can start ramping up your app marketing efforts with teaser trailers and other short video advertising that helps build curiosity. The goal is not to give too much away, but rather to start raising interest and awareness for a more concerted marketing effort later.

Prepare Your Press Kit

Depending on your level of marketing, you should have both physical press kits (PKs) and electronic press kits (EPKs) available for the relevant press and promotion groups. Compile your list of most likely media groups, bloggers, and other notable names and personalities, and make sure your press kit and launch materials cover all the essential points about your app.

Have a system in place to quickly send materials out to groups on your list and respond to others who request a PK or EPK to maximize your media coverage. Remember, these people are doing your work for you.

Optimize Your App Store Page

Optimizing your pages on app stores is a critical, ground zero strategy. According to Sensor Tower, there were about 106 billion app downloads in 2018 alone, with Google Play (76 billion downloads) and Apple App Store (30 billion downloads) taking the lion's share of the market, respectively. In the same way that your website is your storefront, your app store page is your product on the shelf, trying to distinguish itself from all the other competing products.

TIP

When creating an effective store page, think carefully about the title and tweak your description to make it as simple but appealing as possible. Come up with a catchy, pleasing icon. Use screenshots that accurately convey the selling points and benefits of the app. Spend as much time as necessary on all these factors because they can make the difference between an impulse buy and moving on to the next app.

Get Reviews

Even though you need to make your app store page appealing, don't assume that will guarantee a sale. Most people want to know what others think about an app before they buy. Reviews are a critical part of this process.

It's not unusual for customers to research their purchases in advance, and apps are no exception. If you've created an app that you believe many people will enjoy or find useful, encourage them to say so. Your own marketing and promotion of your product's benefits are important, but people already expect you to say nice things about your own app.

An independent third-party assess-ment, such as a random user review or an informed, professional review by a website that specializes in the area your app covers, carries a lot more weight than a "biased promotion" from the software developer. Reach out to customers and reviewers and get those positive reviews lined up.

> **TIP**
>
> The biggest disadvan-tage of marketing with apps is that, according to Statista, 25 percent of users delete apps after using them once. Valuable content and functionality can result in apps being kept longer and used more.

Use Social Media

While not as in-depth as a review on a tech website or blog, a social media post can still have an enormous effect on the popularity of your app. A mix of deliberate, targeted advertising on social media platforms like Facebook, Twitter, Instagram, and LinkedIn can be combined with more traditional word-of-mouth methods, such as promoting and reposting people who use the app.

Once people start talking about an app on social media, the app may begin to gain traction. This helps your app get more visibility, especially if it is combined with effective social media use, such as hashtags.

Use Influencers

Influencers, also called *key opinion leaders*, are just another, more accessible version of the traditional celebrity endorsement. Instead of paying a well-known athlete or actor to pose with your product for a 30-second commercial or print ad, you get a notable YouTube, Twitter, Twitch, or other social media platform influencer to promote your product.

This can be in the form of a blog post, a video on YouTube, a tweet on Twitter, or a photo on Instagram. The important thing, however, is that someone with thousands or even millions of followers is promoting your app directly to their following. The only thing that carries more word-of-mouth influence than a positive referral from an acquaintance is the same thing from an admired public figure. Working out a deal with an influencer is often much cheaper than securing a celebrity endorsement, but it can be far more effective when correctly targeted.

A growing number of influencers are neither celebrities nor subject matter experts, but individuals who review products via social media—typically on YouTube or their blogs. Some do it in exchange for free products and services, while others charge the marketer a fee for a good review.

Monitor Results

Once the app is out and the marketing is underway, that doesn't mean your marketing efforts are over. One thing you should be doing as the launch moves ahead is keeping a close eye on your KPI, or *key performance indicators*.

At the same time, monitor the analytics coming in from your marketing efforts. If you see that some strategies, such as videos, are more successful than others, put more effort into those and start cutting down on or adjusting the plans that are less effective.

TIP

Closely monitor how people are using your app, review the user feedback that is coming in, and be attentive and responsive to that feedback. Address any bugs quickly as they are discovered and documented, and make sure you remain as committed to the app as you were when you were developing it. A useful app will gain more of a foothold if the developers engage with and build a relationship with their users.

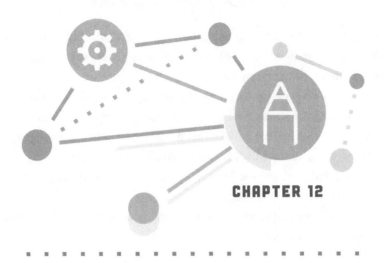

CHAPTER 12

Marketing with Webinars

Webinars have long been an effective content marketing tactic. Your prospects can hear you talk and see your slides right on their computer screens. A typical sales funnel for a content marketing campaign incorporating a free webinar is:

1. Put up a webinar registration page.
2. Drive traffic to the registration page with an email invitation.
3. Hold the webinar.
4. Make a special offer at the close of the webinar.
5. Follow up with emails reminding attendees and registrants of the special offer.

The biggest problem with webinars is that more and more companies are producing them. That means the web is getting cluttered with them, making it more difficult to get attention for your event. Build your visual webinar presentation like a high-quality sales letter, including all the elements that lead to closing a sale.

Plan sales follow-up early. Too often you'll see a lot of work and money wasted on a great webinar or teleseminar because leads are not followed up quickly. Don't make this mistake; it's better to over-prepare for follow-up by automating as much as possible and run reports to inspect the process and track results. After all, the key webinar metric is most often the sales attributed to the event.

In this chapter, I will cover how you can use webinars to help showcase your marketing content.

Eight Steps to Webinar Success

Here are eight methods that can improve your webinars:

1. Use a Topic That Attracts Attendees

Which topic will likely pull in more attendees: a) "How to Buy Our Product Now" or b) "Making Your Business Life Easier Through New Strategies"? If you said b) because it promises a benefit, you're right.

If you test different topics, you'll find that promising an interesting, timely, and educational webinar will pull best. As in teleseminars, your presentation should be "solution-oriented." Give the participants practical ways to solve their problems. This topic should, of course, tie in with the real goal of your presentation: education, lead generation, or product launching.

2. Research to Target the Right People

It would be inappropriate for me to market a teleseminar on "breaking into the ebook writing business" to people who were already successful ebook authors. I would need to search out forums, chat rooms, mail groups, or ezine lists that cater to the beginning ebook writer. Once you find a topic of interest, create a sales follow-up plan, and then build your event marketing plan from there.

3. Temper Your Attendance Expectations

You should expect a show rate of roughly 30 percent of those registered for a free webinar.

If your numbers are significantly below that, make sure you are doing day-of and 24-hour reminders via email. Invite more prospects to your event and invite them multiple times.

4. Use Polling Questions

Most leading webinar platforms allow you to pre-load interactive polling questions into a presentation. You can capture attendee-specific data that may help you tailor this webinar as well as the next one. Ask things like:

- What interests you most about this webinar?
- What is your biggest challenge today?
- Where are you in the buying process?
- Would you like more information on our new technology?

5. Craft to Reach Specific Needs

You can craft a webinar to meet any content need, such as:

- Educational marketing events
- List- or database-building events
- One-to-many sales pitches
- Thought-leadership events
- Client training
- Surveys
- Upsell or resell events
- Thank you or loyalty events

For example, consider holding database-building webinars to restock the top of your sales funnel. Other webinars help educate your prospects and clients over time, which in turn helps you achieve your marketing, sales, and organizational objectives over the long run.

Choose your technology with your overall goal in mind. You'll want a reliable web conferencing solution that is compatible with a variety of operating systems. It should be scalable to the size of your audience and have the features you are looking for: polling, Q&A, and recording. My favorite is Webex.

6. Focus on Live Events First

There are many reasons for this, including the use of polling questions, the chance to answer live questions, and the immediacy and excitement created for participants by a live event.

You can always use a recording of a presentation-only webinar as a sales tool on your website, but the live events truly create relationships and quickly build your business.

7. Inspire and Motivate Prospects

Have your attendees try, buy, or contact you for more information. Also consider a limited-time offer for webinar attendees, to add extra incentive and urgency to your call to action. This can be a simple but effective way of getting more results from your webinars. If you are doing an educational webinar followed by a sales presentation, tell them to stay on for "more information on how they can put the information presented into action with [your product or service]."

8. Speak with Energy

Be enthusiastic. Your exuberance and friendly personality can inspire and motivate your participants. Engage them in conversation and make them feel comfortable enough to ask questions, if you've enabled the chat or Q&A features. Have fun with your presentations!

16 Tips for Webinar Presenters

If you are the webinar presenter, here are 16 rather mundane tips for presenting. These are not flashy, but they are real-world pointers that will help you be a better presenter and make your webinar run more smoothly.

1. *Go to the bathroom.* Ten minutes before you call into the webinar line, hit the head. There are few things worse than having to answer a call of nature in the middle of giving a presentation, because you can't step away from the phone or microphone to do it. And the alternatives are all deeply unpleasant.
2. *Have a box of tissues handy.* And blow your nose thoroughly before you start. It's awfully distracting to listen to a presenter sniffle or snort all the way through their talk.
3. *"Do not disturb."* Whenever I give a webinar, I close my office door and tape a sign to it that reads: "Webinar in progress from [hour to hour]—do not disturb UNLESS you are mortally wounded or the office is on fire." You should also silence your smartphone and turn off notifications on any devices you are using to present the webinar.
4. *The dog trick.* If you work at home and have a dog, have someone take it for a walk or a car ride. Or put the dog outside, far enough away from your office that if it barks, your listeners won't hear it.
5. *Liquids.* Have a big glass of water nearby—large enough to last through the entire talk.
6. *Eat beforehand.* Eat a light snack before the webinar so you can focus on your presentation and not be distracted by hunger.
7. *Bring hard copies.* Print hard copies of your slides and have them on the desk next to your phone. That way, if you somehow get disconnected or lose the video portion of the webinar, you can still work from the print copy. It also ensures that you can read the slides clearly in case the screenshot is low resolution or too small.
8. *Have a backup plan.* You and the webinar provider should have a way to contact each other in case of a technical glitch. I always have my smartphone and the webinar producer's phone number at the ready just in case.
9. *Always record your webinar.* Even if you don't have an immediate use for it, record the webinar regardless. That way a participant who can't get in or gets disconnected can view it later.

10. *Adhere to your time frame.* When your time is up, it's over.

11. *Stick to the plan.* Make sure your slides sync up with the bullet points in your email invitations and registration page. Conversely, make sure every point in your sales copy is covered. If you leave one out, some participants will be very unhappy.

12. *Reference slides by page number.* So make sure to number your pages.

13. *Use the slide bullets to guide you.* Don't just read your talk verbatim from a script.

14. *Repeat questions for all to hear.* Say each participant's question again clearly before you answer it to make sure everyone on the call knows what issue you are addressing.

15. *Avoid offensive language or strong personal opinions.* This should go without saying, but sadly, it needs to be said.

16. *Reuse and recycle.* Leverage your live webinars by offering recorded replays listeners can access via phone and computer.

Rules for Webinar Presenters to Follow

Presentation styles and techniques vary among speakers and are unique to individuals. To help you provide the quality of lecture attendees have come to expect, I recommend following these guidelines:

- Introduce yourself.
- Adhere to your allotted time frame.
- Structure your presentation to follow the advertised agenda.
- Reference page number or slides during the course of the presentation.
- Speak clearly and project your voice fully.
- Use a headset or landline phone to remove outside noise, as a cell phone will pick up any interference. Do not use a cell phone or speaker phone.
- Rely on your expertise and avoid reading directly from the materials.
- Provide balance between your lecture, reference materials, and slides (if applicable).

CHAPTER 13

Marketing with Seminars, Workshops, Speeches, and Talks

Many marketers believe that offering a content-rich "free seminar" to their prospects will boost sagging lead generation and make their company stand out from the crowd. "Organize seminars that involve your products to encourage people to buy more of them," advises consultant Michael Phillips. For example, a clothing store can offer color analysis and wardrobe design. A locksmith can offer a free seminar on how to improve home security.

But beware. The free seminar strategy is not as simple and easy as it appears. In fact, it is fraught with peril. The biggest drawback of using live seminars vs. webinars in content marketing is this: If the seminar promotion flops, you may end up with only a handful of attendees in a mostly empty room. With a too-small group, audience interaction is lessened, and the presentation is less dynamic. Also, the fewer people in attendance, the less successful the content marketing campaign will be, which typically translates into insignificant results. Worst of all, lack of attendance can embarrass you and any other speakers you have at the event. Adding insult to injury, your audience will also know.

Whether your seminar is local or out of town, you have to travel, so presenting the content takes more time. By comparison, a one-hour webinar that starts at 2 P.M. finishes at 3 P.M., held from your office, allows you to immediately go back to work. Also, for out-of-town seminars that involve air travel, there is always the threat of bad weather that can stop you from getting to the venue on time—or even at all.

In this chapter, I will share my tips for making in-person marketing events work to your advantage and help you navigate some of these concerns.

Get Attendees in the Door

Obviously, your purpose in presenting the seminar is to persuade people to buy your product. But if the seminar is a blatant promotional pitch, people become annoyed, or even disgusted. If you present information of genuine value, however, attendees will think well of you and be more inclined to do business with you. They know you will be selling to them, but they want to learn something, too.

Provide Value for Higher Response Rates

Free seminars work well when introducing new products or technologies. They are also ideal for products that require an in-person demonstration, such as software or computer systems. Also, if your product solves or addresses a major problem or issue (for example, computer security), a seminar is a good place to educate your prospects on the subject.

But the mere fact that the seminar is free will not get people running to your door. Executives, managers, and other business

TIP

Copywriter David Yale suggests calling the seminar a "forum" and has gotten good results doing so. I also like "briefing" for a session aimed at executives and managers.

professionals are flooded with invitations to free seminars and don't have time to go to even a fraction of them. Response rates for free seminars in fields where they are common (software, computers, telecommunications, office equipment) are generally not much higher than for paid seminars. Your response rate will probably be anywhere from 1 percent to 3 percent.

You might get a higher response when giving free seminars on a topic that's not usually available. Years ago, Gary Blake, a corporate trainer specializing in writing seminars, sent out a simple letter inviting prospects to a free three-hour seminar on "effective business writing." He got a 10 percent response.

Another way to increase your response is to have a well-known industry expert or celebrity as your featured speaker. One software vendor packed a large ballroom by announcing that Bill Gates, founder of Microsoft, was the speaker. (The invitation didn't even mention the topic or contents.)

The title of your seminar is very important, as it connotes value. "Product demonstration" is least desirable and should only be used when the event is indeed a pure and straightforward demonstration of a system. "Seminar" implies that the attendee will gain useful knowledge. "Workshop" implies hands-on participation and should not be used for most free seminars.

You can invite people to your seminar using a combination of emails (usually to your customer list) and direct mail (DM) (to both your customer list and rented lists). The most effective DM invitation consists of a personalized letter combined with a brochure outlining the seminar's contents and the benefits of attendance. I recommend adding a business reply card (BRC) or other reply element, even though most people will register online. You can use a #10 envelope, a 9-by-12-inch size, or mailings that look like formal event invitations. If your seminar is a breakout session at a trade show, include a ticket in the envelope

> **TIP**
>
> Remember, the fact that the seminar is free is not, in itself, enough to persuade someone to attend. You must write copy that will make the reader say, "This sounds wonderful; I would really love to go. How much does it cost?" *Then* tell them it's free.

good for free admission to the main show. A simple seminar flier is shown in Figure 13–1, below.

FIGURE 13-1 Flier Promoting a Content-Based Presentation

Learn from a Legend

In the world of business-to-business marketing, there are very few legends. One of them is Bob Bly, internationally renowned market communications specialist, teacher, and author of 30 books. Bob's also a member of the New Jersey Chapter of the Business Marketing Association.

So we're proud to announce that Bob has agreed to present his rave-reviewed seminar on "B-to-B Copy Writing" and "Direct Marketing" at a special BMA/NJ seminar.

You are invited to attend.

▮ Topics and Options
At the breakfast sessions, Bob will teach you everything you need to know about b-to-b copy writing and direct marketing. At the luncheon session, his topic will be "How to Enhance Your Web Site."

You can choose to attend either session or both.

▮ A Gold Mine that Costs Pocket Change
You would expect to pay several hundred dollars to attend a seminar of this quality, with a star like Bob Bly. But we are offering this incredible opportunity for well under $200—and as little as $35!

▮ Free Bob Bly Book
Attend the morning seminars and you'll get a free copy of Bob Bly's latest book, "Quick Tips for Better B-to-B Communications"—a $24.95 value!

Attend the luncheon session and you can buy his book for $17.95— a more than 25% discount!

▮ How and When to Register
Reservations due by October 15. Call Sherry Hahneman at (732) 417-5601, fax her at (732) 417-5699, e-mail to shahneman@salessupport.com, or mail coupon below to BMA/NJ address.

Promote Vigorously

You don't have to sell your free seminar as hard as you would promote a paid seminar—but you have to sell it almost as hard. The copy might not be as long as that for a paid seminar promotion, but it should still tell the reader what they will learn at your session. You must convince readers they will learn amazingly valuable information if you want to persuade them to attend. Figure 13–1 is an example of a flier used to promote one of my speaking engagements.

Know What You're Talking About

No matter what kind of presentation you give, you have to know your content like it's second nature. A *content speaker* is a presenter whose mission is to deliver actionable content—tips and ideas the audience can take back to the office and apply right away to increase their sales and profits. This is in contrast to *motivational speakers*, who primarily deliver inspiration, or *humorous speakers*, who primarily deliver entertainment. The content speaker delivers education, first and foremost. Of course, if the talk can also motivate and entertain, that's a plus. But motivation and entertainment are a means to the end of delivering useful content.

I have been a content speaker for four decades, and here are five ways I make sure my content is solid, practical, and actionable for my listeners:

1. I only talk about things I know from my own work experience. The content in my talks is virtually 100 percent experience-based. So when I give examples, I know for a fact that they're accurate, including the results.

2. I only tell the truth, but I don't reveal everything I know. For instance, if a client of mine wants their strategy, campaign, and results kept confidential, I don't talk about them. But staying silent isn't lying—it's keeping my promise and the client's privacy. Whatever I *do* say during my talk is always the unvarnished truth. Nor do I shirk from giving my experience-based opinions, which are often contrarian. If I did otherwise, I would be cheating the audience.

3. I make sure my content isn't dated. I am a student of multichannel marketing, constantly reading, studying, and staying involved in campaigns to keep my knowledge current. I am obsessive about printing out and filing all relevant emails, enewsletters, and white papers delivered to my email inbox daily. So I always have a rich

library of up-to-date data and ideas on my content topic at my fingertips.

4. I tailor my presentations to the needs, learning objectives, and challenges of my audience. For corporate training, where all attendees work for the same organization, I customize my slides with examples of their work—which I have the students submit ahead of the workshop date. For association talks in a particular industry, I switch out the examples and case studies in my slides with examples from their industry or similar ones.

5. I write extensively on the same subjects I cover in my lectures and seminars. Someone once said to me, "Experts don't really know more than other people, but their information is better organized." So in my case, I have written books on the topics of my key presentations, and there are two benefits to doing so. First, writing a book (or articles, white papers, and other content) forces you to organize your thoughts on the topic logically so that part of putting together the talk is already done. Second, the research you must do for a book gives you access to relevant facts, figures, trends, and statistics, which helps keep the talk fresh and current.

So where have these guidelines gotten me? Well, I am not the best, most polished, hippest, richest, or most popular marketing speaker today. But I strive to always deliver content that is specific, up-to-date, tested, and potentially very profitable to listeners who act on it. I think that's what my audiences want. Other speakers focus on entertainment and motivation. I incorporate some of that, but that's the icing on the cake. The cake itself is high-value content, because it fits with who I am and what my listeners seem to want from me. And it's what they likely want from you, too, whenever you give a talk.

Four Presentation Tips

Presentations can either fall flat, thanks to boring delivery and pedestrian slides, or they can be memorable enough to go viral. So how do you take your presentations to the next level? This section delivers four tips on how to create a talk your attendees will remember.

1. Offer a Surprise Ending

Radio commentator Paul Harvey was a master storyteller. His show, *The Rest of the Story*, often took a different look at familiar characters. Consider his broadcast about a down-and-outer named Al.

"Remember these four words," Harvey said. "Al was utterly useless. Al was utterly useless."

He went on, "'I'm nothing but a burden on my family,' Al once told his sister in a letter. 'Really, it would have been better if I had never been born.'

"Al had hit bottom by the age of 22. His parents, impoverished, were no longer able to support him. He needed a job, but nobody would hire him."

Al finally turned to an old friend from school, who got him a job interview at the federal patent office. Despite Al's past failures, the director, Fred Haller, took a chance and hired him.

The story hangs on a surprise ending. After setting up Al as a complete failure, Harvey revealed his full name: Albert Einstein.

You could draw all kinds of memorable lessons from that story. Storytelling works—especially when the ending delivers a punch.

2. Use Self-Deprecating Humor

There are two advantages to making yourself the butt of the joke. First, you know yourself better than anyone else, so you can tell a story about yourself with clear detail. Second, even though the spotlight is on you, you disarm your audience by refusing to brag and instead poking fun at yourself.

One executive recalls that, as marketing director for a New York City television station, she wrote up a stack of index cards to prompt her points for a speech at New York University. As she ascended the stage, she tripped and her cards went flying.

As she gathered them up, she discovered her mistake: "To my horror, I realized I had failed to number them." She told her audience, "Lesson number one of 'How to Give an Effective Presentation': Make sure to number your notecards."

Everyone laughed. She threw the cards back down and said, "Lesson number two: Rehearse and know your subject matter so cards are unnecessary." The speech she gave may not have been perfect, but it came off as more natural, conversational, and engaging than her talks usually were.

3. Establish Desire and Banish Resistance

Canadian author and writing professor Douglas Glover says a story must have "desire and resistance"—that is, a character with a goal and obstacles that thwart the goal.

The same characteristics can make for a good motivational speech. These generally have the theme "I got knocked down, and I got back up," says Rob Friedman, an affiliate consultant for Ragan Consulting Group and former senior director of executive communications at Eli Lilly, the pharmaceutical giant.

He has used the story of Wilma Rudolph, born prematurely in Tennessee with weak, deformed legs. Unable to get treatment at a whites-only hospital, her mother took her to a black medical college in Nashville twice a week, Friedman said. Despite her disability, Rudolph wanted to be an athlete. She was 12 when she first walked without corrective shoes and braces. In September 1960 in Rome, she became the first U.S. woman to win three gold medals in track and field in the same Olympics.

4. Heighten the Stakes

Stories interest us most when something is at stake. It doesn't have to be Gandalf standing on the Bridge of Khazad-dûm roaring at the dread Balrog, "You shall not pass!" Stories with suspense—in which the hero stands to win or lose something important—are inherently interesting.

Consider radio journalist Robert Krulwich's 2011 commencement speech at Berkeley Journalism School, in which he spoke about veteran CBS newsman Charles Kuralt when he was just a 23-year-old cub reporter striving to beat the competition to a story:

"One night—in the middle of the night, on the graveyard shift, 2 A.M.—the bell on the wire ticker goes off and says an airplane has just fallen short of the runway at LaGuardia Airport and is sinking in the East River, right now.

"And Kuralt and the night editor flip a coin for who's going to go. Charles wins and runs downstairs, jumps into a cab and says, 'Take me to

LaGuardia.' The problem is, no sooner are they out of the Midtown Tunnel than the cab gets snarled in some weird pre-dawn, fire-engines-heading-to-the-airport traffic jam. So Kuralt leaps out and starts running through the tangled cars up the highway, when he sees a guy on a motorcycle weaving his way through the traffic.

"So he waves his hands wildly, flags him down, says he's a news reporter, there's a plane in the water, he's on deadline, 'Take me!' And the motorcycle guy jerks his thumb at the saddle on his bike, says 'Hold on,' and then, like a stunt driver, zigzags through the cars to the airport. Kuralt is one of the first on the scene, where he climbs over fences, gets the interviews, and makes it onto the evening news. After which he's anointed 'correspondent,' the youngest ever—at 23."

Whatever else the journalism grads took from Krulwich's speech, that's one story I bet they will remember. Some might even be inspired to commandeer a motorcycle themselves someday.

Three Formulas for Organizing Your Talk

There are three simple formulas speakers can us to make their talks more relevant, memorable, and polished: WIIFM, TTT, and PPP.

The WIIFM Formula

WIIFM stands for "What's in it for me?" You increase listener interest when they get a direct benefit from the content of your talk, and the more tangible, the better. A common mistake in presentations is neglecting or forgetting to tell the audience what's in it for them.

Often when SEMs give a talk, they know the topic but are inexperienced presenters, so the technical details are great, but the big picture is missing: Why should the audience care? What is the implication of the work? What problem is being solved?

The TTT Formula

The TTT formula for making successful presentations is: 1) tell the audience what you are going to tell them, 2) tell them, and 3) tell them what you told them.

The introduction is a preview so they know what to expect. "Tell them" is the body of your presentation. "Tell them what you told them" summarizes your major points.

In PowerPoint, I usually do this by putting a "tell them what I'm going to tell them" slide right after the title slide. The title is "What we will cover" followed up a five-bullet outline of what they are about to hear.

I insert the same slide at the end of my PowerPoint, except I change the title to "What we covered today." Then my wrap-up is to quickly go through the five bullets and reiterate the major take-aways.

Don't assume everyone in your audience knows words, terms, and acronyms, and be sure to define them for those who don't. For instance, during a talk on HAZOP, an attendee said HAZOP had nothing to do with operability. He did not know that HAZOP stands for Hazard and Operability Solution: If you have terminology or data that are presented in units that are not what [your listeners] can recall from undergraduate studies, define these terms and units when you first use them in your talk.

Another common presentation mistake is not evaluating your audience and adjusting to match their interest and knowledge levels. Some technical speakers just drone on instead of realizing that they are not directing their presentation to the interests of the audience.

A small but important piece of advice: End your talk exactly when it is scheduled to end. If you do not, the audience gets restless, and some get up to leave, which makes you look bad.

Meeting planners should prepare three signs and hold up the signs to alert speakers as to the amount of time remaining for the session—ten minutes, five minutes, and one minute. A common reason for going over the time limit is not rehearsing before the meeting. You must practice your talk. And do it aloud at your normal speaking rate.

Another mistake presenters make is having too many slides to cover in the allocated time. Solution: Don't over-prepare. Figure out how much time you spend on average on a slide, divide your time slot by that number, create a PowerPoint with that many slides, and when delivering your talk, keep up that pace.

For a technical presentation, figure two to five minutes per slide. For a nontechnical talk, my pace is one to two minutes per slide. Therefore, for an hour talk, I have about 30 slides. If you have too many slides, and you don't have enough time to go through them all, your audience will be unhappy.

Speakers with STEM backgrounds (scientists, technologists, engineers, and mathematicians) often prefer to divide their content into segments, usually numbered. But many professional speakers, make just one main point. A speaker once told me, "One of those hard lessons that I've had to learn—over and over again—is how much better it is to focus well on one idea than it is to share many.

Arrive at the meeting room one hour early to check on the audiovisual and make sure everything is working. Failure to do so risks the speaker spending the first ten minutes of the meeting working through technical issues with the A/V equipment in front of the audience—a real turn-off.

The PPP Formula

The three Ps formula for speakers: prepare, practice, and present:

1. *Prepare.* This includes selecting a topic, making an outline, researching, creating your PowerPoint deck, and writing speaker notes.
2. *Practice.* Practice aloud, in front of a mirror, and into a digital recorder. Play back the recording to be sure you are not speaking to rapidly or too slowly.
3. *Present.* Make eye contact with the audience, maintaining a good volume, clear diction, good posture, natural gestures, energy, enthusiasm, good pace, and proper voice inflection, meaning to raise or lower your voice throughout your talk to avoid sounding monotone.

An average speaking rate for presenters is about 120 words per minute. At that pace, the typical 30-minute after-dinner talk at an association meeting is approximately 3,500 words or so.

Another tip: Adjust the speed up or down a bit to match the audience. I live in the New York tristate area, and we speak quickly. When I give a training class in Alabama or Tennessee, I slow down a bit. (This technique also works well when speaking over the phone or giving a webinar to people who are located in different parts of the country.)

Get to Know the Audience Better

Another trick of the trade is, before your talk begins, circulate among people who have come to the meeting or session early. Introduce yourself and, if you don't know them, ask who they are and what they do. Also ask, "If you could get one thing out of my presentation, what would that be?"

Then, make every effort to deliver what they told you they want to know in your presentation. Also, as you speak, refer to some of the attendees you spoke with before the start by name; e.g., "I was speaking to Ray and one thing he does to achieve X is . . ." Then share something valuable Ray told you, as long as it was not confidential. This further bonds you with the audience and customizes your talk for them.

Some attendees sometimes leave early. Whether they told you in advance they would be doing so or not, never comment on this in a negative way. Doing so presumes your talk is more important than the task they are leaving to attend and usually it is not.

More Tips for Presentations

Dr. Rob Gilbert is a great motivational speaker and a master of teaching presentation skills to others. At the beginning of a Gilbert workshop I attended on "How to Give a Speech," he told us, "If you get one good idea from this session, it will have been worth the price." In fact, I got at least 41 good ideas on improving my presentation skills, and Dr. Gilbert has generously given me permission to share them with you:

1. Write your own introduction, and send it to the sponsoring organization before your appearance.
2. Establish rapport with the audience early.
3. What you say is not as important as how you say it.
4. Self-effacing humor works best.
5. Ask the audience questions.
6. Don't give a talk—have a conversation.
7. Thirty percent of the people in the audience will never ask the speaker a question.
8. A little nervous tension is probably good for you.

9. Extremely nervous? Use rapport-building, not stress-reduction, techniques.

10. The presentation does not have to be great. Tell your audience that if they get one good idea out of your talk, it will have been worthwhile for them.

11. People want stories, not information.

12. Get the audience involved.

13. People pay more for entertainment than education. (The average college professor would have to work 10 centuries to earn what Oprah Winfrey makes in a year.)

14. You have to love what you are doing. (Dr. Gilbert has 8,000 recordings of speeches and listens to them for three to four hours a day.)

15. The first time you give a particular talk, it will not be great.

16. The three hardest audiences to address: engineers, accountants, and high school students.

17. If heckled, you can turn any situation around ("verbal aikido").

18. Communicate from the Heart + Have an Important Message = Speaking Success.

19. You can't please everybody, so don't even try. Some will like you and your presentation, and some won't.

20. Ask your audience how you are doing and what they need to hear from you to rate you higher.

21. Be flexible. Play off your audience.

22. Be totally authentic.

23. To announce a break, say: "We'll take a five-minute break now, so I'll expect you back here in ten minutes." It always gets a laugh.

24. To get them back in the room (if you are the speaker), go out into the hall and shout, "He's starting; he's starting!"

25. Courage is feeling the fear and doing it anyway. The only way to overcome what you fear is to do it.

26. If panic strikes, just keep talking. The fear will subside in a minute or two.

27. In speaking, writing, teaching, and marketing, everything you see, read, hear, do, or experience is grist for the mill.

28. Tell touching stories.
29. If the stories are about you, be the goat, not the hero. People like speakers who are humble; audiences hate bragging and braggarts.
30. Join Toastmasters. Take a Dale Carnegie course in public speaking. Join the National Speakers Association.
31. Go hear the great speakers and learn from them.
32. If you borrow stories or techniques from other speakers, adapt this material and use it in your own unique way.
33. Use audiovisual aids if you wish, but not as a crutch.
34. When presenting a daylong workshop, make the afternoon session shorter than the morning one.
35. Asking people to perform a simple physical exercise (stretching or a mindfulness activity, for example) as an activity during a break can increase their energy level and overcome lethargy.
36. People love storytellers.
37. Today's most popular speaking topic: Change (in business, society, lifestyles, technology) and how to cope with it.
38. There is no failure—just feedback.
39. At the conclusion of your talk, tell your audience that they were great even if they were not.
40. Ask for applause with this closing: "You've been a wonderful audience. [pause] Thank you very much."
41. If you want to become a good speaker, give as many talks as you can to as many groups as you can, even if you don't get paid at first. You will improve as you gain experience. (Dr. Gilbert has given speeches more than 1,000 times.)

Using a Slide Deck

Using a slide deck is one way to help you navigate the content you are presenting, but it's easy to go overboard. "The most common mistake I see is slides that are overcrowded. People tend to want to spell everything out and cover too much information," says TED presentations coach Paul Jurczynski. Not only are cluttered slides difficult to read, unattractive, and amateurish, but they distract your audience; the attendees are concentrating so hard on figuring out the slide, they are not listening to what the speaker is saying.

In his book *Get to the Point,* Joel Schwartzberg presents his 5-and-5 Rule for making PowerPoint word slides. It says that a PowerPoint slide should have no more than five bullet points with no more than five words per point on average. Explains Schwartzberg: "Not only will bullets keep your conveyances succinct, but they'll also ensure your audience spends more time looking at you and less time reading your slides." If you have more to say, put it on the next slide. Another hallmark of a successful slide: The images work with the words to get the point across more clearly than either could do in its own.

DON'T GO OVERBOARD WITH FONTS AND GRAPHICS

Just pick one or two fonts. Use italics, boldface, underlines, colors, and graphics (e.g., arrows, asterisks) for emphasis, but do so sparingly. Overuse of these devices negates their effectiveness, because as the late copywriter Herschell Gordon Lewis noted, "When you emphasize everything, you emphasize nothing." Make the type large enough so even the people at the back of the room can read your slide without strain.

Keep graphics, charts, line drawings, and other visuals clean, clear, and uncluttered, again so everyone in the room, no matter where they are seated, can read them. Streamline any charts or graphs. *Infographics*, which combine multiple images with words on a single sheet or slide, are popular today (see Figure 13-2 on page 214 for an example). When building infographics, ask yourself these questions:

- What do I want the audience to take away from my infographic?

FONTS AND GRAPHICS, continued

FIGURE 13-2. Sample Infographic

MARKETING RULES of THUMB

The 10-80-10 Rule of You and the Marketplace
- 10% of people won't like you no matter what you do.
- 80% will swim with the tide – they can take you or leave you.
- 10% will follow you devotedly even if you don't deserve it.

The 99:1 Rule of Affiliate Marketing
- 99% of your affiliate sales will come from 1% of your affiliates – the "Super Affiliates".
- The other 99% of your affiliates will sell virtually nothing and are not worth your time and attention.

The 90/90 Rule of Free-to-Paid Conversion
- Of the prospects who will join your e-list for the free content, 90% of those who buy something will do so within the first 90 days of being on the list.
- Therefore it behooves you to induce new subscribers to buy something now.

The 50/50 Content/ Sale Ratio
- 50% or more of your e-mail marketing messages should be pure content.
- 50% or less of your e-mails should be sales messages.

The 0.1% Opt-Out Threshold
- Each time you e-mail your list your opt-out rate should be no greater than 0.1%.

4 Steps to a Happy and Successful Life
1 - Money. 2 - Enjoyable, meaningful work.
3 - Love and friendship. 4 - Good health.

The 25-50-25 Rule of Time Management
- 25% of your time should be spent studying your business or profession.
- 50% of your time should be spent rendering your services or selling your products.
- 25% of your time should be spent managing and administering your business.

Fred Gleeck's Rule of 10X Price
- All products you sell should be worth at least 10 times the price you charge for them.

Name Value
In online information marketing, your list will generate average revenues of a dime to a dollar per name per month.

Doubling Day for Direct Mail
- From experience you will learn how long it takes your mailings to produce half the orders they are going to get - that day is "doubling day".
- On doubling day, count orders received to date and multiply by 2 to predict total response to the DM campaign.

Doubling Day

The Agora Model for Online Marketing
- Your initial marketing should focus on getting subscribers, not selling products.
- Reason: People already on your e-list are much more likely than strangers to buy products you offer.

Jeffrey Lant's Rule of 7
- To succeed in any market you must contact the prospects a minimum of 7 times within 18 months.

To get more FREE tips on marketing, visit www.bly.com/reports

◎ Why is it important for them to know this?

◎ How does it tie into my overall story or message?

FONTS AND GRAPHICS, continued

You may need to highlight key numbers or data points with color, boldface, enlarging, or some other visual treatment that makes them pop.

Maps are another common graphic. Maps show where something is located. A common use of maps is to show the locations of multiple entities (e.g., warehouses, service centers, dealerships) as red dots.

At the same time, many attendees—especially scientists and engineers—love graphs and find them the most credible evidence. Use graphs even when speaking to lay audiences, as people generally believe your supporting evidence when it is presented as a graph or chart.

Don't Be Afraid of Blank Slides

It may seem counterintuitive, but at certain points in your speech or pitch, the best visual is . . . no visual at all. These points occur when: a) no appropriate visual comes to mind or is needed to support the point you are making; b) you want the audience to focus 100 percent on you, your facial expressions, and the gestures you are making for emphasis or dramatic effect; c) you want to give the audience a visual break from a series of slides; d) you want to shift the mood or tempo of the presentation; and e) you want to pause your lecture for an audience participation activity or exercise.

A blank slide is the visual equivalent of a pause, and most stories could use at least one. It is also a "pattern interrupt," meaning it breaks the chain of continuous screen viewing that risks lulling an audience and helps shift them into a more wakeful and attentive state once more. Blank slides should be a soft color, such as light blue; if it is white or black, people will see it and think something is broken.

There is also the question of whether to use PowerPoint at all. Some speakers prefer to talk without visual aids, but for technical presentations, word slides, charts, tables, and graphs are almost always a necessity. But of course, they can be contained in a handout instead of on slides. A few speakers prefer using white boards to PowerPoint. But, at most meetings today, the meeting sponsor requires speakers to use PowerPoint, and the audience expects it.

When your audience is looking at you, make eye contact with members of the audience, one at a time. Doing so increases engagement and attention. Even better, as you are looking at that person, gesture toward them to create the impression that you are having a conversation rather than "making a presentation."

Fewer words per slide enables you to make the type large enough to be read, even from the back of the room—and it should be. If you find yourself for saying, "There's a lot of information on the slides so it makes it hard to read," avoid this by not using slides crammed with content in small type or with images so small, captions and call-outs are in mouse type (three-points or tinier). For slides with graphs, the labels on the X and Y axis and the labels for the curves should be legible.

One workaround is to distribute a handout document for information that would be too small to be seen on the screen from 20 feet away or farther. Put all the too-small-to-read data in the notes and present them when you talk, but only summarize them in the slides. Examples: complex graphs and text-heavy tables.

Your slides or other visuals should be in synch with your verbal presentation, not compete with it. Also, use a common font in your slide deck. The reason? If you upload your slides to another computer—as is sometimes the case at larger conferences where technicians at an audiovisual table use the facility's computers—and that computer doesn't have your font installed, the slides could become nothing but gibberish.

Note: If you find a diagram from another source and make a slide out of it, be sure you understand it well enough to explain it to others. If not, you may be embarrassed during the question-and-answer portion of your talk. Also acknowledge the source in a footnote or in the caption.

Also, use the PowerPoint pointer on your laptop and set the arrow on visible so it is always on screen and easy for you to find at a glance. The problem with laser pointers is that they force you to turn away from the audience. And never gesture at the screen, because your audience has no idea what you're trying to point to.

Practice Your Slides

The easiest way to figure out if your slides really work is to recruit a colleague, friend, or family member and run through your entire presentation with them. Sometimes people can get so carried away with rehearsing their delivery and memorizing their words that they forget to make sure their slides complement and sync up with what they're saying.

Even if you are an experienced and polished presenter, you should rehearse your presentations. You can do this by yourself. Even better, videotape your practice session so you can see just how good or bad you really are. Best of all, do a dry run of your presentation in front of someone else.

Teaching

In the corporate world, if you are an expert in a subject of interest to businesspeople—stress reduction, time management, leadership, success, selling, management, interpersonal skills, desktop design, the internet, safety—you may find a ready market for in-house corporate training seminars on these topics.

Contact corporations and offer your services as a seminar leader. Write to training managers. Or call vice presidents, supervisors, and department managers whose employees may need to improve their writing or other skills. Prepare an outline of your course and a biography highlighting your credentials to send prospective clients who request more information. Design these materials so they can be emailed

TIP

Don't feel comfortable teaching in person? Try an online course! You can offer individual courses or a full series on platforms like Udemy, Coursera, or Skillshare.

or faxed if there is immediate interest. If demand builds and inquiries come pouring in, consider registering a domain name and posting these seminar descriptions on your company's website.

There are a number of available venues for teaching. You can teach adult education courses for community colleges, universities, high-school adult education programs, YMCAs, writers' groups, libraries, and bookstores.

Fees are usually modest. Some seminar sponsors pay a flat rate of a few hundred dollars at most. Others pay you a percentage of the registration fees, ranging from 15 to 50 percent. Bookstores expect you to speak for free, viewing it as an opportunity for you to sell books and promote your business. Another outlet for teaching seminars is at association conferences. Almost every conference features guest speakers who are industry professionals.

Is teaching for you? It depends. If you are introverted and dislike public speaking,

TIP

The most prestigious teaching gig is one that allows you to legitimately use the title *professor* in front of your name. Many local colleges and universities have evening programs for working adults who cannot attend classes during the day. Typically, if you are asked to teach such a class, you are given the title "adjunct professor," which adds to your credentials as an expert in your field. Adding "professor" to the speaker's name further enhances the credibility of your content with the listeners.

you may still be able to teach, but you simply may not want to. In that case, stick to taking courses rather than giving them. But if you are as comfortable at the podium as you are at your desk or on the factory floor, consider giving teaching and speaking a try.

CHAPTER 14

Graphic Design
for Content Marketing

The best design is always one that serves the reader and makes even compli-cated topics more accessible. In fact, the primary objective of the graphic designer should be to make the copy easy to read. Sure, you want pages that are colorful and visually engaging. But readability always comes first.

Copy drives content. Layout, design, and images are important but secondary to the copy at least 95 percent of the time. In this chapter, we'll cover some tips for how you can use graphic design to help get your content marketing noticed.

Seven Secret Weapons for Maximum Response

When good design supports great copy and content, that's the recipe for content marketing success. Here are seven secret weapons graphic designers use to help make it happen:

1. Know who you are talking to. Consider identifiers like age, concerns, needs, fears, and goals. Gather information from your customer service team to find out what other products your customers have purchased or tried and what their daily routine is like.
2. Be clear on what words will resonate with your audience.
3. Understand what visuals, photos, charts, and graphs will get their attention. Do your photos look real?
4. Are your colors a good fit and up-to-date?
5. What fonts, sizes, and styles will really hit a home run?
6. How do your testimonials stack up? Do they sound natural or made-up?
7. Are you using FAQs to your best advantage?

The 14 Biggest Graphic Design Mistakes

Design plays an important role in the success of your content. Long before they read your words, readers will begin judging the value of your content by its appearance.

Design influences reader satisfaction. Satisfaction goes up when your white paper is easy to read and its design projects an optimistic, professional image. Quality design differentiates your white paper from the competition and builds equity in your brand.

Here, according to desktop design guru Roger C. Parker, are the 14 most common graphic design mistakes and how to avoid them:

1. Overuse of Color

The overuse of color does a disservice to readers who print white papers on inkjet printers. Avoid solid-colored backgrounds behind the text. Such pages can cost several dollars each in ink supplies.

It can also send the wrong message. Readers know that color is often used to camouflage a lack of content. In addition, bright colors can create distractions that make adjacent text hard to read. Finally,

> **TIP**
> When in doubt, play it safe. Use the minimum amount of color needed to brighten, but not dominate, your pages.

text set in color is often harder to read than black text against a plain white background.

2. Missing Page Numbers

Many white papers lack page numbers. This presents a couple of problems. First, readers depend on page numbers to track their progress through a publication. They also rely on page numbers to refer back to previously read information.

3. Boring Similarity

The front cover is the first thing your readers will notice about your white paper. It's hard to project a unique image if the cover looks just like the covers of hundreds of other white papers the reader has seen.

The interior pages of many white papers look the same because they were created using the templates built into Microsoft Word. As a result, typeface, type size, line spacing, and text alignment choices are often the same, regardless of who published the white paper. This prevents your white papers from projecting a unique image.

4. Long Lines of Type

Many white papers are hard to read because the text extends in an unbroken line across the page, from the left-hand margin to the right-hand margin.

These long lines of type present two problems. One is that the resulting left and right margins are very narrow. White space along the edges of pages provides a resting spot for readers' eyes and emphasizes the adjacent text. Margins also provide space for readers' fingers to hold each page without obscuring the words.

In addition, long lines of type are difficult and tiresome to read. It's very easy

> **TIP**
>
> Layout, type, and color should project a strong "family resemblance" that not only sets your white papers apart from other companies' papers, but also relates them to your firm's marketing materials, including business cards, letterhead, newsletter, and website.

for readers to get lost making the transition from the end of one line to the beginning of the next. Doubling (rereading the same line) can occur, or readers may inadvertently skip a line.

5. Inappropriate Typeface

There are three main classifications of font: decorative, serif, and sans serif.

1. Decorative fonts like Constantia or Broadway are heavily stylized and great for attracting attention or projecting an atmosphere or image. The use of these typefaces should be restricted to logos and packaging, however, where image is more important than readability.
2. Serif fonts like Times New Roman and Garamond are ideal for extended reading. The *serifs*, or finishing strokes at the edges of each character, help define the unique shape of each letter and lead the reader's eyes from letter to letter.
3. Sans serif fonts like Arial and Verdana are very legible. Their clean, simple design helps readers recognize words from a long distance away, which is why they are used for highway signage. Sans serif typefaces are often used for headlines and subheads combined with serif body copy.

The historic analogy has been that type is similar to a wineglass. You should notice the wine inside the glass (your content) rather than the wineglass holding it (your type treatment). You can easily extend that analogy to all graphic design: Focus on the copy, not the page layout containing it.

6. Wrong Type Size

Type is often set too large, such as 14 points, out of habit. (There are approximately 72 points to an inch.) Type set too large can be as hard to read as type set too small. When type is set too large, you cannot fit enough words on each line for readers to comfortably skim the text.

Conversely, the details that help readers identify each character become lost when type is set too small, and they must squint. Type set too small also requires too many left-to-right eye movements on each line, which causes eye strain over time. The most popular and readable type size is 12 points.

7. Improper Line and Paragraph Spacing

Few white paper publishers take the time to carefully adjust their line and paragraph spacing. Correct line spacing, called *leading*, depends on the typeface, type size, and line length. White space between lines acts like "rails," guiding your reader's eyes along each line.

Very seldom is your software's default line spacing measurement the best choice for ease of reading. Correct line spacing depends on:

- *Line length.* As the line length increases, you will probably want to add more leading between lines.
- *Typeface.* Sans serif typefaces like Verdana require more leading than serif typefaces like Times New Roman.
- *Type size.* Line spacing should increase proportionally with the type size.

Correct paragraph spacing is equally important. Avoid the temptation to press the Enter (or Return) key twice at the end of each paragraph. This creates far too much space between paragraphs. Lines are single space. New paragraphs should be separated by noticeably more space than line spacing within paragraphs, but not so much space that it isolates each paragraph. Spacing between paragraphs should equal one and a half lines of space.

8. Awkward Gaps Between Sentences

Never press the space bar twice after the punctuation at the end of a sentence. This is especially true when working with justified text, where all lines end evenly at the right-hand margin. When word spacing is adjusted to create lines of equal length, each space will expand, and double spaces often create a very noticeable gap between sentences. Sometimes these gaps will be located in adjacent lines, creating distracting rivers of white space running through your text.

9. Difficult-to-Read Headlines

Headlines should form a strong contrast with the text they introduce. Readers should have no trouble locating or reading them.

Never set headlines entirely in uppercase (all capital letters). These are harder to read than headlines set in a combination of uppercase and lowercase type, because words set entirely in uppercase lack the distinctive shapes lowercase characters create. Uppercase headlines also take up more space than headlines set in mixed type.

10. Failure to Chunk Content

Chunking refers to making text easier to read by breaking it into manageable, bite-size pieces. The best way to chunk content is to insert frequent subheads throughout the text. Subheads convert skimmers into readers by "advertising" the text that follows.

Before committing their time, readers often skim each page for clues indicating whether it is worth reading. Subheads attract their eyes and "advertise" the content of the paragraphs that follow. Each subhead thus provides an entry point into the text. They also avoid the visual boredom created by page after page of nearly identical paragraphs.

11. Poor Subhead Formatting

To work, subheads must form a strong visual contrast with the text. It's not enough to simply italicize the subhead text. They should be noticeably larger and/or bolder than the adjacent body copy.

A few more subhead formatting tips:

- ◎ *Typeface.* One of the safest formulas is to combine sans serif bold subheads with serif body copy. To unify your publication, use the same typeface for headlines and subheads.
- ◎ *Underlining.* Never underline subheads to "make them more noticeable." Underlining makes them harder to read because it interferes with the descenders—the portions of lowercase letters like g, p, and y that extend below the invisible line the subheads rest on.
- ◎ *Length.* Limit subheads to a few key words, and avoid using full sentences. Subheads work best when limited to a single line.

Subheads should also be set off by generous amounts of white space, but avoid "floating" subheads, which are equally spaced between the previous paragraph and the next one. Ideally, there should be twice as much space above a subhead as there is between the subhead and the paragraph it introduces.

12. Inappropriate Hyphenation

There are different hyphenation rules for headlines, subheads, and body copy. Never hyphenate headlines or subheads, but always hyphenate text paragraphs. A failure to hyphenate body copy is very noticeable.

Failing to hyphenate justified text can cause awkward word spacing problems. There will be huge gaps between words in lines that contain only a few long words. Spacing in lines containing several short words is apt to be noticeably cramped. The difference will be very obvious in adjacent lines.

When copy is set flush left and ragged right (even on the left margin and uneven on the right margin), failing to hyphenate the text can cause lines containing a few long words to be very short, while lines containing several short words will be very long. The difference can be very noticeable.

At the same time, be on the lookout for excessive hyphenation. Avoid hyphenating more than two lines in a row. If your text shows excessive hyphenation, the type size you have chosen may be too large for the line length you are working with.

13. Distracting Headers, Footers, and Borders

Headers and footers refer to text or graphic accents repeated at the top or bottom of each page.

Often, white paper publishers use the same typeface and type size for both body copy and header and footer information. Page numbers, copyright information, and the publisher's address should be smaller and less noticeable than the main text. Compounding the problem, often headers and footers contain website links in blue. This creates another distraction that can pull the reader's eyes away from the primary message. Large, colored logos on each page can also be very distracting, without adding meaningful information.

Few white papers help readers keep track of their location in the paper and their progress through it. Without section and chapter numbers and titles, it is hard for readers to find specific chapters and topics.

As for borders, pages are often *boxed*, with lines of equal thickness at the top, bottom, and sides. Boxed pages project a conservative, old-fashioned look. A more contemporary image can be created using *rules*, or lines, of different thickness at just the top and bottom of each page.

14. Widows and Orphans

Widows and *orphans* occur when a word, a portion of a word, or a partial line of text is isolated at the bottom of a page or column (an orphan) or at the top of the next page or column (a widow).

The worst-case scenario occurs when a subhead appears by itself at the bottom of a page, isolated from the paragraph it introduces, which appears at the top of the next page. Some software allows you to automatically "lock" subheads to the text they introduce—make sure you use this feature.

When someone downloads a white paper from you, within seconds they will either feel a glow of pleasure or a sense of disappointment. Readers check out the cover and glance at the text, and then either say, "Aw, just another hard-to-read, look-alike white paper" or "Wow! This looks really great!"

Whether your white paper receives the attention it deserves and paves the way for future sales or (worst-case scenario) is instantly deleted or round-filed depends to a great extent on its design.

Quality Control Checklist for Content Marketing

Run through this checklist to make sure you've checked off everything:

- ❏ Run a spell check prior to sending copy out for review. *Every time.*
- ❏ The style of apostrophes and quotation marks should be consistent.
- ❏ Style and spacing for long dashes and ellipses must be consistent as well.
- ❏ Subhead styles should be consistent.
  - ◉ This is a sample of a subhead in sentence form
  - ◉ This Is a Sample of a Subhead in Initial Cap Form
- ❏ Make sure that all lead magnet cover titles are always treated the same—either in italics, bold, or bold italics—they all must match on all components. In the case of web-based designs, you want the titles to also appear the same.
- ❏ Check to make sure that all pages are numbered correctly.
- ❏ Are all phone numbers/fax numbers/web addresses/links/log-ins correct?
- ❏ Do jump lines take you to the proper page? Example: (continued on page 3)

❑ Are "continued on" or (over please) lines used on every page where they are needed?

❑ Are the typeface and type size easy to read? If this white paper is being sent to seniors, is type at least 12 point?

❑ If you have used reverse type (light letters on dark background), is it easy to read? Try to reserve this for text that is at most five to seven words long.

❑ Use appropriate visuals to show, not just tell (see Table 14–1).

TABLE 14-1. Visuals and What They Communicate

Type of Visual	What It Shows
Photograph or illustration	What something looks like
Map	Where it is located
Exploded view	How it is put together
Schematic diagram	How it works or is organized
Graph	How much there is (quantity); how one thing varies as a function of another
Pie chart	Proportions and percentages
Bar chart	Comparisons between quantities
Table	A body of related data

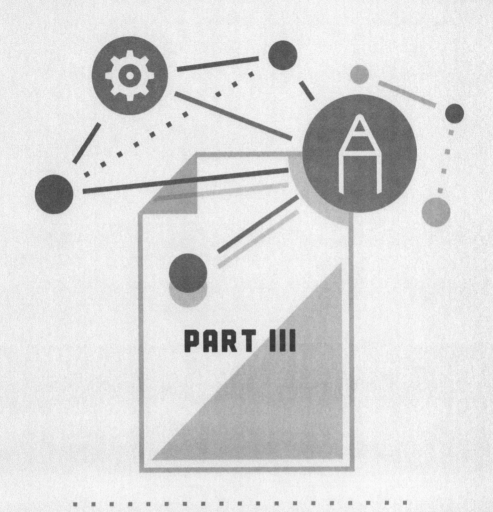

PART III

Converting Content Marketing Activity into Sales

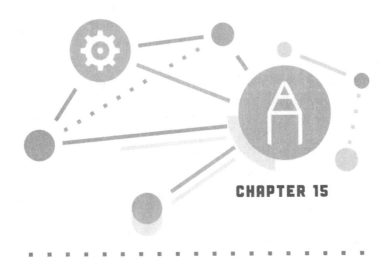

CHAPTER 15

Driving Traffic with SEO

There is more than one way to reach your target audience. I have found over the years that there are many entry points to reach consumers, but some of the best ones are courtesy of organic search. Online, to help your content reach more of the right readers, take advantage of the power of good search engine optimization (SEO). People still use hashtags and search engines to find more information about your website, app, ebook, white paper, or any other content marketing vehicle. Taking advantage of strong SEO practices will make sure that when people are looking for information, they can get to it quickly. That applies to the app store as well as to general search engines like Google.

You should also apply SEO to your marketing efforts. Good SEO on articles and videos using meta descriptions, tags, and other identifiers will help your app and your marketing be more visible and easily found.

Users who come to your site without the use of paid advertising are called "organic traffic."

In this chapter, I'll introduce you to some best practices for driving traffic with SEO and other organic methods.

Shoot for SEO Success

When people Google your pages' keywords, *meta tags* help the search engine find your page. The two most important meta tags are the meta descriptions and title tags. The *meta description* helps Google find the web page. It is usually displayed on the Google Search Engine Results Page (SERP). It gives a concise description of the page contents, not to exceed 158 characters. The keyword should appear at the beginning of the meta description.

The *title tag* is an HTML title for the page, no longer than 60 characters. Again, the keywords should be at the beginning of the meta tag. The main title is given the designation H1 in the HTML coding for the web page.

Google also gives a higher ranking to pages that download quickly. So do users: 53 percent of mobile users will leave a page that takes more than three seconds to load, according to a 2016 report from Google.

Two more tips for raising your ranking: Incorporate keyword and key phrases in your posts, articles, and web pages, and work to build links to other sites.

Use Keywords Judiciously

I recently read an article in a marketing magazine that advised repeating keywords on your site as often as possible, and in multiple places, so search engine "spiders" can find them. But my friend and fellow copywriter Nick Usborne says this advice is not only wrong, but actually harmful.

"This is the worst possible advice you can give to anyone about optimizing their site for the search engines," says Nick. "It's an element of what is referred to as 'keyword stuffing' and is either ignored by the search engine algorithms—or, in bad cases, your page and site will be penalized. Worse still, it results in pages that read very strangely to human visitors.

"Using keywords too often on a page and in the meta tags is worse than not using them at all. The frequency of keywords on a page has nothing to do with whether a spider will find the page."

Since I am not an SEO expert, I asked a number of consultants in this area—and others more knowledgeable than I—to comment on keyword usage on websites. "I think stuffing keywords on a web page is taking the focus off where it needs to be to be successful in any business," says Sean Woodruff, president of ProPride. "That focus should be trained squarely on the customer. Stuffing keywords is a gimmick that is focused on tricking the search engines."

"Yes, search engines are important," says online marketer Susan Getgood. "But it is far more important to have a good website that sells effectively. We should focus on writing good copy that effectively communicates the offer. I expect that keywords appear an appropriate amount in good selling copy vs. some artificial stuffing exercise that doesn't fool the search engines and likely damages your overall communications effort.

"Remember, people do land on your website from other sources—advertising, direct mail, and so on—not just from search engines. It is silly to try to optimize for one source, if in doing so, you end up with a suboptimal website for all the others."

Copywriter Apryl Parcher advises, "When writing websites, it's more important to put keywords in meta tags and descriptions that are only used by spiders and not seen by the average person reading your page, and also to give your pages titles in HTML that truly reflect the page's contents.

"While it is true that words are picked up on your homepage for the search engine description, unless the text block is made into an image, it's usually the first 20 words or so. So make sure that text is what you want people to see when they pick you up on Google. However, you can go all-out in putting appropriate search keywords in your description tags without stuffing your actual copy with them."

"Never stuff a web page with keywords; it's awful advice," says Paul Woodhouse, SEO director at Hive Digital. "You make sure they're in your title and your meta data. Place them carefully in the beginning, middle, and end of your spiel—and in the H1 and H2 tags if necessary."

"If you want to attract search engine spiders and repel your human visitors, then by all means, stuff away," says marketing expert Andrea Harris. "Good web writing is a balance between satisfying the spiders and the humans. But it's the humans who buy your products and services."

"It's not about 'stuffing' copy with keywords," says Richard Leader. "It's about making sure the keywords are in there.

"Some years back, I ran an online training company. Our course outlines were quite clearly course outlines to a human reader—but not to a spider. We realized we didn't once use the phrase 'HTML training course,' for example. So we added it in a few times—and yeah, it looked a bit clunky. But with just a couple of mentions (for example, 'In this HTML training course, you will learn . . .'), we increased our search engine traffic—and our conversions. So my advice is not to stuff but to 'strategically place.'"

"Placing keywords within your site is certainly an important part of getting search engines to notice you," says Joel Heffner, former marketing director for Ideal Computer. "However, my current favorite way to appeal to search engines is to ping entries that I make to my blogs. Search engines appear to love to run to see what's been added to a blog. If you create a link to your blog posts, search engines can find your content more reliable."

So, just how often should you use your keyword on your web pages? In most pages, you ideally want to use the keyword once in the title meta tag, once in the headline, two to three times in the body copy, and once in the meta description. Also, in meta tags and page headlines, put your keyword at the beginning; e.g., "Venturi scrubbers cut energy costs 20%" is better than "Cut energy costs 20% with venturi scrubbers."

META Tags

Obviously, you will include your list of keywords in the META "keywords" tag, but you will also want to use your keywords in your *site title* and in your *description* of your site. There are *three HTML tags* that let you present your keywords, and a few other HTML tags and attributes come into play as well.

The META Description Tag

Search engines permit anywhere from 135 to 315 characters in the META description tag. Since this is what will describe your site to most searchers, make sure that the first 135 characters adequately describe your site.

The META Keywords Tag

This is the obvious place for your keywords. Keep your list of keywords as short as possible, and use both individual words and keyword phrases. A large percentage of searchers enter incorrect spellings, so you might want to include common misspellings of your keywords. And be aware that some search engines' agents are case-sensitive, and you might want to include punctuation variations as well.

The Title Tag

Most search engines use the title tag as the name of your site in the search results listings. It's not a required tag in HTML syntax, but if you leave it out, your site may show up named "No Title." Some search engines include only the first 60 characters of the title, so either keep your title under 60 characters or at least make the first 60 characters meaningful on their own.

Be aware that META tags are not the only factor that affects search engine placement, as Search Engine Watch points out:

> META tags are what many web designers mistakenly assume are the "secret" to propelling their web pages to the top of the rankings. HotBot and Infoseek do give a slight boost to pages with keywords in their META tags. But Excite doesn't read them at all, and there are plenty of examples where pages without META tags still get highly ranked. They can be part of the recipe, but they are not necessarily the secret ingredient.

The HTML Body Tag

The HTML tag also comes into play for many search engines. Rather than emphasizing what you say is important in your title and META tags, some search engines analyze the content of your site to determine its relevance to people who use their search engine. This is most often done by analyzing the words that appear within the HTML tag. These analyses often assign more importance to the first few paragraphs of content, so be sure that the pages you want indexed have strong opening content.

ALT Image Tags

If your site uses a lot of graphics, and you want to attempt to get the content of the images indexed, be sure to use the ALT attribute of the IMG tag. Some search engines index the alternate text that you include in this tag along with the other content on your page.

For years, search engine optimizers have included their important keyword phrases in ALT text for images, feeling confident that many of the search engines considered the contents of ALT text when determining relevancy.

TIP

One more point: Don't "spoof"—attempt to "fool"—the search engines. They're smarter than they were a few years ago, and using the common spoofing techniques of senseless repetition of words, inserting META tags unrelated to the document's content, or using words that cannot be read due to their small size or color. If you do such juvenile things, your website can be banned by the search engine in question!

Seven Ways to Promote Your Content with Organic Search

To repeat: The more people who see and read your content, the more likely you are to generate engagement and interest with qualified prospects for what you are selling. The more qualified and engaged the prospects, the quicker and easier it is to convert them to leads and ultimately to customers. (We cover conversion strategies in Chapter 16.)

As we've just seen, SEO is one effective method of putting your content in front of more eyeballs. Here are seven additional organic search-focused techniques for getting greater distribution, readership, and exposure among your target audience:

1. Research Topics with Quora

Quora is an online platform where people post questions. As an expert in your industry, you can use your knowledge to answer some of these questions while exposing people to your brand.

Quora is also an excellent tool for finding content ideas. People often ask questions there after they've failed to find answers elsewhere. This leaves a space your brand can fill. Research what questions people ask on Quora and then create a blog post or other content that provides a satisfying answer. You can then link to your content in your Quora answer.

2. Leverage Newsjacking

Newsjacking is using a current news story to amplify your B2B marketing and content strategy. It can take many forms. As you create your content, take a look at the major events in the news. This could include holidays, national events, or international news.

Note: Some news, such as natural disasters and terrorism, is unpleasant, and if you have reservations about newsjacking a story, trust your first instincts—and don't.

3. Create Content with an Influencer

Influencers are noted individuals who have become authorities within an industry or who have promotional cache that reaches the social media masses—and who have a social following that matches. Is it effective? Very—as evidenced by the 94 percent of marketers who have used influencer marketing and believe it works. Working together to create content gives each of you the opportunity to add your individual insights and benefit from sharing the content. This kind of partnership gives both of you access to each other's audience base. When you work with influencers, though, it has to benefit both sides, which could mean monetary compensation or some other arrangement. You'll need to work out those details with each influencer.

4. Engage on Free Social Media

Social media has become an essential part of any content marketing strategy. Social media promotion can be done either organically or through paid ads (see number 7 on our list). Promoting your content on social media is not without its challenges. Between complex network algorithms and human nature, it can be difficult to reach and capture your audience's interest. But it's possible, especially if you concentrate on just one or two major platforms. First, pay attention to the quality of your content—take your time and make sure your audience will find it valuable. Studies show that long-form content performs the best on social media, so put in extra work to make it as comprehensive as possible. Another aspect of social media success is your profile. It's no use having amazing content if your profile doesn't support it. An ideal social media profile includes high-quality images, all your information in the right place, and a company bio that showcases its culture.

5. Plan an Event and Promote It Online

Nothing excites audiences like an industry event. Whether it's a conference, trade show, or online event like a webinar, it gives you the chance to connect with your audience and amplify your content. Your presence and participation at such an event leaves a major impression on your audience and brings your brand to the top of their minds. Use this to your advantage by referencing key pieces of content throughout the event. There are a number of ways to promote your content at such events:

- Volunteer for a public speaking engagement.
- Incorporate event-related hashtags in your social posts.
- Participate in a podcast interview.
- Create and publish event-related content.
- Publish key takeaways from the event.

6. Repurpose Your Content

Think of repurposing content like renovating a home: You're taking what you love and making it even better. Take a piece of content that you and your audience savor—perhaps it's a blog post people have devoured or an infographic that has gotten a lot of shares on social media. Then take steps to improve it, such as adding more information and changing the title. You could even transform it completely into another asset, such as a checklist or video. Repurposing bolsters your content marketing strategy and helps pique the interest of new audiences—especially when you tie new SEO keywords to it.

7. Pay to Promote on Social Media

While organic social media is a valuable strategy—especially if you have the audience to back it up—paying to promote your content can give it the extra boost it needs to reach new audiences. Social ads aren't just for gated content campaigns, such as promoting an ebook. They can also be used to promote blog posts, infographics, and videos. Learn all you can about your audience and use that data to target the audiences likely to be most interested in your content. Social media promotion isn't an exact science. A lot will depend on your specific industry and target audience. You may need to go back to the drawing board a few times before you get the right combination that resonates with your audience. But it's definitely worth the effort.

Boost Your Google Ranking with Links

The core principle of links and SEO is simple: Google rewards sites by giving them higher ranking when the sites have a of lot of good quality, valid hyperlinks, both to other sites Google sees as legitimate as well as internal site links (links from one page of your site to another).

Within recent months, Google seems to have tightened the reins on what they consider *a true and valid link*.

Deciphering this new approach can be tricky. What is seen as a *good* link? What is a *bad* link? Once upon a time, any link was a good link, it didn't matter the source. Today, a *good* link is a link from a site that is considered *relevant* to you. When you search for link partners, make sure that the link you post on your site is a positive reflection on your image and perceived status as an "expert" in your field. Linking sites that are not related by industry or common value to the user may actually reduce your Google ranking.

Link Aging

Link *aging* is a factor in the Google algorithm. By looking at how long a link has been in place, a search engine can assign weight and relevance based on time. A new link has little or no value while a link that has been in place for several months has some value, and a link that has been in place for a year may have the most significant value.

What does link aging accomplish? It fights link spam. Many link spammers try to achieve top rankings for their sites by getting hundreds, if not thousands, of links for a site virtually overnight, or by purchasing "ads" on high PR sites for the purpose of getting the link value, where the ad itself is of little or no consideration.

These are methods used simply to make a site be considered "important" in the eyes of the search engine. Link aging essentially makes these linking methods less valuable and less cost effective.

Mass link purchasing is less attractive if the link must stay in place for months before any value can be attributed, which can often cost a significant lump of change, especially considering that the moment you stop paying for the ad, you lose all the value in that link. Search engines are also getting better at detecting links from paid ads as well.

Reciprocal Links

Reciprocal links are links you trade with other sites (you add their link, they add yours) in order to build link popularity. There are many online services and group exchanges, around to help you link up with more like-minded webmasters quickly and easily. I would be very hesitant however to buy links. I would rather take my time to build a solid list of relevant, worthwhile link partners, through old-fashioned networking.

"Mutual linking" is where the content of each site actually benefits each other's sites. If you sell web copywriting services, you may want to recommend other sites for website design and hosting services. This is useful information for your visitors, who are likely to need these services as well. It makes sense for these sites to also recommend your services and link to your site. While it's technically still a reciprocal link, it has a *mutual benefit* for both sites.

Make sure you get links from pages with a Google page rank higher than zero. A site Google rates as "0" (maybe because they are penalizing it for some reason) can only hurt you as a result of linking to it. Download the Google tool bar (http://toolbar.google.com/) with the page rank indicator to make things simple.

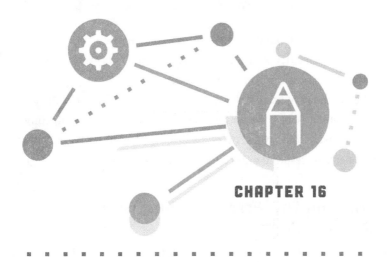

CHAPTER 16

Increasing Conversion with Response Devices

I've talked about how free content offers can significantly increase response rates (as well as build brand awareness, establish thought leadership, and spread your ideas). An *offer* is simply: a) whatever the prospect gets by responding and b) what they have to do to get it. Both elements affect response rates. The more relevant and useful your free content is, the more prospects will request it. Similarly, the easier it is for them to respond, the more they will do so.

The key step in *conversion*—converting traffic to leads or customers—is to provide clear, easy-to-submit response elements through which the visitor or prospect can request your free content. For instance, if you drive 100 visitors to an online response form offering a lead magnet, and 10 of them download the lead magnet, your conversion rate is 10 percent.

Back in the introduction, in Figure I–2, we saw that more than half of marketers consider ROI a top priority. Conversion is a key element of maximizing response, and therefore ROI.

We've already discussed what makes for effective content and lead magnets, which is half the battle when it comes to increasing conversion rates. Now we'll look at the other half: reply elements that make it easier for prospects to respond and request your content.

Information That Prospects Must Give to Get Your Content

Through extensive testing, we have found that the less information prospects must give you in online response forms, the higher your conversion rates will be. A rule of thumb is that for each additional field you require the prospect to complete, the conversion rate declines by 10 percent.

You should follow this habit and have fewer rather than more fields on landing pages with free content offerings. Remember, you can always ask the prospect for additional information later. But first you have to get a response. Without a response, you don't even know if that prospect exists. But once you have the contact information, you can qualify the prospect more thoroughly later on.

When you are building an online list, such as a subscription list for your enewsletter, the only information you truly need is the prospect's email address. Most marketers also ask for names so they can personalize the emails. In lead-generating promotions, where you plan for salespeople to follow up, you should also get a phone number.

These are the only fields you should make mandatory—which you can indicate on the page by marking them with an asterisk. At the top of the

> **TIP**
>
> To capture a mailing address, including street, city, state, and zip code, use a physical lead magnet, such as a DVD or book. Without a complete snail mail address, you cannot ship the hard-copy content and the prospect cannot receive it. A postal address is particularly useful to companies in which their salespeople's territories consist of a specific ZIP code, city, or state.

page, include a legend that reads "* = required field." Prospects who do not complete the mandatory fields are notified, usually in red type, which fields still need to be filled out and informed they cannot access the content before completing them.

To further qualify prospects, you can add a few optional fields that help you determine whether you are getting an inquiry from a qualified lead. Key optional fields are phone number, company name, website URL, and job title.

Do not add too many optional fields to gather qualifying information. When there are more than a dozen fields on a form, it looks too time-consuming to fill out, and your conversion rates will decline.

Visitors who complete the required fields and click Submit have completed their part of the deal. You get their information, and they get their lead magnet. The lead magnet may appear on the screen as an image they can click on to download the content. Or a message might appear telling them to look for an email that includes a download link.

Though they have already given their name and email address, your email may ask them to provide them again to confirm that they did in fact request your content. Requiring the prospect to provide such information twice is called a *double opt-in*. Those that do not are *single opt-ins*.

The danger of a single opt-in is that someone may submit another person's name and email address without their knowledge or permission. When an email or content is delivered to an individual who did not request it, you are in effect sending spam, which can hurt your reputation online or even lead your ISP to shut down your account.

The double opt-in ensures that the person asking for your content is the same person receiving it. This eliminates spam and the problems it can cause for its recipients—and you.

Phone and Chat Responses

Some marketers know that when they can get prospects on the phone, they can convert more of them to customers. They typically add a phone number in large, bold type as a response option on their landing pages and websites to encourage phone inquiries rather than an online response.

LANDING PAGES

Landing pages are similar to shopping carts or response forms. In addition to the fields the prospect must fill out to receive the content, the page contains descriptive copy about the lead magnet and sometimes about your company. The copy highlights the lead magnets to increase downloads.

Another option is a link or icon on the web page to request a live chat that visitors can use as they navigate the website. A live chat typically pops up in a bubble or dialogue box at the lower corner of the user's screen. Whether facilitated by a live human or a chat bot, the "live" chat can answer questions in real time with the site visitor.

Hard Copy Response Devices

These are off-line response elements such as business reply cards (BRC), business reply envelopes, and 8½-by-11-inch reply forms. They are often enclosed or bound into magazines, catalogs, and direct-mail packages.

They can be returned via postal mail. The BRC is already addressed to you, and the postage is paid. (When using business reply mail in your marketing, you pay postage only for the reply cards and envelopes that are returned to you.)

Most reply cards and forms are printed in black ink on white paper. But you can also print on a light-colored stock, such as canary yellow, salmon pink, or light blue, to make it stand out more. Then you can say in your letter, "Just return the enclosed yellow reply card."

Postcards can be filled in by the prospect and dropped in the mail. For full-size reply forms, you include a business reply envelope and an option to fax the completed form back to the sender. You may argue that no one uses fax anymore and the technology is outdated. That's not really true. Health care, finance, law enforcement, and many other sectors still rely on fax communications for security purposes.

Quick Response (QR) Codes

When I was starting out in marketing in the late 1970s, the standard response device in direct marketing was the business reply card (BRC).

With the advent of PURLs (personalized URLs), use of the BRC declined dramatically. Many argued that the BRC was unnecessary: Why waste a piece of card stock when the prospect could just go online? Now the use of quick response codes (QR codes) has further driven a stake into the BRC's heart. Why fill out a BRC with a pen when you simply scan it with your smartphone in about a second?

According to a study published by Pew Research more than 81 percent of Americans are now smartphone users. The gender mix is about 50-50. And, thanks to recent smartphone OS upgrades (most notably the iOS 11 update), many smartphones now come equipped with QR readers.

While QR codes have had their challenges, they are currently experiencing a renaissance, especially in the US consumer market and overseas as a payment system conduit. Juniper Research reports that the number of QR codes redeemed by consumers will surpass 5.3 billion by 2022. Asian markets in particular are seeing a steady uptick of QR code-enabled payment systems for the B2C market.

Although QR codes have been around for years, there are still plenty of people out there who don't know what they are or how to use them. To assist those folks, it's a good idea to provide instructions near the QR code on your printed materials, such as "Scan the QR code with your smartphone;" or include an image of a smartphone pointing to the QR code, or show how the code could take them to a website.

Always ask yourself, "Why would my audience want to scan this?" Rather than just slapping a QR code on your printed materials, think of a reason why you should have one. Perhaps it will make it easier for your audience to access a map or directions, or make it easier for prospects to contact your company or make a purchase. Include that reason on your printed materials to let people know what they'll gain from scanning the code.

TIP

Use a URL shortener, such as TinyURL, to reduce the number of characters in a long URL.

People love special offers and discounts. When you give them a reason to scan your code by offering a discount or coupon, you have a winning combination of technology and incentive.

The page where your QR code directs prospects should be tightly focused on conversion. Make the conversion process (email sign-up, coupon, demo request, and so on) easy and user-friendly. If you are using a form, keep it short. If they are downloading a coupon, provide instructions for how to redeem it. Present them with a thank-you page after they take action. Include social media share buttons on this page to make it easy for them to share your content.

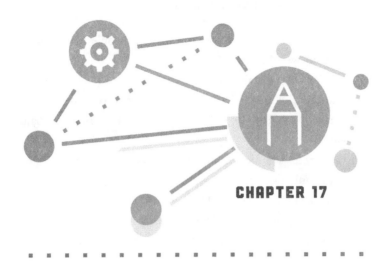

CHAPTER 17

Increasing Digital Conversion with Content

According to a 2019 study by Heinz Marketing and ON24, only half of B2B marketers are confident or somewhat confident that their content marketing boosts revenues. But there's a way they can improve the odds, gain more confidence, and generate more leads.

In my experience, offering a content lead magnet can double marketing response rates.

In this chapter, we will explore how you can increase your conversion rates using the very thing you are creating—content.

Metrics: Measuring Content Marketing Results

Here are some of the metrics you can use to gauge the performance of your content marketing campaign:

- ◎ *Unique visitors*: The number of different people who have clicked onto your website
- ◎ *Page views*: The total number of times your page was accessed
- ◎ *Backlinks*: The number of websites linking to your site
- ◎ *Sources of traffic*: The response to all traffic sources, paid and organic
- ◎ *Bounce rate*: The percentage of visitors who leave your site after viewing only one page
- ◎ *New vs. returning visitors*: The percentage of people who return to your site or page multiple times
- ◎ *Time spent on website per visit*: And the time they spend on each page
- ◎ *Shares by content type*: White papers, articles, web pages
- ◎ *Number of comments*: On blog posts and discussion boards
- ◎ *Number of friends*: Including connections, followers, and subscribers
- ◎ *Opt-in rates*: The percentage of visitors who opt in to your email list
- ◎ *Clickthrough rates*: The percentage of email recipients who click on hyperlinks that connect to a sales page or other web page
- ◎ *Cost per click*: Based on cost of traffic generators, what you are paying per click
- ◎ *Conversion rates*: The percentage of people landing on your page who request your free content or order a product
- ◎ *Downloads*: The number of requestors who actually download the ebook or other content (not all do)
- ◎ *Number of leads*: The number of prospects who complete your online form and who fit your criteria of a qualified prospect
- ◎ *Cost per lead*: If you send out a postcard to 100 people at a total cost of $100, and 5 of them call you to request your free catalog, your cost per lead is $20
- ◎ *ROI*: The ratio of the revenue brought in by a marketing campaign divided by the cost of the campaign

Fifty-eight percent of 500 B2B marketers surveyed by Rapt Media in 2016 said that being able to accurately measure ROI is a major obstacle, and 31 percent said their specific problem is not being able to measure and prove conversion behavior driven by content. In addition, only 44 percent of B2B marketers are clear on what content marketing success looks like, according to a 2015 survey by the Content Marketing Institute.

Planning the Online Conversion Series

One way you can track the efficacy of your content is by setting up an online conversion series. In the *conversion process*, you send a series of emails via auto-responder to people who have visited your page and submitted their email addresses, but have not yet converted to a lead or a customer, because they did not take your primary offer.

Experience shows that the online conversion series works best with between three to seven email messages, though some marketers keep sending conversion emails until the response drops so low it isn't worth continuing.

Many marketers attempt to make a sale with every email in the series. That is, they all have a URL for a page from which the recipient can order the product. Others like the first two emails to be content, promoting the value of the free information and encouraging the recipient to read it—in some cases, they even give out more free content. These are called *free touch* emails, because they touch the reader without asking for a purchase.

Subsequent emails in the series ask for the order; these are called *conversion emails*. In a six-effort series, the first one or two emails might be free touch, and the remainder would be conversion emails.

When the reader clicks the URL link in your email, they could go to a landing page or a transaction page. A landing page has a fair amount of descriptive copy about your product and your offer. It does a strong job of selling the reader on the product's value. A transaction page has a minimal description of the product; it's basically just an online order form.

Some marketers always send email recipients to a landing page, on the theory that the more sales copy there is, the more sales they will make. Others believe that if the conversion email has a lot of sales copy, there is no need to repeat it in a landing page, so they opt for a short transaction page.

The best offer for an online conversion effort is a free 30-day trial of the product. If you can set up your site so that the recipient's credit card is not billed until after the 30-day trial period, that's the best choice. Then you are truly offering a free trial or subscription. By comparison, if you charge their credit card as soon as they submit their order, it is not really a free 30-day trial; it's a *risk-free* 30-day trial. They are paying, but if they cancel within 30 days, they get a refund.

You can experiment with the timing, number, and mix of emails (free touch and conversion) in your series. A typical series might go like this:

1. *Day 1*: Email #1, free touch. Thank the prospect for requesting your free content and reinforce its value.

2. *Day 2*: Email #2, free touch. Encourage the prospect to read the free content and highlight its value. Point out some of its especially good ideas, tips, or strategies.

3. *Day 4*: Email #3, conversion. Tell the prospect they can get more of the same content by accepting a free 30-day trial subscription to your publication. Sell them on the publication and its value.

4. *Day 7*: Email #4, conversion. Remind the prospect they can still become an expert on the topic by getting your publication and accepting your free trial offer.

> **TIP**
>
> Every marketer who wants to generate leads or sales on the internet should try an online conversion series. Just renting an elist of opt-in names and asking them to subscribe won't work; people tend not to buy from strangers online. But offer those same people a free article or report, and they will frequently take you up on it. After all, what do they have to lose?

5. *Day 14*: Email #5, conversion. Tell the prospect the free 30-day trial offer is expiring, resell them on the content you are offering, and urge them to act today. Tell them after that it will be too late.

Write your online conversion series emails the same way you would write other online and off-line promotions to sell your products. Use the same copy, content, and organization: Get attention in the lead, generate interest, create desire for your product, and ask for the order.

There is one key difference: In your lead, always acknowledge that they are hearing from you as a follow-up to the free report or article *they asked you* to send them. This has two benefits: First, they may feel slightly more obligated to read your message; after all, you did give them a gift. And second, if they liked the free content, it automatically puts them in a receptive mood for more of the same—even if this time they have to pay for it.

If you have targeted the right audience, and your free content is of high quality and value, then some readers will be willing to accept a free 30-day trial of your product. And if your product is also of high quality and value, a large percentage of the buyers will not request a refund, and you will have successfully converted free content requesters to paid customers.

Ten Tips for Increasing Landing Page Conversion Rates

The online conversion email series typically sends recipients to a landing page offering more in-depth content or selling merchandise. Depending on whether you are selling a product directly from your landing page, asking visitors to download a free white paper, or promoting a webinar or demonstration, conversion rates can range from less than 1 percent to more than 50 percent. Here are ten keys to creating landing pages that maximize online conversion rates:

1. Build Credibility Early

People have always been skeptical of advertising, and with the proliferation of spam and shady operators, they are even more skeptical of what they read online. Therefore, your landing page copy must immediately overcome their doubt. One way to do that is to prominently display one or more "credibility builders" on the first screen the visitor sees. In the banner at the top of the page, put your logo and company name if you are well-known; universities, associations, and other institutions can place their official seal in the upper-left corner of the screen. Within or immediately under the banner, put a strong testimonial or three above the headline.

Consider adding a pre-head or subhead that summarizes the company's mission statement or credentials.

2. Capture the Email Addresses of Nonbuyers

There are a number of mechanisms available for capturing the email addresses of visitors who click on your landing page but do not buy the product. One is to use a window with copy offering a free report or ecourse in exchange for submitting their email address. This window can be served as a *pop-up* (it appears when the visitor arrives) or a *pop-under* (it appears when the visitor attempts to leave without making an inquiry or purchase). These will both be blocked if the visitor has installed a pop-up blocker. A *floater* is a window that slides onto the page from the side or top. Unlike the other two, the floater is part of the site's HTML code, so it is not stopped by the blocking software.

3. Use Lots of Testimonials

Testimonials build credibility and overcome skepticism, as do case studies and white papers posted on the website. If you invite customers to a live event, ask if they would be willing to have a brief testimonial recorded on video. Have a professional videographer tape it, get a signed release from the customer, and post it on your site as streaming video. Require visitors to click Play to hear the testimonial, rather than have it play automatically; autoplay videos are generally disliked. As noted in Chapter 6, sometimes customers ask the marketers to write the testimonial they seek, submit it to the customer for editing and approval, and then publish it.

The problem with doing so is that testimonials written by the marketers rarely sound as sincere, honest, and enthusiastic as those written by the customer. Solution: Politely ask that they give you their opinion of your product in their own words instead. What they come up with will likely be more specific, believable, and detailed than your version, which might smack of puffery and promotion.

4. Use Lots of Bullets

Highlight key features and benefits in a bulleted list of short, easy-to-read items. I often use a format where the first part of the bullet is the feature, and after a dash comes the benefit. For example: "Quick-release adhesive system—your graphics stay clean and don't stick together." Online buyers like to think they are getting a lot for their money, so when selling a product directly from your landing page, be sure you cover all major features and important benefits in a comprehensive list on your landing page. When generating leads by giving away white papers, you don't need a huge list of features and benefits. But using bulleted items to describe the contents of the paper and the benefits that information delivers can raise conversion rates for download requests.

5. Arouse Curiosity in the Headline

The headline should either arouse curiosity, make a powerful promise, or otherwise grab the reader's attention so they must keep reading. For example, the headline for a landing page selling a program training people to become professional property locators makes a big promise: "Become a Property Locator Today—and Make $100,000 a Year in the Greatest Real Estate Career That Only a Few Insiders Know About."

6. Use a Conversational Copy Style

Most corporate websites are unemotional and sterile: They just offer "information." But a landing page is a letter from one human being to another. Write it that way. Even if your product is highly technical and you are selling it to techies, they are still human beings, and you cannot sell something by boring people to death.

7. Incorporate an Emotional Hook in the Headline and Lead Paragraph

Logical selling can work, but tapping into the prospect's emotions is much more effective—especially when you correctly assess how they are feeling about your product or the problem it solves. Another effective tactic for lead generation landing pages is to stress your free offer in the headline and lead. Example: A landing page for industrial manufacturer Kaydon showed a picture of its catalog with a bold heading above it reading, "FREE Ceramic Bearings Product Selection Guide."

8. Solve the Reader's Problem

Once you hook the reader with emotional copy dramatizing their problem or making a powerful free offer, show how your product or information can help solve their problem. For example: "Now there is a better, easier, and more effective solution to wobbly restaurant tables that can irritate customers and ruin their dining experience: Table Shox, the world's smallest shock absorber." To maximize conversion rates, you have to convince the visitor that the quickest route to solving their problem is taking the action indicated on the landing page, not surfing the rest of the site. That's why I prefer landing pages with no navigation, so the reader's only choice is to respond or not; there's no menu with links to other interesting pages to distract them from the offer.

9. Make It Timely and Current

The more your copy ties in with current events and news, the higher your response rates will be. This is especially critical when selling financial and investment information, as well as regulatory compliance products in fields where laws and rules change frequently. Periodically update your landing page copy to reflect current business and economic conditions, challenges, and trends. This shows visitors that your company is on top of what's happening in your industry.

10. Stress the Money-Back Guarantee

If you allow customers to order directly from the landing page, make sure you have a money-back guarantee clearly stated on that page. All your competitors give strong money-back guarantees, so you must do the same. If your product is good and your copy truthful, your refund rates can be less than 1 percent.

TIP

If you are generating leads, stress that your offer—whether a white paper, online demonstration, or webinar—is free. Say there is no obligation to buy and no salesperson will visit.

Five Ways to Capture Email Addresses of Landing Page Traffic

Most marketers I know who use landing pages to make direct sales online focus on conversion: getting as many visitors as possible to the landing page to place orders.

Other internet marketers, when writing landing page copy, focus not only on conversion but also on search engine optimization: keyword selection and meta tag creation that can increase traffic by raising the site's search engine rankings.

But in addition to all this, savvy online marketers are concerned with a third performance metric: capturing email addresses. If you have a 2 percent conversion rate, then for every 100 visitors to the landing page, only two buy. Of course, during these transactions, you capture the buyers' email addresses. What happens to the other 98 visitors? You will not be able to add their email addresses to your list unless you incorporate a deliberate methodology into your landing page to capture them.

Here are five methods for capturing the email addresses of landing page visitors who do not purchase. Every landing page you operate should use at least one.

1. Ezine Sign-Up Box

This is a box where visitors can get a free enewsletter subscription just by entering their name and email address. You can see an example of a simple ezine sign-up box at https://www.bly.com/ and countless other websites.

The ezine sign-up box placed prominently on the first screen is a widely used method of email capture for websites, but it is less commonly used for microsites and landing pages. That's because if your headline and lead properly engage the visitor's attention, they won't bother to sign up—they'll just start reading. Then, if they lose interest or reach the end but do not order, and instead click away, you haven't captured their email address.

2. Squeeze Page

Also known as a preview page, squeeze pages are short landing pages that require the visitor to register with their name and email address before they're allowed to go on and read the long-copy landing page. To see a squeeze page at work, visit www.clickfunnels.com.

In some cases, the long-copy landing page itself is positioned as a "report" that visitors can read after registering. For this to work, your landing page must be written in an informative, educational style. Many squeeze pages offer a content premium, such as a free report, just for submitting your email address. Those seeking to capture snail mail as well as email addresses make the premium a physical object that must be shipped, such as a free CD.

Squeeze pages work well when your primary source of traffic is organic and paid search. That's because search visitors arriving at your site are only mildly qualified—they have decided to visit based on only a few words in a search engine description or paid Google ad. Therefore they may not be inclined to read a lot of copy from an unfamiliar source. A squeeze page lets them absorb the gist of your proposition in a few concise paragraphs.

The main advantage of the squeeze page is that it ensures you capture an email address from every visitor who reads the full landing page. In addition, they have been pre-qualified, in terms of their interest in the subject, and so are more likely to read through the long copy.

3. Email Capture Sidebar

These are forms built into the main landing page as sidebars, again making a free offer. In a long-copy landing page, the email capture sidebar usually appears early, typically on the second or third screen, and may be repeated one or more times throughout the page. Example: https://www.rocketlanguages.com/french.

The drawback of the email capture sidebar is that the prospect sees it before they get too far in the sales letter, and therefore before you've finished selling them and asked for the order. So the risk is that if your product teaches, say, how to speak French, and the email capture sidebar offers a free French lesson, the visitor will just take the free offer instead of spending money on the paid offer.

4. Pop-Under

When you attempt to click away from the landing page without making a purchase, a window appears that says something like, "Wait! Don't leave yet without claiming your free bonus gift."

The advantage of the pop-under is that visitors see it only after they have read to the point where they are leaving without ordering. Therefore the free content offer doesn't compete with or distract visitors from the paid product offer. The disadvantage is that about 25 percent of U.S. internet users run pop-up blockers on their devices, and many of these blockers will prevent your pop-under from showing.

5. Floater

A floater looks and functions much like a pop-up window, but it's actually part of the landing page's HTML code, and therefore won't be blocked by a pop-up blocker. The floater blocks a portion of the landing page when you click onto the site. You can enter your email or click the floater. Either action removes the floater and allows you to see the complete landing page.

As you can see, all these email capture methods offer some sort of free content—typically a downloadable PDF report, an ecourse delivered via auto-responder, or an ezine subscription—in exchange for your email address. But be warned: The ever-changing Google algorithm penalizes sites with floaters because, until you click out of them, they block the homepage.

Why bother to maximize the capture of visitor email addresses on your websites? There are two primary benefits. First, by sending an *online conversion series*—a sequence of emails delivered by auto-responder—to these visitors, you will have another opportunity to persuade them to buy and increase your overall conversion rate. Second, the best names for your email marketing efforts, far better than rented opt-in lists, are on your house elist. The faster you can build a large elist, the more profitable your internet marketing ventures will become.

How much more profitable? Internet marketing expert Fred Gleeck estimates that, for information product marketers, each name on your elist is worth between ten cents and a dollar per month. For many ecommerce sites, it can be higher. Therefore, an elist with 50,000 names could generate annual revenues of $600,000 a year or more. In other businesses, the sales could be significantly higher.

How to Qualify Prospects Who Ask for Your Free Content

MAD-FU is a formula for qualifying prospects. It separates visitors who just like to download, collect, and look at free content from genuine prospects who may become paying customers. A prospect can be qualified only if they fit M, A, and D, but they are easier to close if they also satisfy F, U, or both. Here is the formula spelled out:

- *Money.* Does the prospect have enough *money* to afford your product? One way to find out is to ask on the online registration form. You list budget ranges, and the prospect can check which is within their range.
- *Authority.* Does the person have the *authority* to spend the amount of money you charge for the product they want to buy? If the prospect is a married couple, often there is joint authority, and either spouse can veto the purchase. When selling to businesses, there are often several people who can authorize the purchase. At a large company, many purchase decisions for large dollar amounts are made by buying committees or teams.
- *Desire.* The prospect *desires* or needs what they are looking for and thinks they can get it from your site.
- *Fit.* The product *fits* what they need and are looking for. For example, if they want a convertible, a hardtop won't do.
- *Urgency.* The prospect *urgently* needs or wants your product now, as opposed to people who are just shopping around and do not intend to buy any time soon.

Goals for Marketing Metrics

Here are some of the key content marketing goals and the percentage of digital marketers who consider them priorities:

- Lead generation—80 percent
- Brand awareness—79 percent
- Engagement—71 percent

And here are the most frequently used content marketing tactics:

- Social media—83 percent
- Blogs—80 percent
- Enewsletters—77 percent
- In-person events—68 percent
- Ebooks and white papers—65 percent
- Video—60 percent
- Infographics—58 percent

Next, we have the most preferred methods of distributing content:

- Email—93 percent
- LinkedIn—89 percent
- Twitter—77 percent
- Facebook—76 percent

And here are the top metrics that content marketers measure to evaluate the performance and ROI of their campaigns:

- Web traffic—78 percent
- Audience engagement—75 percent
- Leads—72 percent
- Sales—57 percent

Some brand managers measure the performance of content marketing by such metrics as page views, time spent on site, likes, shares, form submissions, and downloads.

For senior management, who are much more concerned about ROI, the goal is to increase revenues. And the more you can show the sales and profits produced by your content marketing programs, the more likely you are to get continued support for them—and the better off your bottom line will be.

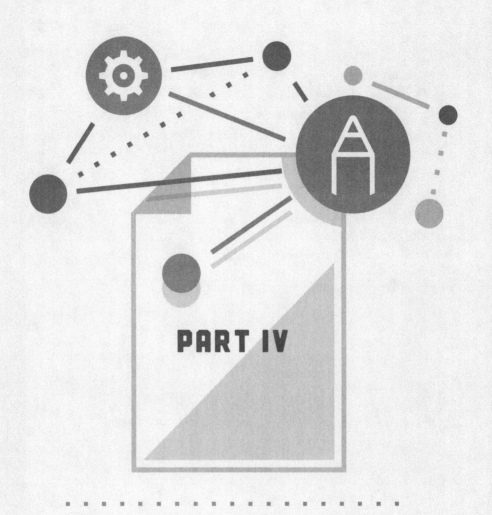

PART IV

Appendices

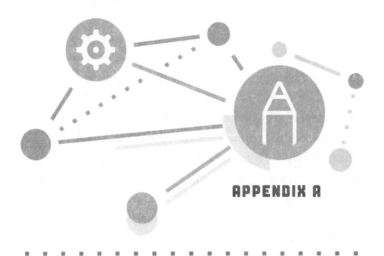

Complying with Copyright Laws When Creating Your Content

Note: Copyright is a legal issue, and I am not an attorney. Consult with an attorney before using content from other sources.

Any published material that is no longer protected by copyright law for one reason or another is in the *public domain*. For written works, that means anything published before 1925. However, the issue is often more complicated.

The U.S. Copyright Office's publication on investigating copyright status states: "The U.S. copyright in any work published or copyrighted prior to January 1, 1923, has expired by operation of law, and the work has permanently fallen into the public domain in the United States."

For various reasons, another large body of works entered the public domain in 1963. Generally this happened because they were not originally eligible for copyright protection or the owner failed to renew the copyright in the last year of its original protection.

Works created before January 1978, but not published with a copyright notice or registered, are permanently in the public domain. Works created on or after January 1978 are automatically given copyright protection—generally the life of the author plus 70 years, or 95 to 120 years, whichever is shorter.

Use of public domain content is in sharp contrast to copyrighted works. Most original works of art—literature, paintings, film, photographs, poems, songs—are protected under copyright laws for a specific period of time. When the copyright expires, the work enters the public domain.

Content may be in the public domain for many reasons other than a lapsed copyright. The work may have been published before there was a copyright law or its protection has expired. Maybe the copyright was lost or never applied for. Sometimes authors or artists dedicate their work to the public domain so that everyone has free access to it. Sometimes the work is ineligible for copyright protection—for example, many government publications.

Attorney Stephen Fishman, in his book *The Public Domain: Find and Use Free Content for Your Website, Book, App, Video, Art, and More*, 8th Edition (Nolo, 2010), states that "Copyright experts estimate that 85 percent of all works of authorship first published in the United States between 1922 and 1963 are in the public domain." He estimates there are at least 85,000 works in the public domain.

There are even works published today that are in the public domain. The U.S. Government Printing Office (GPO) is the largest publisher of information in the country, and most of its work is not copyrighted. This is because government publications are paid for with taxpayer dollars, so the public should be entitled to use them. In fact, government publications often invite you to use their work, as long as you credit GPO as the source.

When work enters the public domain, it is available for anyone to use. One example of this would be the Brothers Grimm's fairy tales, published in the 19th century. Disney was able to adapt the original stories to film because they were in the public domain. Does that give you any ideas?

Copyright laws are specific to the country in which the intellectual property was produced, so if you want to use something from Great Britain, for instance, you'll have to research that country's copyright laws and be sure the piece you want to use is no longer protected. At https://www.gov.uk/government/organisations/intellectual-property-office, for example, you can find information on "intellectual property" use in Great Britain.

It may be more difficult to search records in countries other than the United States. For example, the law on intellectual property in the United Kingdom says that copyright is an automatic right. There are no registers that can be checked to locate the creator or right holder in a work. There are, however, organizations representing copyright owners who may be able to assist you in tracking them down.

But if a country is a treaty party (a country or intergovernmental organization that is a party to an international agreement) of the United States, works created by nationals of that country are eligible for copyright protection in the U.S. as well.

You can learn more about the international copyright laws of other countries at the World Intellectual Property Organization (WPO) website: https://www.wipo.int/copyright/en/.

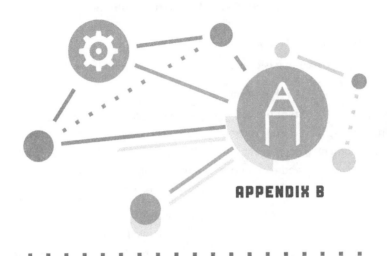

Content Writer's At-a-Glance Grammar and Punctuation Guide

The following tables are a convenient reference when composing your content material.

Grammar At-a-Glance

Tables summarizing basic rules of grammar and punctuation.

	Incorrect	Correct	Why
Subject and Verb Disagreement	In reference to your recent letter, your address on our files are correct. An order form, as well as a postpaid envelope, are enclosed.	In reference to your recent letter, your address on our files is correct. An order form, as well as a postpaid envelope, is enclosed.	The subject of the sentence is "address," not "files." The subject is "order form," which is singular, and so the verb should also be singular.
Problematic Pronouns	John, George, and me met to discuss the job. We met with Mr. Brown, Mr. Smith, and yourself in New York.	John, George, and I met to discuss the job. We met with Mr. Brown, Mr. Smith, and you in New York.	Read the sentence with each subject one at a time. You will discover that "me" should be replaced with "I," and that "yourself" should be replaced with "you."
Dangling Modifiers	After finding the missing report, the search was ended by the administrative assistant.	After finding the missing report, the administrative assistant ended the search.	The modifier, "after finding the missing report," modifies the assistant and not the search.

	Incorrect	Correct	Why
Displaced Modifiers	The payroll teller recommended First Carrier over Federated, whose delivery service is very prompt.	The payroll teller recommended First Carrier, whose delivery service is very prompt, over Federated.	If First Carrier is recommended, it must be the prompt company, not Federated.
Run-On Sentences	Your projected cost for fiscal 2017 is $650,000, however, this figure may vary because of a variety of factors.	Your projected cost for fiscal 2017 is $650,000. This figure may vary because of a variety of factors.	The "however" is the start of a whole new thought with its own subject and verb.
Unparallel Structure	Operators should carry out maintenance activities safely, carefully, and in a detailed manner.	Operators should carry out maintenance activities safely, carefully, and thoroughly.	Use the same pattern of words to show that ideas have the same level of importance.

Punctuation At-a-Glance

Comma ,	Separates dependent clauses. A dependent clause doesn't present a complete thought.	Mr. Smith, a lawyer, was at the party. As I mentioned in my letter, we need to hire three secretaries. We need action, not words.
Semicolon ;	While commas separate dependent clauses, semicolons separate independent clauses that closely relate to each other.	Hundreds of tests are conducted to determine product safety; accidents occur regularly.
Colon :	Announces something that follows. Usually precedes a list, a letter, or an explanation.	Go to the stockroom and bring me these items: pens, toner, and folders. Hospitals exist for one reason: to heal the sick.
Hyphen -	Links words. Usually links two or more words modifying a noun.	This is a state-of-the art course. We need to go through a two-stage process.
Ellipsis . . .	Separates dependent clauses. Often used when only part of a quotation is used.	"I . . . am . . . guilty," he stammered. "This is the best report I've seen . . . you did a good job."

Parantheses ( )	Adds information. Usually the information is of secondary importance.	Acme Co. had excellent revenues (see fig. 5). I'm sending you three checks (No. 1245, No. 1247, and No. 1249).
Dash –	Highlights or interrupts a thought. A dash SHOUTS; parentheses whisper.	The Dow Jones Average closed at 17,000–the rich get richer, it seems–to set a new record.
Apostrophe ,	Shows possession or contraction. Singular nouns ending in "s" get " ' "	The boy's pen is on his desk. We'll see you soon. The employees' rights are protected by OSHA. Mr. Dickens' book is open.

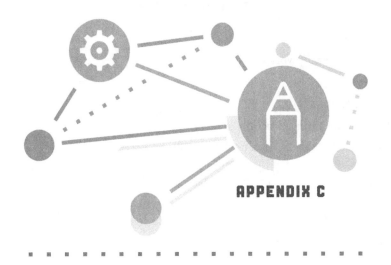

Resources

Courses

AWAI Content Writing

https://www.awai.com/p/is/com

Dozens of Additional Vendors

Bob Bly's Vendor List

https://www.bly.com/newsite/Pages/vendors.php

Ebook Designers

Fiverr

https://www.fiverr.com

Upwork
https://www.upwork.com

Organizations

Content Marketing Institute
https://contentmarketinginstitute.com

PR Distribution Services

(a partial list)

eReleases
http://www.ereleases.com/
Email: comments@ereleases.com
Phone: 800-710-5535
eReleases is a PR writing and distribution service that has more than
30,000 opt-in journalists signed up to receive the press releases they
distribute.

Press Release Network
https://www.pressreleasenetwork.com/
Global online distribution and website announcement services; media
database includes more than 20,000 news recipients, such as editors of
newspapers and magazines and managers of TV, radio, and broadcast
stations. Contact via web form only.

Press Release Writing
http://www.press-release-writing.com/
Email: info@press-release-writing.com
Phone: 877-362-7924
Provider of press release writing tips and services, press release
distribution, and distribution list services. The basic package starts at
$375. Press release writing: $250.

PR Newswire
http://www.prnewswire.com/
Phone: 888-776-0942

PR Newswire is a global leader in news and information distribution services for professional communicators. A membership-based site with an extensive list of services available to members, including monitoring and distribution reports.

PRWeb

http://www.prweb.com/

Contact form: https://service.prweb.com/contact-us/

Phone: 866-640-6397

PRWeb is the recognized leader in online news and press release distribution services for small and midsize businesses and corporate communications.

24-7 Press Release

http://www.24-7pressrelease.com/

Contact form: https://www.24-7pressrelease.com/contact_us

Phone: 888-880-9539

Press releases to wires and media in any industry, with distribution to approximately 85,000 sources, including Yahoo! News, MarketWatch, *The New York Times*, and *USA Today*. Payment is per release rather than by subscription, with higher payments widening your press release's distribution.

Useful Books

Cashing in with Content by David Meerman Scott (CyberAge Books, 2005), trade paperback, $30.

Content Rules by Ann Handley and C.C. Chapman (Wiley, 2012), trade paperback, $19.95. With the exception of a new section of content marketing case studies, pretty similar content to her newer book *Everybody Writes*.

Epic Content Marketing by Joe Pulizzi (McGraw-Hill, 2013), hardcover, $28.

Everybody Writes by Ann Handley (Wiley, 2014), hardcover, $25.

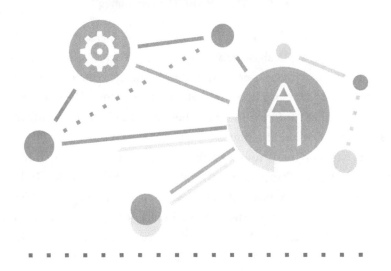

About the Author

Bob Bly is an independent copywriter and consultant with four decades of experience in business-to-business and direct marketing. McGraw-Hill calls Bob Bly "America's top copywriter." He has written copy and content for more than 100 clients, including Kiplinger, Boardroom, Agora, KCI, Nightingale-Conant, IBM, AT&T, and Medical Economics.

A prolific content writer, Bob is the author of 100 books, including *The Digital Marketing Handbook* (Entrepreneur Press) and *The Copywriter's Handbook* (Henry Holt). He has published more than 100 articles in *Cosmopolitan, Writer's Digest, New Jersey Monthly, City Paper,* and many other publications.

Bob writes regular columns for *Target Marketing*, a trade publication covering the direct-marketing industry. His free enewsletter, *The Direct Response Letter*, has more than 65,000 subscribers.

Bob has given lectures on marketing to numerous organizations, including The Optical Society, General Electric, National Speakers Association, Learning Annex, American Seminar Leaders Association, and the American Society of Journalists and Authors. He is a member of the Specialized Information Publishers Association and the American Institute of Chemical Engineers.

He has won numerous awards, including a Gold Echo from the Direct Marketing Association, an IMMY from the Information Industry Association, two Southstar Awards, an American Corporate Identity Award of Excellence, the Standard of Excellence award from the Web Marketing Association, AWAI's Copywriter of the Year, and ETR's Lifetime Achievement Award in Marketing. He was voted one of the 50 most influential people in sales lead management by the Sales Lead Management Association.

Bob holds a B.S. in chemical engineering from the University of Rochester and has taught copywriting at New York University. Prior to becoming a full-time freelance writer in 1982, Bob was a marketing writer for Westinghouse and advertising manager for Koch Engineering.

He can be reached at:

Bob Bly

31 Cheyenne Drive

Montville, NJ 07045

Phone: 973-263-0562

Fax: 973-263-0613

Web: https://www.bly.com/

Email: rwbly@bly.com

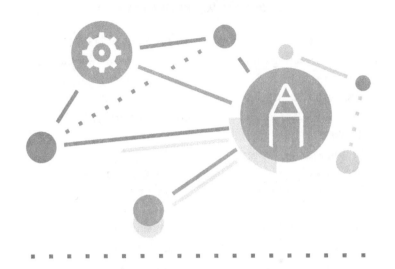

Index